THE TEN
PAINS OF DEATH

The Ten
Pains of Death

by

GAVIN MAXWELL

ALAN SUTTON
1986

ALAN SUTTON PUBLISHING
BRUNSWICK ROAD · GLOUCESTER

Copyright © Gavin Maxwell Enterprises Ltd, 1959

First published by Longman Ltd 1959
This edition published 1986

British Library Cataloguing in Publication Data

Maxwell, Gavin
The ten pains of death.
1. Sicily—Social life and customs
I. Title
945'.8092'5   DG865.6

ISBN 0-86299-289-3

Cover picture of Sicily; Spectrum, London

Printed in Great Britain

This book is dedicated with profound affection
and sympathy to the common people of Western
Sicily, who know the ten pains of death.

To wait for one who never comes,
To lie in bed and not to sleep,
To serve well and not to please,
To have a horse that will not go,
To be sick and lack the cure,
To be a prisoner without hope,
To lose the way when you would journey,
To stand at a door that none will open,
To have a friend who would betray you,
These are the ten pains of death.

Second Fruits,
Giovanni Florio, 1591

Contents

Acknowledgment

We are indebted to Messrs. Sheed & Ward Ltd.
for permission to quote material from *Moral and
Pastoral Theology* by Henry Davis, S.J.

Plates

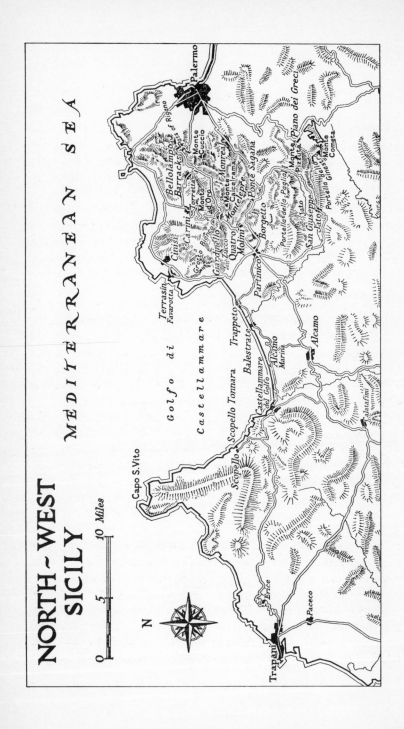

NORTH-WEST SICILY

MEDITERRANEAN SEA

N

0   5   10 Miles

Capo S.Vito

Golfo di Castellammare

Scopello Tonnara

Scopello

Trappeto

Balestrate

Castellammare del Golfo

Alcamo Marina

Alcamo

Calatafimi

Erice

Trapani

Paceco

Terrasini
Favarotta

Palermo

Barracks of Rigano
Bellolampo

Monte Cuccio

Monte Monreale
Monreale

Cinisi

Carini

Montelepre

Monte d'Oro

Monte Caccamo

Ponte Sagana

Grotta Bianca

Zucco

Gardinello

Quattro Molini

Partinco

Borgetto

Portella della Pagliá

Iato

San Giuseppe Iato

Monte Pizzuta

"Piano dei Greci"

Portella Ginestra

Monte Comcca

PROLOGUE

SOME explanation may be desirable of how this book came to be written in its present form.

I first went to Sicily in 1953, with the idea of throwing a truer light upon a figure who had gained world notoriety, the 'bandit' Giuliano, whose life had ended in very mysterious circumstances in 1950. It took me the best part of three years' research to collect the material for a book that was necessarily inconclusive, but during those three years I had become both horrified and fascinated by Western Sicily; horrified by its desperate poverty and misery, and fascinated by an intensely individual people whom I had come, a very little, to know, to understand, and to feel for.

I wanted to know more and understand more, not of the visible splendour of Greek and Roman remains, nor of the glories of Byzantine and Baroque ecclesiastical architecture that so many unwearying pens and cameras have described; not of past conquest and reconquest that over the centuries has blended the blood of three continents into the turbulent fluid that fills Sicilian veins; but of the living swarming suffering mass of humanity that fills the island today.

It was not very easy to see how to do this. Sicilians are an intensely secretive people, and at the end of my third year I was still, to most of my acquaintances, a stranger, to be trusted with only a little of the truth either about themselves or anyone else. I decided that the only approach would be through some group who were in some way isolated, among whom I could quickly become inconspicuous and where outside interference would not constantly remind the people of my novelty and renew distrust.

Finally I hit on the idea of going to live at a *tonnara*, one of the great tunny-fish traps that are manned from March until June by a crew of some fifty men. The trap, consisting of two vessels and a complex structure of net chambers, is static a mile or so off shore; the crew man the trap in day and night shifts, and when they are ashore they sleep in a kind of barracks and loaf about and talk and cook their own food over fires of sticks. This, I thought, would be an ideal atmosphere in which to learn much that would normally be inaccessible to a stranger.

I should not have to invent a reason for my presence, for to me every detail of their work would be intensely interesting.

Such a *tonnara*, extremely isolated and with no road to it, existed only a few miles from Castellammare del Golfo, a town which I had come to know during my earlier visits to Sicily. Scopello, the *tonnara* was called; it is not amongst the greatest *tonnaras* of the island, but a very ancient one. There was a barracks, a small '*palazzo*' where one of the owning syndicate lived during the summer months, and a number of unused buildings beside it.

With the owner's permission I took up residence in one of these unfurnished 'wings' in March, and I lived there right through an extremely bad tunny season until the whole trap was dismantled and taken ashore in July. During that time I had no visitors from outside and seldom left Scopello, so that day by day I gained the acquaintance, and in some cases the friendship, of men who had little to do with their leisure but to talk. Both their inhibitions and their native attitude of somewhat predatory curiosity broke down under the constant familiarity of my presence, and after a while many of them treated me much as they would have treated each other, though all felt I must have been a little insane to choose these conditions when I could apparently afford others.

From stories that they told me of their own lives I conceived the idea, before the inherent risks struck me, of writing a book composed entirely of autobiographies told to me by members of this group. I felt, however, both that identification of the narrators would be too easy and that a series of exclusively male biographies from one occupational background would be too limited in scope. The territory that I knew best, indeed the only territory that I knew well, was the country lying between Palermo and Castellammare del Golfo some forty miles from it by road. This is mountainous at first, with dense villages clinging to the hill slopes, among them Montelepre, the home town of Giuliano. Beyond the mountains lies the long plain of the gulf that stretches away to Castellammare; in many of its villages I had acquaintances, and, in a few, friends. From the villages of the hills and the plains I collected other stories, but it was a slow business, because the difficulties of dialect, more especially among the aged and the toothless, were formidable. (The relationship between Sicilian and Italian—or the lack of it—may be seen in the Chapter Notes.) Finally, a few of my friends who were literate offered to help me—to transcribe direct certain life stories that I wanted and to send them on to me. To them I owe an enormous debt of gratitude, and I regret infinitely that in their own interests I cannot give them public recognition.

It may seem strange that during all the time I was in Italy I knew little of Danilo Dolci or of his work, and what I did know had been thoroughly garbled and biased through the Italian government Press. Dolci, who is now often spoken of as Sicily's Gandhi, had been living in Sicily for some time then, had given up his career as an architect to the detailed study and the hope of betterment of Western Sicily's appalling social conditions, and had spent much of his time in gaol after arrests upon entirely frivolous charges. This was, and at the time of writing still is, the Christian Democrat Government's attitude towards the greatest social reformer that Southern Italy has ever seen, and because of this intense repression most Sicilian peasants are afraid of having anything to do with Dolci, even to admitting that they know anything of his work or that they think it praiseworthy. The nearer one comes to Dolci's chosen town of Partinico the more noticeable is this silence, so that his reputation is much greater abroad than in the island to which he has given his life. It was only when one man whose life story I wanted to record told me that he had 'already given it to Dolci' that I realised how pathetically slowly I was plodding in the footsteps of a master. This story, it seemed, had been published in Dolci's book *Inchiesta a Palermo*, but when I tried to buy this in Palermo I was told that it had been withdrawn from circulation while Dolci and his publisher stood trial for obscenity on its account.

Thus it was not until I had left Sicily, and an expurgated edition of the book had appeared in Italy, that I was able to read the work and to appreciate how thoroughly Dolci had covered much of the ground I had been exploring. My first instinct had been to abandon my own book and to translate his, but that project came to nothing, for at the time it was impossible to find an English publisher for the full work, and Dolci understandably wanted no abbreviation. He very generously gave me permission to use his statistics if they should prove of value to me, and I resumed the writing of my own book. Because of the different scope and *locale* of our works I have not availed myself of his offer.

Since then Dolci has found an English publisher, and it is no more than fitting that his book should appear in English in advance of mine, for to its creation went time and effort beside which my own labours were as nothing.

As my aims were less strictly socio-economical than his, I have tried to present a somewhat broader picture of life in Western Sicilian villages than was necessary for his purpose, and to bring into the witness-box, too, a few of the 'upper-dogs' against whom the voices of the oppressed are so continually raised. Thus my book covers rather more ground, less thoroughly, than Dolci's, and anyone seriously interested in the subject should regard mine as, perhaps, a postponed introduction to his.

The preparation of this manuscript has presented formidable difficulties. To begin with it has been necessary, in so far as could be contrived, to protect the identities of those who have, wittingly and unwittingly, contributed their stories and their outlooks. To do this I have shuffled them among the double handful of towns and villages in the area, so that no character appears in his or her true *locale* although preserving the appropriate milieu. None, of course, carries his or her own name. These assurances I gave to those who contributed knowingly, and, wherever one's personal sympathies may lie, it did not seem fair to withhold an equal protection from those who were persuaded to talk without knowing to what use their words would be put.

Beyond this there has been the problem of expurgation that, without the certainty of political persecution with which Dolci had to contend, has been difficult enough. When a Sicilian's reticence does go it goes completely, more especially on those subjects of which he has been taught to believe that Northerners disapprove. At the forefront of these is sex. Every Sicilian is utterly convinced that his sexual urges and necessities are many times stronger than those of any Northern Italian, and probably hundreds of times stronger than those of anyone inhabiting countries still further north. There is absolutely no evidence to support this belief—indeed I met one Sicilian doctor who had been shaken to his foundations by the Italian edition of the Kinsey Report—but its existence undoubtedly adds a quota of impatience towards the sanctions of a Church that will not take the 'fact' into account. When his reserve has thawed a Sicilian likes to talk about sex; what he says is often illuminating, and important to the understanding of his outlook, but in the English language it is very difficult to preserve with any decorum the spirit of what he says. The vocabulary of Sicilian sexual slang is voluminous, and in most cases the nearest English equivalents are, to most ears, unequivocally offensive. The method I have adopted is to use a less jarring English word and to place it between brackets to show that this has been done; it is not a wholly satisfactory solution, but where the original word or phrase is of semantic interest I have preserved it in the relative appendix. The Sicilian language, with its innumerable dialects, contains words from the languages of nearly all the island's past occupiers.

It would have been impossible to omit these passages altogether and still give an even approximately truthful picture of the people; already, perhaps, too many of them have been eliminated. The visitor who first comes to know Sicilians at all well often thinks them obsessed with sex, and fails to take into account that he is dealing with a people whose intense poverty has always made this one of the very few pleasures they can afford. Because it is so important to them it is impossible for the acuter among them to escape the conclusion that the mystic sanctions imposed upon the subject by the Church are part of a vast plan to keep them in subjugation, a view strongly reinforced by the avowedly political activities of the priests.

This book attempts to give a picture, however necessarily incomplete, of conditions as they are among rural communities in Northwestern Sicily and, more important still, of how the people really think and behave. Its purpose is to be objective, and it is uncommitted to any political party; no profound political knowledge is required as a background to reading, and the intricacies of Italian politics have been no part of my study.

Virtually only one party has been in power in Italy since the war; the Christian Democrats. This party, wholly linked to the Vatican, adopted the cross as its party sign, and there are many Western Sicilian peasants who will cross themselves when they see it; at election time they will automatically vote for it both because it is variously known as the Party of God, the Party of the Madonna and the Party of the Cross, and because the priests are, by instruction and conviction, active political agents. The two crosses of Christ and of Government are by now inextricably confused.

A peasant who does not belong to this party is treated as a moral leper by all in authority. A slogan that I have seen carried at election time 'Vote Christian Democrat or starve' seemed not so much a prophecy as a threat all too often put into action.

It is said that there are three rulers in Sicily—the Church, the State, and the *mafia*, and of the last it is more difficult to give a clear or concise picture. The *mafia* is a unique criminal organisation that probably grew out of a kind of perpetual resistance movement while Sicily was conquered and reconquered no less than sixteen times in recorded history. Once it may have had laudable or useful aims, but now its activities are almost wholly criminal, and its network extends through high commerce and even into government circles. When I wrote *God Protect me from my Friends* I knew less of Sicily than I do now, and I understood less of the *mafia*. Any faint sympathy I may have seemed to exhibit towards that body I recant absolutely. Broadly, it is a 'protection racket' on a grand scale, such as was run in Chicago in the 1920's—many American gangsters were emigrated Sicilians who started a new kind of *mafia* in the States—and where the *mafia* holds sway it is impossible to own land, or enter trade, or do business, or be a successful criminal, without paying 'tax' to the organisation; the *mafia* takes its percentage on practically all money that changes hands. All produce is under *mafia* control—fruit, meat (assisted by employed or semi-employed gangs of cattle-thieves), and even water, for water is a precious commodity that in the summer months is always rationed. Western Sicily is the true home of the *mafia*, and there are half-a-dozen large towns and surrounding districts entirely under its control. No Italian government other than Mussolini's seems to have made any real effort to stamp out the *mafia*; he rounded up many of them and put them in *confino*, that is to say exile on the prison islands such as Lipari and Ustica and Pantelleria. Unfortunately as soon as the war was over the Allies were at pains to liberate these men as 'political prisoners', unconvicted of individual crimes. A *mafioso*, a member of the *mafia*, brings his sons up as *mafiosi*, so that the status is largely hereditary, and there are famous *mafia* families who conduct long-term feuds between each other, involving murder and counter murder until one side is either wiped out or put to flight. Besides the true *mafiosi* there are circles who have much dealing with them, and who are often called *più o meno* (more or less) *mafioso*; these, in *mafia* strongholds, can form a surprisingly high percentage of the population who are not actually destitute.

According to official statistics, which we may assume to be conservative, half of the inhabitants of the island, nearly five millions, are destitute or semi-destitute; classed, that is, in terms implying that they live at or below subsistence level, and the figure is increasing every year. Nearly half of all those millions are illiterate. (There are large numbers who are not placed in the category because they can, with difficulty and letter by letter, write their names.)

Many children believe that Mussolini is still the ruler of Italy, many more that Italy still has a king. Some (more understandably) believe that Germany won the war; others that America is an island off the coast of Britain; that Winston Churchill was a kind of tomato worth more than theirs; that Anthony Eden (who visited Castellammare by naval vessel while I was there) was King of Egypt. None of these misconceptions is the least surprising among people for whom there is no written word, and who are too much preoccupied with trying to remain alive to listen to talk on such idle subjects.

Every now and again some English newspaper reports a major crime in Sicily—usually a kidnapping or murder. When it is a kidnapping it is usually the size of the ransom that makes the item international news; when it is murder it is often the third or fourth of a chain of connected killings that would not individually have got further than the Italian Press.

To anyone who knows any part of the island at all intimately, these reportings seem curiously isolated and arbitrarily selected, for crime in Sicily is as much part of everyday life as street accidents are in a capital city. Sicily, and especially Western Sicily, is a land of violence and banditry; a land in which even the good and the honest have by necessity something to hide.

In Western Sicily one can fairly easily make a division between 'big' crime and 'small' crime. A murder may be in either category, but a kidnapping or a large-scale robbery is always 'big' crime, because it cannot be carried out without the co-operation of *mafia*. But the total number of true *mafiosi* is very small—possibly under a thousand—and for the almost unbelievably high crime rate among the bulk of the population one must look to quite different causes—to a degree of need and deprivation not easy for the average Northern European to understand. All repressive measures attack the symptom rather than the disease.

'When the babies cry we steal for them' is a sentence I have heard very often; and while it certainly is not always for the babies that they steal, there is at the heart of their attitude the sullen violence of the oppressed, who, because Sicily also contains rich men, are bitterly conscious of their under-privilege.

'What choice have we? The priests tell us to pray, but does that get us money?' So it comes about that there are whole large communities in Western Sicily where eight out of every ten adult men have served more than a year in prison, and a further four per cent are *fuorileggi*—outlaws identified as having committed crimes for which they have not yet been arrested. Probably ninety per cent 'criminals' in all.

It is impossible to speak of employment or unemployment in the sense in which we are accustomed to use the words, for the majority who find work at all are paid by the day, hired in the small hours of the morning at a labour mart, and the average number of those days will rarely be more than one hundred and twenty in a year—more often about one hundred. The rate of pay for a day's work for an agricultural labourer, which is the nominal work of half the island's employed, is arbitrary and competitive, but rarely exceeds the equivalent of 8s. 6d. That means a maximum legal earning of little over £40 a year to feed and clothe a family whose size may not, under religious sanctions, be limited by contraception. The population, already at starvation level, is increasing at a rate of more than sixty thousand a year and the increase in the number of families classified as destitute runs almost exactly parallel.

That is the social background from which these stories come, and against which they should be judged. It is the reason why few Sicilians feel inclined to look northwards and say 'Friends, Romans'. The union with Italy in 1862 brought no material benefits to the island, and the people's way of life and outlook has remained unchanged for perhaps a thousand years. To the eyes of northern Italians Sicily has always appeared a disreputable, illegitimate and criminal relation. When the President of the Italian Republic visited Sicily in 1958 he said he had seen things that had 'frozen his ability to smile'.

CHAPTER ONE

The Killers

WHEN I first came to Scopello I thought only that it was the most beautiful place I had ever seen. I had become accustomed to this country as I knew it in the late summer before the grape harvest, when the flowers were dead and all the land was parched and rustling, brown and yellow under a hard cobalt sky. I had not believed that a million million flowers and acre upon acre of verdure had powdered into the pale crumbly earth and vanished; I had not believed that this paradise could exist.

I had come as far as I could by car, if the vicious bundle of senile decay that I tried to steer about Sicily that year could possibly be described as a car. (Appalled by the cost of hiring *topolinos* in previous years I had this time disastrously decided to buy my own transport in Palermo on arrival and sell it before I left. It was not a happy experiment; indeed it would be easy to write a separate book about my adventures with that malign twenty-five-year-old harridan of a Ballila. I do not remember her ever completing the shortest journey without some greater or lesser disaster; though her most spectacular improvisation was perhaps the spirited discharge of a front wheel carefully aimed at a traffic policeman on her first entry into Castellammare del Golfo. This was a variation upon her already deep-rooted vice of hooting spontaneously, long and loudly, at the sight of a *carabiniere*; in desperation I had cut the horn wires, so that now I was unable even to warn the policeman of the approach of the wheel that I saw scooting away in front of me.)

I say I had come as far as I could, because there is no road to Scopello *tonnara*. The road, or rather track, is some five hundred feet above the sea, and it ends in a tiny semi-deserted village called Scopello di Sopra, which could be freely translated as Upper Scopello. Until a very few years ago there were some three or four hundred people living at Scopello di Sopra, but because they nearly all had relations in the United States, or Canada, or Brazil, or Australia—(and, if the truth be

9

told, because many of them had bettered their lots by smuggling contraband into Scopello *tonnara*)—the greater part of them decided to escape from the squalor of life in Sicily, and have emigrated. Now there are only some fifty people left, and they too dream for most of the time of escape.

There is a little *piazza* of crazily uneven paving-stones and loose boulders, with an unadorned stone fountain at its centre; above, the bare stone mountains climb steeply into the sky, and below, the land tilts abruptly seaward. Already, when one leaves the last of the scarecrow houses and begins twisting one's ankles among the big loose stones of the track, one is on a gradient of one in four; looking back, one is aware of having skirted a cliff upon the very lip of which Scopello di Sopra is built. And immediately one is looking down on the sea a mile below, a sea of purple and blue and peacock green, with a jagged cliff coastline and great rock towers or *faraglioni* thrusting up out of the water as pinnacle islands, pale green with the growth of cactus at their heads. The track winds down on the line of least resistance, through vines and bamboo clumps and scattered olives standing in low green corn, and everywhere there were flowers of a myriad colours; thistles of blue and of yellow and of purple, and poppies, and many, many, whose names I did not know. Where a slope of ground has been cultivated in the past the thistles grow thick and even, like a crop. They are not scattered and of uneven height as in English fields, but close-marshalled as corn, their delicate tops presenting a blue blanket to the sky. (Later, in the still weather of the summer, when the earth cracks and gapes and the flowers die, the thistle-down falls to the ground to form a carpet of glistening silk around the pale crackling stems, and twittering puffs of gold-finches rise in a flurry from the thistle fields.)

Among and over the flowers flitted thousands of brilliant butterflies, and great yellow-banded bees a full three inches long, and humming-bird hawk moths hovered above scarlet, trumpet-shaped blossoms. Over the ground flickered darting lizards of electric green; here and there were fat giants whose bodies, of an even more vivid colour, were more than a foot long—and more than once a long black snake streaked away straight as a flame-thrower from under my feet. The air was heavy with the sweetness of aromatic leaves, of thyme and mint and of a low, red-leaved shrub whose pungent fragrance clung to my clothing as I brushed through it.

A pair of kites wheeled overhead, and clouds of jackdaws chattered round their rock nesting-places on the cliff behind and on the *faraglioni* below me.

I met no one between the village and the *tonnara*, and I heard no sound but the birds and the insects, the slow, lazy thudding of deep-toned cattle bells somewhere out of sight, and the clear ventriloquistic trill of water running from a hidden spring.

When I reached the foot of the slope I was fronting a bay, with high rock outcrops at each side. There was a curtain wall between myself and the sea and scattered buildings beyond it; to the left the square pink villa that they called the *palazzo*, with a ruined tower on a rock spur rising high above it and older, whitewashed buildings at its flank; and to the right were long low houses, barracks and storerooms, with a single cottage at their extremity.

Roberto, the custodian of the *palazzo*, came forward from under the shade of an arch while I was wondering which way to turn. He was a man of vast girth, with the face of a good-humoured villain, and the rolling foot-splayed walk of a Turkish *pasha*. Most of his teeth were missing, and during all the time I was at Scopello I found him largely incomprehensible. We skirted the *palazzo* on the seaward side with the wavelets scrabbling gently on the gravel at our feet, past a little jetty and on to the foot of a broken stairway that led up the rock. Above us was a dazzling whitewashed building with the blank windows of long disuse, and above that again the dizzy rock turret with the crumbling Saracen tower at its summit.

Roberto led the way up the stone stairway, along a little ruinous terrace and into the building. The door opened straight onto a steep wooden staircase; when we were half way up this there was a tremendous clatter of wings and hysterical cackling, as a hen, disturbed at roost in my bedroom, shot past Roberto in full descent and struck me squarely in the face with both feet. (When I returned to Castellammare and explained my scratches to an American-Sicilian who prided himself on his command of English, he replied 'Ah, so you were invested by a crazy hen'. *Investire* is the Italian for 'to strike'.)

My bedroom was white and square and utterly devoid of furniture; one window looked out over the jetty and the sea and the other to the courtyard of the *palazzo*. I sent messages of gratitude to the owner and went back to Castellammare; the next day I got my luggage sent down

by mule from Scopello di Sopra, and moved into the room that was to
be my home for many weeks.

There were only two resident families at the *tonnara*; Roberto, the
caretaker of the *palazzo*, had a wife and a small daughter, and at the
cottage beyond the barracks lived the family of Galante whose reigning
member Angelo was responsible for the stored gear during the off-
season, working during the tunny months as a member of the crew.
Angelo was about thirty; he had a pretty young wife and a four-year-
old daughter of a curious, simian beauty, an unmarried sister of about
his own age, and a mother who might well have been taken for a
centenarian, but was, I believe, in her late sixties. I never heard her
referred to as anything but *la nonna* (the grandmother). In the cool of
the cobble-floored kitchen with its great cone-shaped oven she would
sit and cough and tell her beads while the hens clucked round her small
hard chair; she would put her hands into an attitude of prayer and
gaze long at the cheap print of the Madonna and Child upon the wall,
and mutter to herself 'If St. Joseph wills it my cough will get better,
if St. Joseph wills it'. She would break wind with an extraordinary
volume of sound and go on telling her beads and praying to St. Joseph,
no wit abashed. Apparently he never did will that she should get
better.

In this house I ate my meals, and here members of the *tonnara*
crew came when they were off duty to sit and gossip and drink the wine
which the Galantes sold, but at the beginning I was much alone; I
belonged neither to the *palazzo* nor to the *sciurma* (crew). *La nonna*
was frail and weary, but she would exhibit a terrifying energy in
making me understand her stories, shouting and gesticulating and
miming until she was satisfied that I had taken everything in.

She told me that the sea beyond her door was beautiful but that
it was terrible too, that last winter the waves had crashed over the roof
of her house and smashed the windows; that in that same storm she
had seen in broad daylight a big fishing boat of eighty or more feet
in length crossing the bay, and that it was there one moment and gone
the next. There were eight men and two boys aboard her, but not
one of their bodies was ever found; only the wheelhouse of the boat
came ashore near Castellammare. She told me that she remembered
when long ago the Saracen towers on the rocks had been joined by an
arched bridge, and how the bridge had fallen during a great tempest,

and with it had fallen ancient skulls, each with a spike driven through it from front to back.

It was the worst tunny season for many years. A mile and a half out at sea the huge trap was manned night and day, but few fish entered it, and an air of heavy despondency descended on Scopello *tonnara*. After a few weeks of this a brand-new effigy of St. Francis was set in the niche on the second *faraglione*, and the *rais* or chief of the crew (an Arab word going back to the days when the Arabs carried on the same fishing from the same place more than a thousand years ago) would demand hats off and a cheer for St. Francis after a miserable catch of a hundred or so *bisi*, big blue mackerel, and a sword fish, had strayed into the trap. The response from the crew was half-hearted and rebellious, and one voice audibly shouted 'B . . . him!' '*E sia lodato*' intoned the *rais*—('*inculato*', muttered a voice near my ear)—'*il santissimo sacramento*' responded the crew, and the same voice whispered venomously '*San Francesco!*'

It would have been unreasonable to expect men working night and day for a weekly wage of £3 and a bonus of fourpence per tunny to have found compensation in the pure beauty of the scene as that unprofitable catch was taken, in the unbelievably intense blue of the shoal of *biso* as they had scudded round the death chamber just below the surface. Even the swordfish, a dull greyish brown on land, had seemed a deep royal blue as he slowly circled the limits of his condemned cell, prodding with his sword at the solid rope wall. The rope-mat floor had lifted to the surface and the blue of the darting *bisi* had turned to a glittering dazzle of silver fish and white spray as they stranded and sputtered, to be ladled out with a long-hafted landing net, half a dozen at a dip. Among them had been flying fish; only one had soared high enough to rise over the encircling boats to freedom; the others had leapt in rainbow parabolas to fall right into the scuppers.

At the end of that fruitless season each *tonnara* received a compensatory payment from the government, in some cases as much as ten million lire, but the crews received nothing.

There were only four topics of conversation among the men with whom I gradually came to spend the greater part of my time. These were sex, money, politics and religion, in that order, though the last three are in Sicily so closely inter-related as to form a convenient target for single attack. One day, being alone with Buonaventura and

Carlo, and finding that after half an hour the talk was still running glutinously in the familiar channels of the first subject, I cut clumsily into some libidinous details of Carlo's adolescence.

'Carlo,' I said, 'is it true that more than eighty per cent of all Castellammare's adult men have served prison sentences?'

Carlo stopped abruptly; he had been, as it were, on the verge of climax, and found it difficult to refocus his attention after this un-warrantable interruption. He held a hunk of stalish bread in his hand from which he had cut careful cubes with a short square-bladed knife and chewed them ruminantly as he talked. He adjusted himself politely to the change of subject and swallowed his mouthful.

'Eighty per cent? Eight men in ten . . . yes, I suppose that is true. What can you expect when people are so poor? When the babies cry for bread and there is none to give them, a man must steal. Or when the winter comes and the babies cry because they have not enough clothes, then a man must steal or they will die with a pain in their lungs. They are mad who say that a man should let his babies go hungry and cold—if a man doesn't steal then it is because he hasn't got enough guts to. Isn't that so? Would you let the babies die?'

'No, I don't think I should.'

'Of course', he went on, 'it's the priests who are behind it all.'

I saw that it was impossible to escape the tentacles of the original four subjects—there was no aspect of human behaviour that they could not stretch to embrace.

'There are too many people and too little to support them, there-fore they are poor and therefore they steal. But why are there too many people? Because the priests rule. They tell the women that it is a sin to avoid having a baby, and that they will go to hell if they do as the Americans do and take precautions . . . By the way, have you got any of those *preservativi* with you? No? A pity . . . but it doesn't matter . . . Anyway, as I said, the women believe the priests and so they go on having a baby every year and so there are too many people and they are all poor. And *why* do the priests want this? That's easy, my friend—it is because a poor people means an ignorant people and an ignorant people means a superstitious people whom the Church can rule easily.

'See, the poorer the people the more religious they are, and people say this is a beautiful thing—they do not see that it is a cause and effect that has been arranged. For me, I would take every priest in the country and drown him out there in the chamber of death—that would be a *mattanza* worth seeing! They are hypocrites, they are worse than any politician, because they can rule only by fear, and would tell a man that he must not even think—it is a sin even to question the rubbish they teach. . . .'

His voice was silenced by an enormous hunk of bread which he thrust suddenly into his mouth like a gag. For a moment his face wore an expression as outraged and frustrated as though someone standing behind him had clapped a hand over his mouth. I seized the opportunity.

'Surely there are good priests and bad priests, like other men? And have they really harmed you, any of them?'

He gulped down the bread and answered with his eyes on the ground. His voice was dull and bitter.

'Harm? The whole tribe stinks like rotten fish. I know them. At the time I went to my first confession I believed them and I thought *Il Signore* guided them. My parents were very religious. That priest told me that things were sins that hadn't worried me before . . . things I must not do. Two years later he seduced my sister.'

I said, 'He was a man, Carlo, the same as anyone else, and the sexual side of life must always be difficult for a priest.'

He paid no attention. 'Hypocrites, hypocrites, all of them. They will persuade a dying man that he must leave his possessions to the Church instead of to his children. In that way there are always more poor, more slaves. And where does the money go? Some to him and the rest to the treasures of the Vatican, to vaults of gold and diamonds and emeralds and rubies—treasures past counting, all hoarded and useless when they could cure all the poverty and misery of our people for generations, perhaps for ever. How can the Pope be a holy man when he lives in a palace and everything he touches is made of gold? Was not Jesus Christ a poor man and a friend of poor men? See the photographs of the Pope and the Vatican in the illustrated papers this week?—gold, gold everywhere, even a gold telephone, while babies and cripples starve. Power, that's all they want—hypocrites, hypocrites!'

He was silent for a moment; then he went on slowly. 'Six years ago they killed my wife while I was away in Tunisia. They said it was her or the child that had not yet seen the day—they could not both live. They said the mother must die for the child. So she died, my

Mariannina, sacrificed for a child that only lived nine days, for a child they coveted so that they could twist his mind and teach him their ways. You aren't a Catholic, you can't understand these things because you haven't seen how they work. You cannot understand. They rule all Italy, like Russia rules other countries that still carry their own names—the Vatican rules us through the Christian Democrat Party and the priests. You would understand if the Church and the State were joined in your country.'

'As a matter of fact they are. The longest word in the English language is all about it.'

'Ah? In Italian it is *precitevolissimemente*, I've been told. But what you say can't be true—you wouldn't find a town in England where eight men in ten had been in gaol. It's the work of the Church, the Church has brought it about through the centuries.'

'If it is true that one man in three in Castellammare has committed murder would you say the Church was responsible for that too?'

'One in three . . . Perhaps it is true. If it is, then it is still the work of the Church, because the Church is behind all the unjust laws that govern us and drive us to desperation.'

Buonaventura spoke for the first time. 'There is a difference between murder and killing, Gavin. Most men that are killed here—not all, but most—are killed because they deserve to die. Men kill here when it is just to do so. Not the *mafia*—I'm not talking about them—but the common people.'

'It seems to me,' I said, 'that just as you make all the priests black you make all those who are not priests white. You won't admit either a good priest or a bad Castellammarese except for the *mafia*.'

'Of course it is true that there are many bad men in Castellammare, very many, but they don't pretend to be saints—they aren't hypocrites. Carlo is right about that, there are many hypocritical priests, though he exaggerates. I have known good priests, sincere men, who I've been sorry for because of all the rubbish they had to try and believe . . . But of just killing I will give you examples, and you shall judge for yourself.

'I will tell you two stories, and in each case I knew the man you would call the murderer. In the first that I shall tell you I knew both the killer and the killed. It is a very simple story. They were two young men of about the same age who had grown up together and were comrades. One of them, Giovanni, was a boy with a big heart and open ways; the other, Leonardo, was very reserved and sly, and he used to play dirty tricks on people. Everyone knew this, but Giovanni would never hear a word against him, and they were always together. Perhaps it was because Giovanni was big and strong and Leonardo was small and weak that he wanted to protect him—Leonardo had lost an arm when the Americans bombed Palermo. Anyway, when Giovanni was nineteen and Leonardo was twenty, they both fell in love with the same girl—or perhaps Leonardo fell in love with her because Giovanni had. At first they quarrelled about it, but after a time Leonardo played the martyr, and told Giovanni that he would give the girl or anything else in the world for the sake of their friendship, and that Giovanni was to trust him when he said she was out of his mind for ever. Well, Giovanni married her. They had been married a year and had no children when Giovanni was called up for the war. Leonardo stayed at home because the doctors didn't pass him. Giovanni fought in North Africa and was taken prisoner at Tobruk, and he wasn't set free for years. All the time he thought only of his wife and of the day when he should get back to her; they wrote many letters to each other, and when he read what she wrote he felt almost as if he were holding her in his arms. Then, after a year or so, her letters got fewer and fewer, and at last stopped altogether. He became desperate with anxiety; he wrote to his family and his friends for news of her, but when they replied they avoided the question and only said she was well and her letters must be going astray. At last I wrote to him and told him the truth—that his wife had gone off with Leonardo and was believed to be living in Partinico. His mother made me try to excuse her; the bride was young and had got used to having a man and it was a long time to wait and so on and so on, but she only wanted me to say that because she was afraid of what was going to happen—she knew what they deserved.'

Buonaventura cocked an eyebrow at me. 'I told you it was a simple story,' he went on, 'and already you see the end. When Giovanni came home he found them, not in Partinico but Corleone, and his wife was pregnant by Leonardo; also he had given her a sexual disease. He killed them both with a knife and he mutilated the bodies. It was just—they deserved to die, but now he's serving a life sentence in the Ucciardone at Palermo. That is not just.'

Carlo grumbled, 'It is too simple a story to tell to a *scrittore*, and besides you did not recount it well. Tell Gavin the story of Il Volpe, and tell him all of it. If you tell it well perhaps he will make it into a book.'

'Il Volpe. Yes, that is a good illustration, a very good illustration, and the story is not simple. I will tell it very carefully.

'This did not take place in Castellammare, but it was not far away, and the dead man is buried near here, very near. You will take us there in your car one day, and we will lay a wreath of snakes on that monster's grave.

'Il Volpe was a man who appeared amongst us at the time when the island was occupied by the Americans and English. We called him Il Volpe (the fox) because he had red hair and he looked so cunning— *molto furbo*. We only knew his real name later on, and we only found out his nationality after we—after he died.

'He wore civilian clothes, and it was believed that he worked in some way for the military government. He was not an old man, probably under fifty, but in some ways he was like an old man—he talked slowly, and whatever he was doing he moved slowly, walking, eating, or even taking a cigarette to and from his mouth. He may have thought quickly, but if he did it wasn't quite quick enough.

'He was much alone, Il Volpe, and he was seldom in the company of other foreigners. He'd been about for two or three months when he took up Mario. Mario was a pretty boy of about fourteen, with fair hair and a mouth like a girl's, the kind that's always a big success with foreigners who come to this country. Times were terrible then, far worse than they are now—there was no food to speak of, and no money to buy it if there had been. Men would sell their souls for a loaf, or commit murder for a kilo of *pasta*. There was the *intrallazzo* (the black market) but only the big-shots had money to buy from it, and the poor starved and died. Mothers had no milk, and they watched their babies grow thin and die in their arms.

'Mario was the eldest of six children, and his father was in gaol— the *carabinieri* had caught him trying to make a lira to feed his children by carrying black market *pasta*. His mother thought St. Joseph had answered her prayers by sending Il Volpe, who gave Mario clothes and money. Mario went to live with Il Volpe, to clean his shoes and cook the food and do the work of the house, and he had good shirts to his back and no longer went barefoot. Mario became fond of Il Volpe in a way, though he sometimes found him cold and evil-tempered, and they were together for all that spring and summer. No one was the worse, and Mario and his family had something to eat for a change.

'But Mario had had an admirer before—a young man called Gino who had gone to fight in the army of E.V.I.S., the irregular troops who had been gathered to fight for an independent Sicily. When the politicians ratted on the irregular troops and their army was left without serious hope many of its men came home, but often after hiding in the mountains for a time first. Gino was among these, and when he came home at last he didn't like what he found.

'You will have noticed that we Sicilians are very jealous people—half the murders in Sicily are caused by jealousy. At first Gino wanted to kill Il Volpe, but his friends persuaded him that it would be unwise, for Il Volpe was said to be working with the army of occupation. So Gino went to the house—Il Volpe was out all day—and spoke with Mario. He instructed him what he should tell Il Volpe when he came home that evening: that the situation was ended, and that Mario would leave that night. Gino did not want to tell Il Volpe this himself, because as yet there was no amnesty for E.V.I.S., and he was afraid of Il Volpe's connection with those in authority.

'Mario was frightened, and also he didn't want to go back to having no food and no clothes; he cried, but in the end he agreed to do what Gino said.

'After Gino had gone, you may imagine what poor little Mario felt while he was waiting for Il Volpe to come home. He had never realised before how frightened he was of the man, and a dozen times he was on the point of going to look for Gino to tell him he couldn't do what he'd promised. But he was a brave boy, and he waited, praying to the Madonna and all the Saints and angels to give him courage. At last he heard Il Volpe's foot on the stair, and he pretended to be very busy about the room.

'Mario said afterwards that Il Volpe saw at once that something was wrong, but when he found the boy tongue-tied he just sat on the bed and watched him as he tidied the room, saying nothing. After a long time he said,

' "You seem very busy tonight, Mario. Better leave that work till tomorrow."

'It was only then that the boy found it possible to speak. He straightened up and faced Il Volpe and blushed and gulped and said, "Tomorrow I shan't be here." He had meant to go on, but he couldn't get any further. Il Volpe just looked at him for a moment or two, and then he asked quietly, "Anyone ill at home?" Then, when Mario didn't answer he said, "Take your time, no hurry."

'Mario got it out at last. "I can't come here any more. I'm going home tonight and I'm not coming back." He was crying as he said it.

'Il Volpe asked, still very quietly, "Any special reason?"

' "No . . . Yes . . . I must go, that's all. You must understand."

' "You're quite certain nothing can change your mind?"

' "Certain, quite certain . . . Now, I must go now—you mustn't try to stop me."

'He ran to the door, and when he had his hand on the latch he turned and said, crying, "Goodbye . . . I beg you to forgive me." I told you he'd become quite fond of Il Volpe, and he still trusted him.

'So when Il Volpe said "I understand that you must go—I won't try to stop you, but there's something I want to give you", he came back into the room with the tears wet on his face.

'Now Il Volpe had an unusual watch of which he was very proud. It was a large gold wrist watch with many hands and things, and it must have cost a lot of money. Mario had often admired it, but he was not a greedy boy, and he had never asked for it as many other children would.

'Il Volpe unstrapped this watch from his wrist and held it out. Mario said afterwards that he was smiling, but looked very sad. He said "I want you to have this, to remember me, and to show that I have no ill-feelings. *Per ricordo*. Take it, to show that you bear no ill-will either."

'Mario didn't know what to do. I've said he was a boy with a good heart, and he felt he couldn't take this great gift at the moment when he was leaving and causing grief. He was crying with pity for himself and all the world, and he tried to explain, but Il Volpe wouldn't listen. "If you take it," he said, "I shall not feel so badly, and I shall know I am giving you something of more value to you than my affection, which is useless to you now."

'In his distress Mario couldn't even find the words to say thanks, and he ran from the room with the watch in his hand. When he reached the street door he put the watch in his pocket, because he guessed what Gino would do if he saw it. He was feeling angry with Gino now, and sorry for himself and Il Volpe. He decided to go home first and hide the watch before he went to find Gino. He dried his eyes and tried to look as if nothing was wrong. His family lived more than a kilometre distant, and he ran all the way. He told his mother that he'd come home because Il Volpe had gone away for a while, and he made it all sound quite natural. His mother wanted to know if Il Volpe had given him any money to live on while he was away, and he said no and that he hadn't liked to ask. She cuffed him for that, and set up a great wailing.

'Mario hid the watch under the mattress he had shared with his two brothers, and went out again to find Gino at the *quattro canti* where he had said he would be.'

Buonaventura paused to light the stump of a cigarette, and when he went on his voice was meditative, almost languid.

'He never reached the *quattro canti*. He was arrested by the *sbirri* (police) as soon as he turned into the main street. Il Volpe had gone to them immediately after Mario had left the house. He had told them that Mario had worked for him as houseboy for many months and had been well paid, but this evening, when Il Volpe had gone down to the sea to bathe and left his watch in the house, he had come back to find the boy gone and the watch missing. He had made enquiries in the street and had heard that the boy had been seen running in the direction of his home.

'They took Mario to the *Ufficio di Sicurezza Pubblica* for questioning. When he said that Il Volpe had given him the watch they slapped his face and twisted his ears. Then they did worse things to him, and he told them all the truth except for Gino's part in it, for he did not want them to find out who Gino was and what he'd been doing during the past year. Then the *sbirri* said "If this foreigner gave you the watch, why are you not wearing it openly?" And Mario couldn't answer, because the reason was Gino. He told them he'd taken it home for safety because he was afraid of being beaten up and robbed of it—but then they asked him where he had put it, and he couldn't answer because he saw that if he said it was hidden under the mattress it would seem proof that he'd stolen it.

'They kept him while they sent to search his home, and the searchers found the watch and then they ill-treated him because he had lied to them.

'Mario was sent for trial and convicted of stealing the watch. Il Volpe was there to give evidence; at the beginning Mario looked at him as if he believed he might still save him, but Il Volpe kept his eyes turned away from the boy even when he identified him; he never glanced at him once. He said he blamed himself for having put temptation in the boy's way, that he should never have left anything so valuable as the watch lying in his room while he was out.

'The President of the court spoke much of the boy's ingratitude to his employer, and sentenced Mario to six months' imprisonment in an institution. He had always been a happy boy—that was one reason why everyone liked him—but now as he was taken out of the court he looked lost and stupid with misery, almost simple-minded. I saw him. I was there.

'You may wonder why Gino did not come forward to explain. It was not that he was a coward, but that it would have done no good. They would have discredited his evidence because of his part in E.V.I.S., and also put him in prison for the same reason. There is no justice in the law, but there was the power of justice in the hands of Gino.

'I am betraying no secret, for Gino is a common name, and in any case it is not his own.

'Gino killed Il Volpe. Perhaps you would say "murdered" him, but for me killed is enough. He did not kill him pleasantly; afterwards he said that the rage in his heart had been too great for him to make Il Volpe suffer as much as he should have done—Gino wanted to strike and strike and strike again, and so Il Volpe died too quickly. Gino gave his eyes and his *coglioni* to a tame raven, and then he buried the body at the foot of an olive tree, where the big roots divide and the ground will never be dug.

'It was nearly four months before the newspapers reported that he was missing, and it wasn't until then that we knew his nationality. We had always thought he was a Swiss, or a traitor German perhaps, but he turned out to be a South American, Costa Rica or somewhere. Anyway, he's part of Sicily now. The papers said he was a geologist— I hope he's finding some interesting stones where he is now.

'Well, Gavin, did Il Volpe not deserve to die? Was it not justice?'

'One thing first,' I said, 'that's two murders for which even you can't blame the Church. As for justice, Il Volpe did something that I personally could never forgive; I might say he "deserved" what happened to him, but what is justice?—What does the word mean? Can you explain it?'

'That's easy. Justice is *un occhio per un occhio, un dente per un dente,* "an eye for an eye and a tooth for a tooth." '

'Then according to you Il Volpe "deserved" only to go to prison for the same length of time as Mario, and to suffer as much unhappiness as he had. And Gino "deserved" to be killed painfully because he'd killed Il Volpe painfully. And in any case your idea is concerned only with punishment for evil and not with rewarding good.'

Buonaventura was looking shocked and bewildered. 'You mean to say,' he exploded, 'that you don't think Il Volpe deserved to die? That's absurd! Do you mean that?' He grew red in the face.

There was to be no delicate fencing; he had hacked straight to the weakness of an argument unsupported by certain conviction. I made my escape on an intellectual plane, he on an emotional.

I said, 'I don't know; I would have felt as Gino did—but I do know that the word justice is as crazy as any of the Church doctrines you call rubbish, and always will be until someone can either explain it or apply it in a way they'd accept if applied to themselves. There's no justice in nature, and if we invent an idea and a word for it then we ought to be able to explain what it means before we start killing in its name. Say that it seemed best to kill Il Volpe, or that Gino killed him because he wanted to, or that vengeance is necessary, or anything else you like, but for Christ's sake don't use that crazy word.'

'But it *was* justice,' blurted Carlo. 'And as for rewarding good, Gino sold the watch and a ring and other things of Il Volpe's and gave all the money to Mario when he came out of prison. The ring had a diamond, and Mario still had some of the money left when he got married five years later. Wasn't *that* justice? Poor Gavin, you are so educated and so intelligent, and *simpatico* too, but there are things you can't understand. There are times when it is better not to think too much.'

Buonaventura yawned widely. 'On Sunday you shall take us to look at Il Volpe's grave.'

Two years later I discovered that Buonaventura was 'Gino'. I saw Mario and his wife and their four small children; Mario had no work, and the money from the watch and the ring had long been spent. His wife was pregnant again.

CHAPTER TWO

'Marriage à la mode'

THE days went by and the sun grew hotter and I saw the flowers begin to crumple and fade and the summer come back as I had known it. When there was no-one to talk to I would go to the edge of the sea and watch the moving surface; in the height of a Sicilian summer to be at the edge of the waves is as if one experienced for the first time in all one's life the coolness and glitter and the purity of water. All the magic of the element is fixed by contrast; behind is the pale soil, cracked and crumbling now, the vegetation dusty and rasping, then a tumble of white boulders and a strip of fine shingle. The shingle and the rocks are too hot for bare feet to touch. To be in the sea itself would be to lose the contrast.

Because as the season advanced we were forced into the shade and thus into greater privacy, I found my companions ever more ready to speak freely. It was like the Arabian nights; there were not a thousand and one, but if there had been they would not have become wearying, for I was learning more and more about human beings.

Buonaventura had his fingers broken by a tunny's tail, and retired to Castellammare, but Carlo had decided that I was to be trusted, and used to introduce me to his friends with that recommendation. The first time I met one of these, Enzo, he was warm with a litre of the dark sour Scopello wine, and told me much not only of himself but of several of his luckless fellow crewmen.

'Of course we are all criminals, Gavin,' he said cheerfully, 'how can you be a man and not be a criminal? It doesn't make you less *good* to be a criminal. Take Salvatore who you were talking to this after-noon—you wouldn't think he was a criminal, would you?'

Salvatore was a giant, a great hulk of flesh and muscle who, like half of the other members of the crew, could neither read nor write; his round unshaven face held a babyish innocence and friendliness.

'Well,' Enzo went on, 'it's not his fault that he's not a murderer—he just happens to be a bad shot. He couldn't kill his own son-in-law at five yards with five rounds.'

'Why did he want to?' I asked lazily. I had found that apparent uninterest was the best stimulus to loquacity.

'Well, it's a long story, and it's really about things an Englishman wouldn't understand. Do you know all about engagement and marriage in Sicily?'

'A bit, but tell me more.'

'You must be patient—it'll take time to explain, and you have to understand what made Salvatore angry before his story would make sense to you. This is the way we do it in Sicily.

'In each town marriage is part of a tradition—it's one of the most important events in human life, and it's a subject of most careful attention. But while the traditional function of the wedding remains almost the same from town to town, the details are different even between one village and another and not only different but often contradictory. There's a common root from which the different traditions of particular districts branch.

'In Sicily there's no fixed age at which you can marry, but there's the most usual age, which is almost always from 20 years upwards. In fact the majority of marriages are after the age of 21, because in Sicily a youth is absolutely under the thumb of his family up till that age. He achieves a certain independence after he's finished his military service, and not until then can he tell his parents he wants to get married. But by that time he's chosen his girl—a pretty girl and a good house-wife, religious, and above all who has never been in love with another man. Usually he's loved this girl for several years, without letting his parents know anything about it. These hidden engagements are called *ammucciuni*.

'We needn't go into details as to how a youth falls in love in Sicily and how tradition affects him—it's an interesting story but too long.

'The famous old Sicilian proverb says "Man is a hunter", and he's got to find his prey. In a Sicilian town the circumstances in which a youth falls in love are always the same; almost, you'd say, traditional. The most truly traditional of the ordinary circumstances is when the girls go to church. A girl very rarely appears alone on the street, not even when she goes to church; she's always accompanied by her mother or a younger sister, or by some older woman. The boys talk among themselves only of the physical attractions of the girls, but sooner or later a youth feels something more than this—he feels the need to see one of them again, to be able to look at her better; the need, really, to be in love with her.

'So the long story of the engagement begins—an engagement which in Sicily traditionally lasts between five and ten years. The youth will pass down the girl's street every evening as soon as he's finished his day's work, usually accompanied by some trusted friend, and hopes that his eyes will meet those of the girl he loves. When that happens he feels certain that the prey is almost his. Then he must make his own intentions known to the girl—there is still much work ahead.

'Every evening at the same time the girl will show herself, apparently indifferent, in front of her door or on her balcony; and he will pass by in his best clothes, and pass and repass until the girl's eyes can no longer make him out in the dark.

'Jealousy is deep rooted in Sicilian character, more especially in matters of love, and in fact the youth won't have many friends with him, for they too might look at his girl, and then you never know. He will go either alone or with one trusted friend, and he keeps an eye on him too, no matter how much he trusts him.

'Now he must make his love known to the girl. It's not an easy matter, and it's not possible without the help of neighbours, or a woman friend of the girl's, or, very often, of the parish priest. The youth in love is up against a hard struggle, and not without risk. He must cultivate the girl's neighbours and find out from them if there are other claimants, and if the girl has ever been touched by another man—and if she has the matter can go no further. He must propose to the girl—but how? Through whom? It's a story that goes on month after month, often for a year, until at last he's found a safe hand to carry a letter—probably not written by him—which always finishes with the words *ti vogghiu beniri* "I love you", and the great step has been taken.

'The reply comes after perhaps a month, after she's consulted with her friends and with the parish priest, and if the advice is favourable she too will end her letter *ti vogghiu beniri*.

'The two now love each other—in the evenings they look at one another and smile; every now and again they exchange letters, but always from a distance, for there are long years to be passed before he may approach his girl. They are secretly engaged; neither dares to say anything even to their own families, even though all the family knows all about it already—as a matter of fact the whole town often knows all about it, but the family's always got to make its weight felt, and quarrels and rebukes would begin.

'The years pass; the youth must do his military service, and when that time comes the boy can say to his father that he's in love and that before he goes away he must give the "word" to the girl's family. The "word" is a kind of permission that the youth's father asks of the girl's family—that they won't pledge her to anyone else while he's serving, and in return the youth's father promises that as soon as his son has finished his service he and his family will come and "ask the marriage". "Asking the marriage" means that the youth's parents ask from the girl's parents permission to marry their son to his daughter.

'Well, he finishes his military service and comes back to the town already of age; he takes up his work again, and first of all he fixes the "appointment" with the family of his fiancée—he fixes, that is, the day on which his family will go to the fiancée's family to "declare" the marriage.

'This declaring is a real traditional function. The youth's family invite their nearest relations to be present at the important happening that is taking place, and the girl's parents do the same. So on the appointed evening all the youth's intimate friends and his relations go together to the home of his fiancée; they walk in double file, the mother in front with her betrothed son. The fiancée is waiting before her door with her father. Greetings are exchanged, and the guests seat themselves in the positions assigned to them by custom. The two young people sit at the middle; at the youth's side is the girl's mother and at the girl's side the youth's mother, all outside the house, and all the other guests sit inside the house. The benedictions begin, thanking Heaven and the Saints, then good wishes to the betrothed couple, and so on. At last the long-awaited moment comes—the youth's mother gives a ring and many other presents to her son, and he, usually very embarrassed, places the ring on his fiancée's finger, and then gives her the other gifts. Then the girl does the same, and all the guests applaud by clapping their hands. The engagement is now official, and everyone celebrates it with wine.

'Now begins the period of official engagement, which will last from three to five years. The youth may go to his fiancée's house every evening, but he must sit at a distance from her—between him and her will be her mother and her grandmother and the rest of the family. They make small talk and joke, but always at a distance. Every Sunday and on days of *festa* the two families will go out together, the youth's mother with her future daughter-in-law, and the youth with his future mother-in-law, and behind them all the rest of the family, brothers, cousins and so on.

'During the time of the engagement the youth's working to get enough money for the wedding, and the girl works at home preparing her trousseau, all of which she customarily sews herself.

'After three or four years of official engagement it's sometimes, but not always, permitted to the couple to sit side by side, but never to kiss each other, or so much as to touch each other.

'Now they can begin to talk about marriage—the girl has almost finished her trousseau, and her fiancé has earned a fair sum working, and there's nothing left to do but to get the documents through and get married. When this decision has been taken another six months will go by before the wedding.

'And so here we are at the week before the wedding day. The two families fix between themselves the day on which the dowries of the engaged couple are to be shown to the public. Usually the girl's dowry is shown first. The families send invitations to all their friends and neighbours, and to their more distant acquaintances too, saying that on such and such days the dowries will be on show. Everyone comes to see the dowry, and everyone leaves some present at this show.

'The dowries are on show for three or four days, and on the last day they send for the priest to bless everything; the linen is put into the appropriate chests, and everything is carried to the house where the couple are going to live.

'The wedding day comes at last. The wedding's almost always in the morning. All the guests assemble at the house of the bride or the bridegroom, according to who's invited them, and wait for the couple to be ready. Then the bridegroom's mother, with her son at her side, and all her guests behind her, repair to the house of the bride. Here a change takes place—the bridegroom stands with his mother-in-law and the bride in front with her own father, and behind them in pairs follow the bridegroom's parents and relations and friends.

'A group of children dressed in white go in front of the bride, then a little girl carrying a bouquet of artificial orange blossoms which will

afterwards be given to an altar; and behind the bride there are sometimes unmarried girls, but that doesn't always happen.

'The long procession moves down the street until it reaches the
church, all the townspeople ranged along the street watching the
wonderful procession, and the girls look at the bride and dream.

'After the religious ceremony there are kisses in the church. Only
the women may kiss the bride and the men the bridegroom—there
are tears in the eyes of the young couple and of their parents.

'They leave the church again in double file, the bride and bridegroom arm in arm in front. All the guests go to the house of the
bridegroom, where there is a real feast. According to the family's
means they give the guests beer and sweets and so on. Sometimes
there's dancing too, but the unmarried girls can't dance or they would
have been "touched" by a man. The youths look at the women and
the girls, dreaming of a wedding like this one, and often they fall in
love because of it.

'After the feast there's a photograph taken, which will be jealously
preserved in their new home.

'To wait so many years for something that only takes place on one
day!

'Well, that's what ought to have happened with Salvatore's daughter
and son-in-law, but it didn't. I've told you all the stages of what
ought to happen so you can see what a shocking thing it is if someone
takes the law into his own hands and how angry the parents would
get if all this tradition was flouted—and of course it would mean
flouting the family itself, which you can't expect them to like.

'Salvatore only had one daughter, but she was very pretty. Such
eyes, such breasts, such a behind—she was really *bona*. That's a word
we use to mean very very attractive in a sexual sense. There'd been
two other daughters, but they'd died during a typhus epidemic years
ago, and there were two brothers who'd been in Giuliano's band—both
of them are in prison now. So the one daughter, Pietrina, was all
Salvatore had left, and he wanted her to make a good marriage.

'You know his son-in-law—he's the young chap in the crew who's
got a twisted hand, it doesn't bend properly. That's where his father-
in-law shot him; it was meant for the heart, but he's no good with a
gun, as I said.

'Three years ago this young man Andrea fell in love with Salvatore's
daughter. He went through the first stages in accordance with

tradition; he got his letter ending *ti vogghiu beniri*—she didn't write it herself because none of that family can read or write; she got it written by a *spicciafacende*[1]—but the marriage was never "declared". Salvatore just put his foot down and said no, and he wouldn't give way an inch. No-one really knew why, and it must have been because he wanted a richer son-in-law, for there was nothing much against Andrea. He could read and write and he had a job as a garage mechanic and he'd never been in trouble with the police, which is saying a lot here.

'But Salvatore made up all sorts of reasons, that he wasn't earning enough money, and that he went regularly to the brothel even while he was secretly engaged—and that was silly, because everyone goes to the *casino*, and more particularly while they're engaged, because then a man wouldn't be human if he could keep his mind off it. At last Salvatore found a real reason, and one that nobody could say was silly. He found out that forty years ago Andrea's great uncle had killed a member of Salvatore's family, and after that he had quite a lot of people on his side.

'Andrea had got to know a maiden aunt of the girl's while he was courting, and through her he begged and pleaded, but it was no use. Salvatore said if he saw Andrea looking at his daughter again he'd kill him. It was about then he got hold of a pistol.

'When Andrea understood that he was really up against it he decided to see how much the girl really loved him. He went to the aunt secretly and told her his plan, and he found her on his side, for old spinsters often have a soft spot for lovers. She was to carry a message asking whether the girl would run away with him. She did this, and when she came back she not only told him that the girl had agreed but she had even arranged the time. Andrea was to be in a *viccolo* (a narrow alley) near to the aunt's house at midnight three days later, and the girl would meet him with what possessions she could carry in a bundle.

'Andrea was overjoyed, and just at that moment it didn't seem to matter that he would have to leave his job and go into hiding. He approached a man we call Uncle Gaspare, who lives in Castellammare —he was once a rich man when Mussolini was in power, but now he's poor like everyone else, and he likes to help people; perhaps it makes him forget that he's not powerful any more. Uncle Gaspare had a little bit of land about six kilometres from the town, with a little two-

roomed house on it, and he said Andrea and his new wife could go
and live there out of sight until things quietened down, and he also
got hold of an old priest to marry them, and he lent them a mule to
get from the town to his property.

'Everything went exactly as planned, and four days later the two
were set up as man and wife in that little house. Andrea had been
saving money for a long time, and now he had enough to last them a
few weeks. After that he hoped he'd be able to come back, because
when a thing has actually happened the parents are sometimes prepared to forget it so as to avoid public scandal.

'But things didn't look like settling down at all. Salvatore went
on raging and shouting and swearing vengeance, and his family and
Andrea's family insulted each other with very bad words and there
was war between them.

'Andrea heard of all this, and he didn't know what to do. The
money was running short, and what was worse the girl began to fret
and to say she hadn't known she was going to be shut up there forever.
At last Andrea thought that if he could give her some present, something that women like, it might make all the difference.

'So he decided to go to Castellammare and buy her a bottle of scent.
He couldn't go openly in the day-time, but as you know, the shops
open in the small hours of the morning, so that the women can do their
shopping when there's no men about. He thought he could go in then
and buy the bottle and get out quick, and if anyone did happen to see
him in the town they wouldn't know where he'd gone afterwards.

'He left on foot about two in the morning, and he was at the top of
the hill above Castellammare when the sun came up over the Montelepre hills. You know the way the road comes down that hill in a series
of hairpin bends, and whenever the bend's to the right you can't see
round it. Well, he came down to just before the last bend without
seeing anyone. After that there's only a hundred yards of straight and
you're in the town.

'He came round that last corner, and there right in front of him was
Salvatore's brother, leaning on the wall and looking out over the
harbour. He turned his head at the sound of footsteps and he saw
Andrea and he took to his heels and away down the road like a frightened rabbit.

'Andrea knew that he had gone to fetch Salvatore, and he was in two
minds. One half of him wanted to go on and the other half wanted to

run away. He started back and then he felt ashamed of himself and turned round, but by that time he had the corner to go round all over again, and he could hear voices and footsteps beyond it.

'But he went round it, and there fifty paces below him were Salvatore and his brother, and Salvatore had a pistol in his hand and he was coming up the hill as fast as his fat would let him.

'Andrea's heart was thumping like a steam engine and the sweat was running down his legs, but he decided to walk right on just as if those two didn't exist. He went on down and they came up to meet him puffing like pregnant donkeys.

'There were only five paces between them when Salvatore upped with his pistol and started blazing away. The first four shots went God knows where, but the fifth hit Andrea in his left wrist. He screamed, and clutched it with the other hand, and the blood started spurting all over the place and spattered his white shirt, and he was waiting for the last bullet to finish him off, because now he could have touched Salvatore from where he stood.

'But do you know what Salvatore did? He dropped the pistol on the ground, yelling "Oh, my son, my son, what have I done to you?" and he threw his arms round Andrea and started kissing him on the cheeks and begging forgiveness. "Forgive me, forgive me," he blubbered, "you come of a fisherman's family like mine, and all we fishermen have big hearts, big hearts for forgiveness! Forgive me as I forgive you—and marry my daughter with my blessing! Oh, my poor son, my poor son!" And the brother started kissing him too, and all three of them were covered with blood and tears like three babies.

'And it's true, Salvatore *has* a big heart, and he's a good man even if he can't read or write, but you see it wasn't his fault that he didn't kill his son-in-law, and then he'd have been a murderer and spent all his life in jug.

'And now, Gavin, I think I deserve a cigarette.'

The sun was beginning to go down behind Cap St. Vito, and the jackdaws were chattering to themselves as they settled down to roost among the prickly pears on the *faraglioni*. An Egyptian vulture came sailing by, his evil yellow head glancing rapidly from side to side. Enzo threw a stone at it and missed only by inches, though it was thirty yards away. 'Vulture,' he said. 'In the mountains, when there's trouble, the *sbirri* police, watch them and the ravens. They see

them gathered together in the air, and they know there's an unburied
'body.'

I took advantage of Enzo's loquacity. 'Enzo,' I said, 'Rosario walks
with a limp. Once I asked him why, and he said he had corns, but
today he wasn't wearing shoes, and he's got a big scar like a bullet
wound right in the top of his foot. How did he get it?'

'You are very inquisitive, Gavin, but all the same I think you are
our friend, so I will tell you. He wouldn't tell you himself, so you
must not betray me. He is a fool, is Rosario, or he would never have
got that wound. He's not so bad—he's always making jokes or pulling
someone's leg, but he's not intelligent. So he gets himself shot in the
foot and he's got corns for the rest of his life.

'He's poor, very poor. It's true he's not married, although he's
thirty-four, but he likes to smoke, and he never has work except in the
spring when he's here at the *tonnara*. So last year when he had no money
at all he and a cousin of his got together and they thought how they
might make a bit. There's an old couple who live about four kilometres from here; they're both more than seventy years old and they
live all alone—they've got a little house and a vineyard that's bigger
than most hereabouts. They hadn't got much money, but they'd got
some old family silver that they kept in a chest in their bedroom.
Rosario had heard about it because his uncle had worked in the vineyard the year before and had seen it himself. Well, you'd think that
was a sitting target if ever there was one. And he had to get a bullet
through the foot!

'It was like this. Rosario and his cousin had it all worked out how
they would get into the house and into the bedroom, very quietly
when the two old people were sleeping, and Rosario would open the
chest while his cousin stood guard covering the bed with a sub-
machine-gun. The chest, you understand, was near the door of the
room, at the opposite end from the bed.

'Well, when they got into the room they could hear the old man
snoring away quite peacefully and his wife breathing deeply beside
him. The chest was standing just inside the door, under the window,
and Rosario started to work on it at once, while his cousin stood
between him and the bed, covering it with a sub-machine-gun. That
cretin Rosario had hardly got started before he dropped something
on the floor with a clatter. The old man woke up, and in less time
than it takes to tell he'd struck a match and had the candle lit beside the

bed. He sat up in bed in his nightgown and nightcap, peering across the room to see what was going on.

' "Don't move!" said Rosario's cousin "keep your hands in front of you and don't move, or you're a dead man!"—but he was trembling all over, because it was the first time he'd ever done anything like this.

'The old boy was a tough one, right enough. He sat staring from behind a moustache like a *disa* broom for a moment or two, while Rosario went on fiddling with the chest, and then cool as you please he bent out of the bed and picked up a slipper and threw it as hard as he could at Rosario's cousin, who had just half turned his head to speak to Rosario.

'The shoe caught him fair in the face and spun him half round towards Rosario, and as he staggered he tightened his finger on the trigger and the gun started going like a motor-bike. There was a yell from Rosario and there he was hopping about on one foot and clutching the other in his hands and bawling like a stuck pig. His cousin took to his heels, and Rosario flopped down on the floor and nursed his foot and started crying like a baby.

'The old man was laughing fit to bust. He and his wife bound up Rosario's foot and gave him a lot of wine to make the pain less, and then their labourer, who'd waited long enough after the shooting to feel safe in coming to the house, set off to get the *carabinieri*.

'That's how Rosario got his corns. The old couple pleaded for him in court and because of that he only got four months, although he had been inside twice before. Corns!'

The following week, by a curious coincidence, Rosario's cousin was in the news again. He was found shot through the stomach on the road near to Scopello di Sopra. He was conscious but in great pain; he said he'd been shot by an unknown man whom he'd never seen before. But he broke down under questioning by the *carabinieri*, and told quite a different story. He'd been carrying a pistol to impress his girl-friend in Castellammare, and he had been on his way to meet her there. Caution, however, had over-ruled his instinct for *panache*, and, frightened of being searched by the police, he had decided to unload the pistol and to hide it before reaching the town. While trying to unload it he had shot himself through the stomach. After the first minutes of shock he'd realised that he might escape the penalty for carrying unlicensed firearms if he claimed an unknown assailant, so he had thrown the pistol into the heart of a prickly-pear bush near where he lay.

'Mad,' summed up Enzo, 'absolutely mad. First he shoots poor Rosario through the foot and then he shoots himself in the stomach— it's not prison he needs, it's the madhouse.'

CHAPTER THREE

Bus from Scopello

IT is only two years since the bus came to Scopello di Sopra; before that anyone who wished to buy provisions or clothing had to walk the four twisting miles to the main Trapani-Castellammare road to get a bus. But the advent of public transport came too late; the doors and windows of the greater part of the houses are bolted and shuttered, the faded paint crackling and peeling from the woodwork under the grill of the summer sun. Here and in Castellammare there are houses that have stood empty and untended for half a century or more; their anomaly in this densely populated island where housing is a perennial problem is at first sight striking. They have, however, as great a human significance as any home enclosing a swarming vociferous Sicilian family, for they are anchors. Their owners, long since emi-grated to the United States, to Brazil, to Canada or Australia, would no more think of selling them than of selling their identities. However prosperous these families may be in the countries of their adoption, some *disgrazia* may overtake them and make it necessary to return to Sicily, and then how would they fare without a home? Or when the parents are old and their children, no longer identifiable with the naked urchins who played and scuffled and defecated in the dust of the little *piazza*, have ripened in the forcing houses of the great cities of the New World into the sleek maturity of swell apartments and convertibles, forsaking their native language and calling their own children 'junior', the pioneers may weary for the sights and sounds of their own childhood, and come home to die within sight of the shrines of saints and madonnas, in an atmosphere where respect and envy for their superior status in this world is pleasantly combined with a reassuring faith in their qualifications for the next. These empty shells of houses are at once sanctuary and temple, extending beyond the practicalities of life into a world of superstitious spiritual comfort, into resurrection itself. *O Madonna, Santa Madonna, madre di Gesu Cristo e di tutto il mondo, ho tornato qua per morire nell'ombra della sua santissima mano!*

In the shadow of the archway to the great courtyard that had once been the country establishment of a wealthy judge, I sat on a stone block waiting for the bus. The exact times of arrival were arbitrary and erratic, and I had arrived very early, perhaps nearly an hour too soon.

For a while I glanced idly through the pages of the illustrated paper whose pictures of the Vatican had so outraged Carlo, and of the *Giornale di Sicilia*, and was struck afresh by the strange form of advertisements inserted by those seeking employment. In the place of such expressions as 'excellent references', such as are familiar in English newspapers, there was the recurrent phrase 'can read and write', and 'no criminal record'.

In the illustrated paper some popular product was running a series of advertisements which dealt with what behaviour was good etiquette. The current photograph showed two men seated at opposite sides of a café table; one of them was leaning forward with an expression of eager brashness and the other was looking acutely uncomfortable. The legend ran 'Is it etiquette to ask a man what his politics are? *No*, it is *not* etiquette; it might cause him the greatest embarrassment, especially in a public place.' But the ad-man had not, apparently, thought that this truth might cause any embarrassment to the Christian Democrat Government, and apparently it does not.

At length my eye was caught by half a column in *Giornale di Sicilia* which seemed to me to epitomize Sicily. It read:

CARETAKER OPPOSES ENTRANCE OF STRANGERS

Insults and stone-throwing and three persons actually shot—Four wounded and many arrested

Yesterday afternoon about 6.30 a party composed of men, women and children penetrated to the side of the cliff at the Transport Aerodrome of Addoura, near Mondello, with the obvious idea of having a bathe in peace and quiet, not knowing, or pretending not to know, that in that area there is no admittance for the purpose.

The sound of children's voices at once attracted the attention of the caretaker of the airfield, who, amazed to see these intruders, at once asked them with courtesy to retrace their footsteps. From this started an argument, which, owing to the behaviour of these unexpected guests, assumed a lively tone. But the caretaker would not allow himself to be influenced, and, faithful to his duty, firmly repeated his request to leave the airfield. At length the party understood that there was nothing to be done, and retired; not, however, without insulting the caretaker, who, regretfully and for the sake of peace, did not reply in kind.

That seemed to be the end of that, but in fact it was only the beginning. The menfolk in charge of the party had misunderstood; they were convinced that they were only required to leave because they had entered from the sea side rather than by way of the normal entrance gate. So they made a half circuit of the field and reached the gate, where, finding it shut, they began to make a terrific din shaking the bars.

The caretaker was a short way off, with his niece near to him. Considering that as far as he was concerned he wouldn't dream of opening the gate no matter how much these violent men battered against it, he let them carry on for a bit. They would get tired of it, and clear off, he thought. But all of a sudden the members of this adventurous excursion began to hurl even more furious insults at the caretaker. And they did not stop at that: they began to throw stones at him, ignoring the fact that there was a woman close to their target. One of the many stones struck her on the shoulder. So the caretaker ran to fetch an old gun that could only fire one barrel, the hammer of the other being broken, and returned to the stone-throwing group. The caretaker fired a shot into the ground, meaning only to frighten these inconsiderate men. It had, however, the opposite effect; they only intensified their shower of stones, insisting on their right to enter the field. A heavy stone hit the head of the caretaker's wife, who had come out to see what was going on and was standing at her husband's side. The poor woman fell to the ground with a shriek of pain, and blood began to flow copiously from her head.

At this her husband momentarily lost control of himself, and rushed to the room where the rifles of the members of the shooting club were arranged in storage; thence he emerged with an efficient weapon and let fly two rounds, still in the direction of the ground. As fate would have it several bits of lead, ricocheting, hit a woman in the heel and two children in the legs. The group now disbanded, and the woman and the two wounded little ones were taken shortly afterwards to the first-aid post of the establishment, where the medical officer of the guard examined their bullet wounds, pronouncing them curable in some ten days s.c. [*senza complicazione*—without complications].

The *carabinieri* of the Mondello police station hastened to effect the arrest of some of the group, while others took to their heels. The caretaker, too, was arrested. His wife was taken to the first-aid post, where she was treated and pronounced curable in seven days s.c.

Praise the Lord and pass the ammunition, I thought, and I composed myself to wait for the bus. Before me was the ruggedly paved open

Scopello tonnara

The outlying *tonnara* buildings under the Saracen tower,
where the author and a few of the crew lived

space with the drinking trough at its centre, twin jets of brilliant
water spouting into the stone basin, the sound cool as cave music under
the blind heat of the sun. This intense heat intrudes like a disturbing
noise into the small peaceful sounds of the still landscape, the trill of
the flowing water, the ruminative but querulous notes of the hens as
they scratch in the loose dust, the choked bellows-braying of a distant
donkey. Somewhere down the path to the *tonnara* a light tenor voice,
replete with mimicry of every trick of the grand opera, sang a ribald
Sicilian parody of La Donna è Mobile.

> La donna è mobile
> In letto stava
> Con dito police
> Se le minava.
>
> Viene il marito
> Povero e pazzu
> Gli leva il dito
> mette il gazzu
>
> In questa notte
> Naque un papazzu
> Chi si a chiamatu
> Testa di gazzu.

The grossness of the words is swallowed in the joyous carefree voice;
all that is crude and violent in Sicily seems not intrinsically ugly but
only vivid threads in an all enveloping mantle of sensuous colour.

Beyond, the mountain ridges rose pale and chalky against a hard
empty sky. A mare and her leggy mule foal came to drink at the
trough; the mare drank delicately from the spout itself, letting the
clear water play on her tongue and palate before plunging her muzzle
deep into the basin; the foal whinnied into the water, blew a cloud of
spray into his mother's face, pranced precariously on splayed legs, and
suddenly sought the udder. Next came a diminutive grey mule
dragging a cart-load of brushwood the size of a house; on the very top
of this structure, some fifteen feet from the ground, sat a hunched,
beaky figure like some fabulous bird brooding on a giant nest of sticks.
The donkey drank long and deep while the bird figure at the summit
remained utterly immobile. I had hoped that he too would be thirsty;
the descent, for a flightless bird, seemed to present insuperable problems,

and I was curious to know how he would compass it, but he remained
apparently unaware of his surroundings and the whole grotesque
ensemble moved off without so much as a flick of the twenty-foot
reins.

The next visitor to the *fontana* was a girl of about eleven, carrying
in her right hand a large black hen swung by the legs. She ran purpose-
fully, gleefully, across the uneven paving, scattering the squawking
poultry with her bare brown feet. At the edge of the fountain she
held the hen aloft as though for some ritual sacrifice, then plunged it
deep under water. After some seconds bubbles began to break the
re-forming glass of the surface; she peered down at her victim intently,
her delicate lips parted in eager anticipation. Suddenly she whisked
the dripping fowl from the water, held it at the level of her face, and
addressed it in an undertone of rapid Sicilian. The bird looked neither
moribund nor much afraid; it appeared reduced to a fraction of its
former size, and wore an expression of outraged surprise. Three times
the ritual was repeated, then the girl scampered back across the yard,
still swinging the draggled bundle of feathers by its yellow legs, and
calling to an unseen ancestor '*L'hu fatu, nonna, l'hu fatu!*'

For a moment I thought I had witnessed the preparation of some
evil magic; in the dusk of a windowless room where the sun shone
white on the walls outside some shawled and toothless hag would
slash at the sodden feathers of the throat, rip the belly of the still
twitching carcase and mumble over the omens of the displayed
viscera. Omens for the girl's marriage, perhaps, or for her initiation
into stranger mysteries. I allowed the fantasy more rein; this, surely,
was the key to the riddle of the desolate and almost deserted village:
one by one the families had fallen prey to the witches coven at its core
and driven by fear or by dark spells had taken refuge in far countries.
The priest was powerless. In face of a force whose rituals were ancient
before his own were formulated, he closed his eyes to the image of the
dusty and cob-webbed confessional, he no longer preached from the
pulpit to the empty pews. Once in his own vestry he had found . . .

'You know what the girl was doing with the hen?'

A very old man had sat down upon a stone block at the other side
of the archway, and was trying to light a cigarette stub without setting
fire to his voluminous moustache. The whole withered skin of his
face was pitted deep with the old scars of smallpox.

'No,' I said, 'I found it very strange.'

'So I saw. One can tell from your face what passes in your head; that is rare in foreigners, I have found. There were many here in Sicily at the time of the war, Americans, Germans, English, Italians from the north . . . I never knew what they were thinking, except when they wanted ordinary things, food, wine, a woman or a boy. And mostly they took what they wanted. We are a poor people. It is not right that there should be so much poverty and misery. Me, I own nothing, nothing—not even this,' he touched a spade leaning against the wall beside him, 'is mine. I use it for others, but it is not mine. Nothing is mine except,' he paused and spat, 'these clothes, which belonged to my dead brother, may Our Lady protect him. But you wanted to know about the hen. She wished to hatch her eggs, and so she wouldn't lay any more. The treatment with the water shows her that this would be imprudent.' The cigarette burned his moustache and he spat the stub to the ground. He rose slowly and shouldered the spade. '*Ai, ai* . . .' he said vaguely, '*arrivederci.*'

After he had gone the little *piazza* was empty for a few minutes. Now I had a vivid picture of the wet hen pondering her imprudence. Every two or three minutes, with a roar and a swoosh and a flash of silver, low-flying aircraft streaked by overhead, an annual race round the airfields of Sicily. Presently there was a light click of hooves, and a small jackass entered the square, ridden side-saddle by a lanky young man with a red bandanna twisted round his head. At his heels, which dangled to within an inch or two of the ground, followed some half-dozen small children. One of them trailed a tortoise from a string attached to its hind leg. The man dismounted and drank while the donkey drank, then he looked round him carefully as though searching for something. Finally he led the donkey to a corner of the *piazza* where some heavy square blocks of building stone had been dumped in such a way as to form a kind of raised platform two or three feet above the cobbles. Onto this platform, by coaxing and pushing, he raised the donkey. When at last the animal stood squarely but apathetically upon it, he passed a length of rope through the halter so that some three yards hung loose on either side of the head. One end he drew tight round the branch of a fig tree; then he looked round for something to fasten the other to. Finally his eye lit on me where I sat in the shadow of the arch.

'Will you hold the other rope for me?'

I went across to him. 'Certainly. But what are you doing?'

He grinned. 'We are going to make a mule. The mare should be here any minute now. Here she comes . . .'

Round the corner of the road came a compact chestnut mare, led by a child and followed by more children. The first group of children, who had arrived with the donkey, set up an excited piping:

'She's here! She's arrived! We are going to make a mule!'

Other children came running from nowhere; the old man came out from among the houses and leant on his spade. Soon there was quite a little crowd, chattering in pleased anticipation. The mare was transferred from the child to a man, and her crupper reversed to the edge of the platform. The jackass plunged and reared; gasps of envy and admiration came from the small spectators. Overhead the silver aircraft tore past unheeded, the children had eyes only for the ass and his willing helpers; they could never become aviators.

When it was over they led the mare away and I tossed my end of rope to the young man with the red bandanna. Suddenly from among the children a voice spoke shrill with indignation and disappointment:

'*Only once!* But *I* can . . .'

The donkey's owner stopped and aimed a pebble at the boy's bare shins.

'*Non vantare! È adulto e tu sei un sicchareddu senza spachimi!*'

The audience began to drift away in little groups, discussing the performance in an animated way reminiscent of a film première audience emerging from the foyer. I returned to my seat under the arch. The donkey, his brief moment of glory and significance over, was unthroned from his little stone dais and led to share the shadow of the archway; his owner, breathless and complacent as though he had himself played the major rôle, slumped down on the block where the old man with the spade sat, and asked for a cigarette. In front of us the child with the tortoise squatted in the dust and employed all his ingenuity to get the best from this promising but unrewarding toy. It took all of two minutes for the tortoise to extrude a withered and wary head, another half minute before the legs began their ponderous and pathetic efforts at escape. When it had walked to the limit of the string the child became puzzled, to allow it to go on would be monotonous, to pull it back by the string would mean another patient wait while, hidden by the shell, the hooded head slowly built up enough confidence for further excursion. The tortoise's potential for brisk entertainment was low; I didn't know whether I felt sorrier for it or the child.

'There should be two of them,' remarked the young man beside me, 'for a race. With obstacles.'

'Where did he get it?'

'Up there by the tower.' He pointed to the crumbling pinnacle with the ruined watch tower at its summit. 'They are everywhere in the mountains. Not on the cultivated ground, only in the mountains. . . . You are English? There are plenty of tortoises in England?'

'Yes, English. No, no tortoises.'

'*No tortoises?* It isn't possible! You *must* have tortoises. . . . What wild animals are there in England? Many lizards?'

'Very few. But,' I added defensively, 'we have many other animals —rabbits, hares, foxes, deer, seals.' I could not think of the Italian for badgers, otters and other impressive additions, and found the list petering out thinly.

'No porcupines?' he cut in sharply.

'No, no porcupines or tortoises.'

His eyes flashed. '*No porcupines or tortoises! Ei, Giacomo! Viene qua!*'

A sad-looking middle-aged peasant who had been watering his horse at the fountain came wearily across to us. 'Giacomo, this Englishman says that in his country there are rabbits, hares, foxes, deer, and seals, *but no tortoises or porcupines!*' The speaker seemed outraged besides astonished; then he turned to me as one who reasons patiently with a child. 'Listen—there are neither tortoises nor porcupines in Palermo; as I told you they live only in the mountains. So I think you will find that there are no tortoises and no porcupines in London, but plenty in the English mountains. You should look. Both are very good to eat, and besides that tortoises are very good for medicine—often the doctor prescribes a drink of raw tortoise blood.'

I was saved further protestations by the long-delayed arrival of the bus. It rolled ponderously into the little square, very new and vast, shining with chromium, and trailing expanding cumulus-shaped clouds of white dust behind it. It looked grotesquely out of place in its surroundings, as anomalous as a television aerial would have appeared above one of the little houses cowering under the sun and the pale mountains. As befitted its modernity, it was treated with the reverence due to a temple. The three passengers, none of whom was bound for Scopello, had to dismount, as transit passengers must dismount from an aircraft at airfields short of their destination, and no passenger might board the bus during the length of its regulation ten-minute halt. The driver went to the fountain and drank and sluiced his face, and presently he was deep in conversation with the owner of the donkey. I caught a word here and there '. . . tortoises . . . Englishman . . . porcupines . . . English mountains . . .' The bus conductor swept out the floor of the bus religiously; when the broom reached the doorway it pushed nothing in front of it but a single blade of straw and a spent match. When the ten minutes were up the passengers were allowed to re-enter, but most of them did so by the wrong door and were turned out again. There was a door at the front and a door at the back; the one at the front, the conductor explained reverently, was for passengers entering, that at the rear for passengers dismounting. Although they were actually inside the bus when their mistake was discovered, they climbed down again and trooped round to the front.

At last the whole ritual was complete, the driver slammed his door, started the engine, and ground into gear. Below me, as I sat at the window, was the red bandanna and shiny black hair of the donkey owner. As the bus swung forward to turn, his face lifted to me for the last word no Sicilian can resist.

'In Sardegna there are tortoises so big that a man can ride on their backs, and they live for hundreds of years!'

The bus surged on, stopped, reversed, and came by him again. I crossed to the other side and called down to him through the open window:

'Then why bother to make mules?'

My last sight of him was the laughing mouth, the white teeth in the brown face and the shine of his dark eyes as he guffawed helplessly. '*Bravo!*' he called, as the retreating bus jolted out of the *piazza*, '*Bravissimo!*'

The bus had only travelled a few hundred yards over the villainous little winding road from Scopello when it was brought to a halt by a yell from the conductor, '*Ei, ferma, ferma*—what's all this meat?' The driver hauled the bus to a standstill and looked wearily over his shoulder. 'What meat?' he asked. The conductor lifted a huge blood-stained paper parcel. 'All this meat,' he repeated helplessly. '*Cretino!*' replied the driver with greatest good humour. '*San Giuseppe cornuto*, is it my job to look after the parcels? *Mamma mia!* It is the meat for Signor Ponte at the *tonnara*. Perhaps you would like me to turn the

bus and drive back? or perhaps you'd prefer me to get out and walk
back with it? . . .' He shrugged his shoulders and lit a cigarette.
Between puffs he went on, 'Well . . . you must find someone to take it
back. What are you going to do about it? Mother of God, have you
no eyes in your head . . .?' The conductor's eyes ranged vaguely
round the horizon. Far down the slope towards the sea they came to
rest on a little group of cattle whose deep-toned bells thudded lazily
in the shade of an olive tree. The conductor dismounted nimbly.
Cupping his hands he bellowed at the full pitch of his lungs, 'Ne-
e-e-e-e-nè!' (In Sicily all names are called like this, a long dying
fall to the last syllable.)

A small figure detached itself from the dappled shadows and began
to plod wearily up the hill. Five minutes later the boy stood by the
bus door, clutching, somewhat rebelliously, the bloody packet of meat.
'He eats meat every day, that man,' was all he said by way of comment
on the situation. The conductor turned to me: 'Give Nenè an English
cigarette for his trouble, Signor?'

Who, I wondered, was Nenè, this smallest and most insignificant
figure in a landscape with figures?

'Hey! . . . hey! But you're writing—what are you writing? You
mustn't write down what I'm saying to you—no! If you want me to
go on you must save that pen and paper—who knows what you want
to do with what I'm telling you?[1]

'I'm telling you certain things because it's a relief, and because it's
so nice to when one can confide things in someone who won't go and
betray you in the town.

'I am poor[2] . . . what harm is there in being poor; there are rich and
there are poor, and I am poor because God wants it that way. He wants
it that way.[3] I was born on the . . . on the [Nenè bit his fingertip]
15th of January, 1945. They say there'd been a war; the great war,
but I didn't think about it at that time. My father went to the war, he
went . . . he went to Africa—God it was hot[4] and to quench their thirst
they used to drink their own urine.[5]

'I am the youngest of two brothers, but there are two sisters younger
than me, Mariannina and Rosa, who at home is called Rusidduzza,
and she's always ill and cries the whole time, and she never gets better!

'In my family[6] only the men work, as the women must stay at home
and do the domestic chores and take care of the hens. There are three
of us who work, myself, my father, and my brother Arasimu [Erasmo],

but we're poor[7] all the same, because they don't give us much money, and it's not enough for my mother, who keeps it at home.

'We[8] live almost always in the country—you never see us in the town except in the winter. In the country the women must work too, even if it's not the same kind of work as the men! My mother gets up in the morning at six, opens the windows, puts out the hens, and then makes us get up. It's cold in the morning in the country, and we hate getting up[9]. We sleep three in one bed, myself, my brother Arasimu, and my sister Mariannina who is sixteen, and when it's very cold we wouldn't want to get up ever![10] In the morning before dawn[11] my father and my brother Arasimu go to dig. To my father they give 600 lire a day, and he digs until the evening when the dusk comes, and to my brother they give 500 lire, because he is nineteen and will earn more when he does his military service,[12] as is usual in this town. I can't go to dig, because I'm not good at it and I'm a little unwell—I have weak kidneys[13] and I wet my pants sometimes.

'I'm a cowherd[14] at Don Paolo's, my employer—he's rich and he's got a lot of cows. I have to stay with the cows in the mountains from the morning till the evening, taking them to graze and milking them in the evening, and do you know how much Don Paolo gives me a week? 1,050 lire. He says that's 250 lire a day. In the winter Don Paolo takes the cows to the town, and there he gives them hay, and no more grass, and I stay unemployed, and become a carrier on the roads, at the service of everybody, and I eat dried figs and locust beans[15] to satisfy my hunger, like the animals. There are plenty of cowherds hereabouts, but some of them own their animals—not like me. My brother envies me because he goes to dig, and I only have to take the cows to pasture. But do you understand, really?—do you understand that it's also hard work to look after[16] animals, which don't reason? Look, look here [showing me his forehead] here I got a kick from a cow, a kick that needed three stitches. And look here [showing me his scarred hands] here I got a bite from a calf while I was giving it grass.

'They don't give me anything to eat in the mornings; my mother gives the bread to my brother Arasimu and to my father, who go to dig, while I go—to take a stroll with the animals. And every morning it's cold, even in the summer, and I have to go to Monte Rozzu and then to Monte Casteddu, to cut grass for hay and to guide the cows, and there's hunger, hunger, so that if it wasn't that sometimes I put a cow's teat in my mouth[17] I should be quite empty.

'Yes, I do as a little calf does, I take the teat and suck it, and the milk comes out. In the evening I leave the cows at Sugareddi, and when Don Paolo isn't in the *campagna* I go home—always in the country— as our house is outside the town. Now that it's summer my mother makes us *pasta* there almost every evening, *pasta* with *smuzzatura* [wild cauliflower chopped up with its leaves; when in seed it is called "*sparaceddu*"] and *tinniruma* [boiled water-melon shoots], and with tomatoes that my father or my brother scrounge from the tomato beds.[18] The table we eat at is small, and my mother and father and two sisters eat at it, while I and my brother Arasimu eat on the ground. My father and mother eat together from the "*spillongu*" [a large plate of oval shape, usually of china, or of aluminium or clay] and my father takes the *pasta* from the centre and my mother from the sides, and they mustn't turn up their noses[19] at eating from a single plate, because when a man and a woman are married they have to sleep together, eat to- gether; yes, even sleep in one bed—you too if you marry will have to eat with your wife and sleep with her in one bed. In bed they make children,[20] but it isn't true what they tell babies, that God sends sons from heaven—they're made in bed.

'Just now when I'm hungry in the country I eat grapes[21] and prickly pears[22] as now it's summer, but when the owner of some *campagna* sees me he boxes my ears and reports me to the *carabiniere*.

'We don't see butcher's meat[23] ever, as it's dear, and is for the rich. On feast days we eat the flesh of hens, of rabbits, and of kids, which is also good, but it is the meat of the poor.

'And that's the life I lead,[24] which would be fine if it lasted all the year round or if there was more to earn, because as far as I'm concerned I love the country.

'While the animals graze I pass the time playing my flute and singing, lying in the shade of a rock or a tree. All the herd boys like me have flutes—we make them ourselves out of thick bamboo stems and when we make a good one we keep it for ever. I can do bird-songs on my flute, too, and you can have a wonderful time doing that, getting the birds to answer you one after another. I play herd songs[25] a lot of the time, and when I meet another herdboy we play part songs.[26] I can sing hundreds of verses of songs—I love them—and I've learnt dozens and dozens from other herdboys I've met in the mountains. The songs go on for ever, and there's as many verses as grains of sand on the seashore.[27] One learns more every day and makes up more every day

—I could sing right through the night until dawn without repeating a verse twice.

'The songs are beautiful, but a lot of them are pretty dirty—if I'm singing in the evening when there's a lot of *contadini* coming home from work and they hear me singing those ones they tell my father and he tells me off. This one starts off all right:

> Turn to me my lovely one and hear me sing
> For my voice will touch your heart.
>
> When you were born a rose was born
> Whose perfume reached to my very home.
>
> Your eyes are like two burning torches
> And when you look at me I turn to fire.
>
> I looked to heaven and saw the stars,
> You too my love are a star to me.
>
> Your eyes are like two lanterns
> That light the darkness of a cave.
>
> If I thought that with me you too would cry with pain
> I would not want to marry you.
>
> My love, my love, what have you done to me—
> My beautiful one, you would betray me.
>
> Blossom of velvet blossoms
> Love unreturned is time lost forever.
>
> Do not leave me
> Or I shall kill myself
> You know that for you
> I am driven to madness.

'But then the lover gets angry at being left, and after a bit he's singing very dirty words. First he sings:

> Before I loved you I loved a hundred others—
> You only passed the time for me.[28]

[Beyond this point the verses are unprintable in English; I have left them in Sicilian in the appendix.]

'Then there's songs you sing in alternate verses with someone you can hear but most times can't see. These are called *botta e risposta*. We herds don't often meet each other in the mountains—each of us takes his animals to different places because there's not enough grass to go round, but we can play games together even if we're far apart. You hear the voice of another herd singing far away and you wait for the right moment and answer him. If he hears you start up alternate verses[29] like this:

I sing: Who are you that's singing up there?
You sound like a yapping puppy.

and he answers: And who are you wailing away down there?
You sound as if you had toothache in every tooth.

I: You know nothing about singing—
You'd better go and learn at school in Palermo.

He: You say I don't know how to sing—
You'd better go to school at Monreale.

I: Don't you come round here again—
Everyone says you're a cretin.

He: It's you that's got to quit this valley—
Everyone knows about you.

I: When you were born behind my door
I thought you were a still-born bitch-pup.

He: When you were born in the middle of my street
There was an awful stink of dung.

[Gradually these verses too become increasingly obscene, until they end in a perfect orgy of sexual abuse and sexual boasting. Nenè quoted twenty-seven verses, all of which I have preserved in the appendix.[30] He went on:]

'But that would be too short for a real *botta e risposta*; I've left out a hundred verses in the middle. If one of us stopped as soon as that the other would think he'd had an accident. Sometimes I've sung a

botta for the whole night—one's voice sounds better at night. We
don't take offence at what we sing to each other—if we did we wouldn't
sing them, or else we'd go and beat each other up. If you're clever
enough you can invent new verses, but you have to make them rhyme
properly.

'But to work in this way is terrible, and surely not even dogs ought
to lead this life.

'I suppose my trouble is[31] that I'm not educated; I don't know how
to read or write, and perhaps that's why everybody takes advantage
of me. In my family only my brother Arasimu knows how to write
and read, and now my sister Mariannina a bit, because she's done evening school. My brother Arasimu is the big shot[32] of the family, and
feels himself quite the gentleman. They won't send me to school,
because I went to the *campagna* when I was six[33] and began work
washing dishes for Don Paolo's men, and pasturing the cattle. I wanted
to go to school, but my father told me that only women went to school,
that men must work, and I didn't understand because I was small, and
I was happy. But now I see my friends who know how to write, and
they call me fat-head[34] and donkey-calf[35]. When they play at betting
or something, four or five of us boys, it's always me who has to pay.
As you know, we sit in a circle, and one of us says a ditty composed
of each part of a word—that is, a part of a word for each of us in turn:

> Little donkey
> of my school
> you are him
> and the straw
> of my donkey
> you eat it
> all of it, you.[36]

And the 'you' is always me, because they're in league, and I get red
in the face and have to put up with it.

'I know[37] how to write my signature—Don Paolo taught me, as
he's fond of me a little. One starts like this—I do it for practice, and
not like someone who knows how to write. First one begins with
the letter C, which Don Paolo told me is like half an egg, and then . . .
then . . . and this is my christian name—the name begins with the letter
N, it's like two spades propped up, and then the E, which is a little
egg with two feet, like this (shows). You do this twice, and it makes

Nenè (etc.). I know some Italian words, because Don Paolo taught me them—it's true that Don Paolo pays me little, but he's fond of me because, . . . because[38] he's fond of me.

'Don Paolo isn't married, and he's rich, and everyone says he's a queer, but it's not true. He says he hasn't got much time for women; it doesn't mean much to him[39]—but better leave these things alone, things one doesn't talk about[40].

'I . . . I . . . really . . . no, it's not right . . . no, I shall go to hell if I talk to you about these things . . . I . . . I swore to Don Paolo and to the priest, and the priest told me that I mustn't tell these things to anyone, on pain of hell.[41] Don Paolo . . . Don Paolo . . . but you truly won't say anything to anyone? Nothing, please, because I should become despised by everyone in the town, and Don Paolo too. Please; if not . . . because . . . because Don Paolo's fond of me . . . One day when I was ten and I was at the farm where I used to wash dishes, Don Paolo was in the cowshed and he called me, and—a thing he'd never made me do—he made me milk the cows. I was pleased, because at that time the only person there who was allowed to milk the cows was Zu Aspanu. And then Don Paolo . . . [follows a description of his seduction by Don Paolo]. Then I began to understand, because one does understand these things by oneself—and Don Paolo told me some things too. If Don Paolo hadn't told me I'd have known just the same, because we boys talk among ourselves the whole time.

'I've been with Don Paolo five years now, and I still sleep with him sometimes, but in the summer because in the town in the winter it's dangerous.

'But Don Paolo spends the nights with Maria, who is married to Mastro Pietrinu, and lives in Via Roma. And I know that men can't stay with women, because they have a furnace there, lit, and we burn ourselves. I've seen the furnace too . . . because I saw my sister Mariannina. Once I saw her in the cowshed with my brother Erasmo, and she was stretched out on the straw and he was lying on top of her. And they saw me, and they told me not to talk, and Erasmo said that if I talked he'd kill me. But brothers and sisters oughtn't to do these things between each other! And then in the evening my sister Mariannina said to me that if I didn't talk she'd let me do the same and she took me to the cowshed and took off her clothes and then I saw it.[42] But I didn't do anything with her—because one doesn't do those things with one's sister, or God punishes you afterwards.

'I can't go to the brothel yet because I'm too young, and I (masturbate); I do it every day, but I'm frightened of doing it because you get illnesses that way—you go soft in the head and die, like Signora Rosaria's son.

'But when we play that kind of game it's always me who wins. Once at the Grotto Bianco, there were five of us boys—myself, Giuseppe the son of Don Agostino, who's a cowherd too, Francesco, whose father is in prison, and Pasquale's son—yes, he was there too, whose father is now a *mafioso*. We had gone to gather snails,[43] because there's a lot of them on the mountain above, and it came on to rain hard. We had a (masturbating) race, and the winner would take all the others' snails, and I won, and I took home six kilos of snails, just like that!

'But I've only talked about these things to two people—to Father Giacomo who is my confessor, and to you—I'm trusting myself to you. Every time I confess I feel like killing myself, saying these things to that man who looks at me with two huge eyes and comes out with "now my good chap". But one has to go to confession, as Jesus Christ said so, and my mother tells me that the priest has studied and that he is a saint. I take oil and cheese and chickens to the priest, and the freshest eggs, because he says he prays to God for us—but we never get rich. I don't know anything about church things—I only know the Hail Mary and the Lord's Prayer, but I go to Mass every Sunday as it's compulsory. But I'm pardoned for not going if I'm in the *campagna*.

'Don Paolo says Mass serves a very good purpose, because on Sundays all the girls come out and go to Mass, and the youths go too and they fall in love[44] and get engaged and then married.

'Father Giacomo is rich and earns a lot, because for saying a Mass he wants 700 lire, and then every month he gets help from America—clothes, *pasta*, flour and tinned milk, and he divides it among the poor. To us he gives a kilo of flour and some milk—but to the Communists he gives nothing because although they're really poor he says they have another God!

'But in the winter when I'm unemployed neither Father Giacomo nor the Member of Parliament gives me work, and I have to scrounge —I have to sweep out the church for 25 lire [about 4*d*.], or the cinema for 50 lire [8*d*.]. I go to the mountains to make herb soup and to get "*scupazza*" [grass for making brooms], as I make brooms and sell them for 50 lire each. Now I would like to go to school in the evenings, but if I did I'd lose 50 lire a day, because in the winter I sweep out the cinema every evening.

'Perhaps I have no luck—I was born unlucky, good for nothing;[45] I carry a horseshoe [above the door] but it brings me no luck. Sometimes I say one of Donna Rosaria's prayers[46] because she talks with the spirits, and she says that when I'm grown up I shall be lucky. I believe in these things—there *are* spirits,[47] and to send them away one needs red ribbon or salt. A spirit can be a snake or a lizard, because when one kills a lizard and the tail flips about that's a spirit that wants to come out, and then one must say this, "Go away from me, because I am a son of Mary"[48] and the spirit goes away. Snakes, lizards, and the "San Giovanni" lizards, the big green ones, are souls of people who can't enter into heaven, and so one shouldn't kill them—and frogs are souls too. How tricky this life is![49] I believe in these things because I'm afraid of them. But are they true? *Ma!*

'That's all about me—I'm only Nenè. If you want a better story talk to that guy who brought the mare to make a mule this morning— the one with the red handkerchief.'

And so in due course I sought out the young man with the red bandanna, and after a little further acrimony about tortoises he told me as much as he wanted me to know.

'What's my name?—I haven't got one—do you understand?—As far as you're concerned I'm just the guy with the red handkerchief.

'And what am I going to tell you about my life? I've got plenty of things to tell, fine things and ugly things, repeatable and unrepeatable, so it's no good my promising to answer your questions as if I was at confession. When I was a kid I was brought up to tell everything to the priest, even the most trivial things. When I was at confession I used to tell that when I had a shit in the country I didn't cover it with earth, a thing that at that time I thought was a sin. It's very different now, now that I haven't confessed for many years, but if I had to confess now I'd know which sins to tell!

'But I'll be frank with you and talk sincerely, because one can tell some things to a friend one trusts.

'I was born twenty-nine years ago, in Montelepre in Via Bellini. There were four of us in my family, my parents, myself and my sister. We weren't all that poor, just so-so. The house where we lived was in the Vadduni quarter, which isn't the quarter of the really poor, apart

from the fact that the whole town's poor. However, with my father's
work as a blacksmith we went ahead honestly.

'I was always a rebel, always a trouble-maker,[50] but in the family
they were fond of me—I was the only son.

'Our house where my father worked was small. Life went on day
by day; we ate, and in the evening we slept in a big alcove off the
smithy. Smoke and stink of coal and black ash on the ground were the
things you knew the house of Mastro Ciccio, my father, by.

'I went to school, though I helped my father at the smithy when I
was free. I worked the bellows[51] and put shoes on horses, mules and
donkeys—and once I hurt a mule and he gave me a kick on the
head that needed stitches, seven of them. My father didn't want me
to go near the smithy any more, and didn't want me to learn that
trade.

'At school I was a flop—I reached the fifth grade, elementary, when
I was fourteen, already able to father children—! I had no trade; the
fifth grade meant nothing.

'My school life was useless and shameful. My nature was rebellious,
and the teachers didn't know how to control me—the opposite,
because my teacher used to give me a good mark if I went and got eggs
for him, which I often used to steal, from my mother; he praised me if
I brought him lemons, oranges and fruit, which could be found in a
garden near the school and which I used to steal. That's what they
taught!

'I learnt to steal, and I can tell you that once you start you never
stop![52] At school I learnt a lot of shameful things in moral ways too.
At school I learnt to (masturbate) and do you know what I used to do?
While the teacher, an old man with spectacles, was glued to his newspaper, and I was sitting at the back bench, I used to take out my cock
and—it was a big one[53]—I used to bang the desk with it, and the teacher
used to say "Who's there? Gaglio [the boy next to me] go and see
who's knocking!" We used to (masturbate) every day in that class.
One day I was in the lavatory experimenting with a little girl of eleven
when a teacher saw me—he laughed, and ticked me off lightly; he
didn't punish me, and we tried it other times and succeeded!

'In spite of the priest's warnings, (masturbating) was fine and still is
fine, although we started [going with women][54]—but it's always that
way. Sometimes in the class half of the thirty pupils would be (masturbating) while the teacher would be reading the newspaper—what a

The kitchen-living-room of the Galante family at Scopello tonnara

One of the *tonnara* crew

life! And then they wonder that one grows up to be a thief, badly brought up, etc! The wood of a tree takes its shape when it's small. [55]

'What did I do when I left school? There was the war . . . I was beginning to understand some things, but by then it was a little late. And when my father had to close his smithy and go to the mountains to make herb soup to satisfy his hunger, then I understood that I ought to do something for myself and for the family. Things were going wrong!—as I found out the first evenings I had to go to bed empty. My father was very honest, and with threats and warnings kept me far away from my other friends who found easy ways of living. I knew that at Zucco there were American soldiers, and I went there to work and to find something to take home. Those were already the first steps in my unhappy life. The Americans gave me cigarettes, tinned meat and chocolate, and I had to wash their pots and pans. But that wasn't enough for me. There were three of us boys, and to take something home we took to stealing from the camp and picking the soldiers' pockets. The Americans were unused to the place. With a litre of wine, which they liked, and certain promises which I leave you to imagine, we would get one of them outside the camp, and then with fists and blows on the head with clubs we would rob him of all he had and send him back to the camp almost naked.

'That's what I did at first, but hunger, want and unemployment were growing; my mother died after a long illness, and I was left with my sister and my father, not really old, but quite without hope. If I had wanted to work honestly I couldn't have—there was no work, not even in the town. A lot of us speculated with their sisters—they took them to Zucco and made them tarts for the Americans, but I didn't want to sink as low as all that! The only other way to live was to give myself over completely to the way of life I'd begun. There was plenty of demand for that kind of work, specially in Montelepre.

'Giuliano had already formed his band, and was looking for youths, [56] and paid them well. It was Taormina who introduced me into the band. Giuliano himself gave me a fine lecture, telling me that if I failed him he would rub me out without pity. And he was capable of it! I was sent with Passatempo; they sent me to the San Giuseppe zone, where as a matter of fact his brother-in-law Sciortino was in command.

'I must say it—I took part in robbery, kidnappings, and shooting against the *sbirri*. By now my name was on the black list, though they hadn't got much on me.

'I could easily come to the town at night; I used to cheer up my father, and I often used to spend comfortable nights in the town with—it doesn't matter who. I had used to know her, and came to love her—and it's thanks to heaven and the French letters I used that I haven't got a battalion of children now!

'Then came my sister's misfortune. She was seduced by a so-and-so who's now in Brazil; but if I'd got my hands on him!

'My life with the band went on until one night as I was coming into the town I was arrested by the *carabinieri*. I'd been betrayed—I thought it was the girl I used to sleep with, but I knew later that it was my sister's seducer—he wanted to get rid of me, and it was easy for him to escape. I went to prison, and my sister stayed with my father, who was the butt of everyone. Then, after the *sbirri* killed my father, they kept her in prison for eight months, and in political exile for four months. I was in prison for seven years—luckily they hadn't got crimes to charge me with, even if I'd committed them, and after many trials, including Viterbo, I was set free but with a criminal record.

'The *sbirri*, accursed race, will have to account to God for what they did to me. How many things they made me say because I couldn't bear the torture! If I hadn't taken part in something, I had to say I had. They used to say, "Is it true that you were in such-and-such a place?"—and I used to say, "Yes, yes"; "Is it true that you did this, or that you took this or that road?" and I said, "Yes, yes—it's true." And perhaps I'd had nothing at all to do with the thing they were talking about. But you'd had it if you said no—you always had to say yes. If I said no they beat me, and they forced salt and water down my throat through a rubber tube—and if I insisted they burned my flesh with a red-hot iron. They beat me, they starved me, they gave me electric shocks in my fingertips and balls which hurt enough to kill, so I was forced to say what wasn't true. Do you know what they used to put in the papers? "The bandit so-and-so, in the course of close interrogation carried out by the *carabinieri*, confessed that on such-and-such a day he was at such-and-such a place, etc. etc." In the course of close interrogation! Even savages don't go in for such vile tortures. Progress! They boast that they're civilised people and then turn the clock back five hundred years!

'I'd made some money living the life I had, but I couldn't buy anything with it or put it in a bank, so I asked a friend who wasn't incriminated to buy some land in his own name and—always acting as if it was his own—to put a sum in the bank. We all lived in the hope of being free, so we promised ourselves that we'd be big-shots—and that way I should have been a landowner and have gone to work that land as soon as I was free.

'The man who I gave several million lire to doesn't recognise me any more, he doesn't want to give me so much as one lira. I can't talk, but that money is mine!—I can't say anything or I should be arrested again. What does that man deserve—who takes advantage of me! There's a lot of people in the same position as me—there were plenty who got rich on our blood while they stayed comfortably at home.

'Five years of sacrifice, risking life and health, sleeping in caves, and at the end of it all I don't own so much as a lira of the money I made with blood and sweat and terror! Our trade was a dirty one, but we never touched so much as a hair of a poor man's head—it was the rich who had to pay.

'I came out of that life worn out and disillusioned. I had suffered a lot in prison. What should he have deserved, that man who used my absence to take possession of my money? What? But I didn't do it; I'd come from a place where life was hell, and I couldn't face going back there.

'And I'm here now—I'm not ashamed of being an *ex picciotto* of Giuliano's band. When I came out of prison I felt the need to wander. I worked for a few months, then I looked for a girl, a poor girl of course, but honest, and although I met with obstacles I found her. We ran away[57] because to get married properly you need a lot of money, and that's the best way out for people who have none. We had a baby, a daughter, who's now two years old, and a boy who's just three months.

'What's my work? What do I do? What can a man like me do. When I first came out of prison there was a little work in the town. I had to go to Father Giacomo's house—those black crows[58] are the bosses, and you have to kiss their hands to get a little work. There was work at some dockyards at 500 lire a day—then that finished. All of us were unemployed.

'I'm not a Communist, nor a Christian Democrat either. Political parties lead to ruin—that poor Turridu (Giuliano) died for them. I haven't got any steady trade. I'm a farm labourer when I do that work, a vegetable gardener when I'm employed at it, a manual labourer when I dig house foundations, a thief when there's nothing to eat, a "*disaiolo*" when I got to the *disa* [a grass used for stuffing mattresses]—

the *disa* is in the mountains, and one cuts it with a scythe; one can do about 70 kilos, and earn round about 600 lire. But one can't always do that, because the *disa* finishes early. I'm a woodcutter when I go to cut firewood; I sell the wood at 5 lire a kilo, and I can make from 400 to 500 lire a day. I haven't got a mule so I have to hump everything on my shoulders, which, believe me, are sore by the evening. And when I'm fed up, when I've got no money for the family, then I become one of those who lead the low life—I become a criminal.

'I have to close my eyes and forget my past and what I've done! If we were all right, if there was something to live on or if we had work, what need would there have been to do certain things? . . . In the country there's always something to take home, and there we steal. Not big robberies—we steal because we're hungry. We do other things too—what do you expect . . . we write anonymous letters to people who have money, rich people—but never to a poor man! There are five or six of us. We send a letter to someone saying that if he doesn't send such-and-such a sum it will be so much the worse for him. The money has to be left at such a place, and two of us go to take it, and if it's there we divide it according to how many of us there are. I never let myself be seen—I stay in the town and do the intelligence side, watching to see if there are *carabinieri* on the move, and if our Mr. X. is at home, etc.—I'm the spy in fact. If all goes well we divide the sum. If we ask 100,000 lire we get 50,000 lire, which isn't even 10,000 lire each. When things go wrong, like three months ago, when two of our boys were arrested as they were taking the money, one knows that the man who's been threatened has told the *carabinieri*. We all risk our lives, some more, some less—I've got a wife and children, I've been in prison, and I try to risk less. We don't do any kidnapping[59] because you want an organised band for that and to be in with the *mafia*—who are always the bosses! . . . But we'll give those things a miss.

'I'm unemployed just now—there's been no work for two months. The children are ill with influenza—my wife's doing laundry work, but she's not very strong.

'The high-ups keep us like this—they like the pleasure of seeing the people suffer. Now there's going to be elections—they'll open the work centres and the priests and big-shots say they'll give us work and help the poor—they give us *pasta*, and want us to promise our votes. That lasts two months and then it's all finished. In their speeches they

say they're on the side of the poor and always provide work—they
don't say they keep us whole months without work, without assistance, empty and hungry, that to eat we have to fall back on herbage[60]
and snails. But they don't do that—they don't even know what
herbage is! But all the same it's worth millions to them!

'But the people are fed up, and are going to lose faith in all of them.
One goes to church because our fathers taught us to, but if our children
were not brought up the same way . . . The faith is corrupted by
now . . . I *believe* because one has to believe, but if we had to follow
the example of the priests we should all be cursed in the eyes of God.

'The blood of the poor has always tasted sweet—but for how much
longer?[61]

'That's all about me, and quite enough too. There's a lot more I'd
have liked to have told you if I dared. And don't forget, I've no name
—I'm just the guy you saw by the *fontana*—the one with the red handkerchief who gave the Englishman the reins to hold when we were
making a mule. And the mare wasn't mine and the ass wasn't mine,
and the mule won't be mine. I got 300 lire for it.'

CHAPTER FOUR

Castellammare del Golfo

THE rigid formality of procedure at the bus stop in Scopello di Sopra was in striking contrast to the general laxity that supervened as this fabulous vehicle plunged and trumpeted towards Castellammare; it was as though a state coach had been taken over by a band of rowdy students on a spree. Over the driver's head a large notice, intermittently obscured by the chattering heads of his friends who had gathered round him in animated conversation, announced, 'It is forbidden to speak to the driver.' Another, over the front seat nearest to the door, on which sprawled a moon-faced child eating green figs from a basket, read, 'Reserved for persons wounded during the war or at work.' At first sight this appeared a sensible and humane decree, though a little frustrating for the born cripple, until reason asserted itself and examined the implications. Wounded while fighting for Fascist Italy, or against Fascist Italy? Wounded by the Allies or the Axis? Or perhaps, more simply, wounded before or after September 1943? And would those wounded by the various branches of police while striving to live through that war have qualified?—would Salvatore Giuliano have been accorded that seat, or any of the *carabinieri* whom he maimed in his civil war for an independent Sicily? But I realised that to a Sicilian mind these things would be no more than talking points; no matter for whom he had fought the wounded man would remain *il povero ferito*, and as much would call from an easy sentimentality a gush of shallow pity that would dry up only at the mention of money.

To reach Castellammare from Scopello one must first rejoin the main road from Trapani. At first it is single-tracked and villainously potholed; there is a low hedge of sisal cactus between the road and the fields that stretch down towards the sea. At one point the sisal was crushed and flattened and the ground littered with small pieces of paper. These were the traces of a motor accident whose aftermath had been the subject of much whispering at Scopello during the past week. A Fiat 500 shooting-brake, driven by a well-known Castellammarese, had swerved to avoid a goat and had overturned, disgorging in doing so a truly phenomenal number of cigarettes, and that within a few hundred yards of a Customs Police station that had been set up to deal with smuggling along the Scopello coastline. There were almost three hundredweight of contraband cigarettes in the car, and had the Customs Police wanted to give complete co-operation the length of time that it had taken to clear up the mess had made it impossible. The penalties for smuggling cigarettes (which are a State monopoly in Italy) are in direct proportion to the weight of the contraband goods, and three hundredweight represented a fine that no one could face with equanimity. At last, I was told, a working agreement had been reached between the driver of the car and the *finanzieri*; they would report one hundredweight and pocket the remainder themselves. This was locally held to be a gross example of pusillanimity on their part, and surely worthy of retribution.

As the road nears Castellammare it runs high above the sea; the cliffs are on one side and inland the mountains rear stony and barren. At the beginning of the corkscrew descent to the port the town lies spread below as though one saw it from an aircraft. Like most Sicilian towns and villages it has no suburbs, no scattered dwellings that gradually merge into the surrounding country; its edges are sharp and defined, and one is either in the town or out of it. There are two small bays, the nearer of which is the harbour; they are divided by a sharp rock promontory which is entirely built over, and on whose extreme point stands the cliff castle that dominates the whole town and gives to it its name. It was that crumbling castle that had been my home when I had stayed in Castellammare in previous years.

Like most Sicilian towns, Castellammare has few motorable streets; the rest are usually steep and narrow, occasionally interrupted by steps. Sometimes they are irregularly set with cobbles, with an 'overcheck' of long pale stones in the Spanish manner, but more often they are a confused mass of ditches and loose pieces of rock, some as large as footballs.

It is a town of extreme contrasts, in which the middle ages and the mid-twentieth century meet face to face, and the extremes of tradition and emancipation, more especially at summer week-ends when there are visitors from Trapani and Palermo, present an effect almost of farce. From my eyrie in the castle I had watched Castellammaresi women come down to the sea to bathe and swim fully dressed in their everyday clothes, and to meet, while so floundering, bronzed visiting nymphs in bright Bikinis and Schnorkel masks. But these were strictly birds of passage, for until last year there was only one hotel in all Castellammare, and it was not of a kind that tourists find inviting.

Some 19,000 people live in the town, about 4,500 families, of which more than a quarter have but a single room for communal sleeping and eating, and more than another quarter have a single room and an alcove. None of these houses has water; it is rationed in Castellammare, and the 'fountains' from which it may be carried in earthenware pitchers run only for three hours a day, six days a week.

More than a third of the inhabitants are illiterate, and another fifteen per cent are semi-illiterate, which usually means that they can write—or rather 'draw'—their names. Schooling is compulsory up to the age of fourteen, but the law is not enforced, and most of the poorer people cannot afford to be without their children—many go to work in the fields at six or seven years of age, or get a few lire a day by running errands for a shop or *trattoria*.

These illiterates and semi-illiterates speak, and understand, very little Italian, and complain that they cannot understand a word of the politicians who at election time speak from the balconies at the centre of the town. They cannot, likewise, read the political posters that form a patchwork quilt on almost every wall. The law permits political posters on any building other than barracks or municipal offices, and the slogans of twelve parties mouth silently at each other wherever the eye may turn. As posters are pasted up henchmen of opposing parties skulk furtively at the street corners, waiting until the bill-sticker is out of sight to tear them down. Poor lads, 'tis little matter how many sorts they sow, for only one will grow.

Despite financial help from the United States and from U.N.O., and despite the continuous reign in office of a single Italian party almost since the war, destitution and illiteracy are growing steadily both in Castellammare and in Sicily in general. The official statistics for Castellammare itself are illuminating:

	Destitute families	Persons Male	Female	Total persons
1954	615	856	1170	2026
1955	736	1066	1415	2481
1956	853	1318	1691	3009
1957	960	1473	1842	3315
1958	1018	1488	1935	3423

In these figures, however, are not included any family whose head is known to be a Communist or any other person notoriously against the Christian Democrat Government, and a large number of opposition followers are among the destitute. In round terms probably at least a quarter of the entire population is without any adequate means of support.

Half of the whole 19,000 are officially engaged in agriculture, and thirty-five per cent are smallholders, *contadini* owning a small piece of land, whose produce (tomatoes, wine and olives) do not, after the deduction of taxes, yield more than the barest living, though none of these families is classified as destitute. The others, who do not own any land, are labourers hired by the day. They congregate in the small hours of the morning at an open-air labour mart that irresistably suggests a slave market, and the bigger landowners take their pick, governed by size and strength and also by the lowest figure for which a man will do a day's labour. If, as often happens, his family is on the edge of starvation, he may be compelled to work for little more than half the average wage, for he cannot afford to refuse it. A prospective employer will look a man up and down and feel his biceps and chest for all the world as if he were at a fat-stock sale.

These men who are employed by the day get a maximum number of some 120 days' work in the year, at a salary of about 700 lire, which is equal to about 6s. 6d. To qualify for the daily family allowance of 120 lire for the wife and 150 for each child he must have completed a statutory number of days' employment; often he is cheated of this because he has no work or because his employer represents him as casual labour.

Of the other half of the population, that is not even in these broadest senses engaged in agriculture, fifteen per cent are fishermen. Though Castellammare gulf was once a rich fishery, these men are not, in fact, any better off than their fellow townspeople, for during a full half of the year the sea is too rough to let their little gaudily painted fishing boats out of harbour. Even in summer there are many days when the *sirocco*, the hot gusty wind that blows up out of Africa, whips the sea into long green rollers in which a boat of twice that size would not live. Illegal methods of fishing, too, impoverished the waters after the war, and there is also much piracy by unlicensed vessels fishing inside the limit. Dolci has said that the problems of Sicilian fishermen warrant an entirely separate study.

In these conditions of extreme poverty the majority of Castellammaresi, and of the people of the neighbouring towns and villages from
which these autobiographies are taken, are accustomed from childhood to a dietary regime which would appear incredible to a northerner.
Few people ever eat in the morning. Their first meal of the day is
eaten in the early afternoon, and is usually a hunk of dry bread which
they have carried to their place of work. On their return home at
night they will eat, if they are not completely destitute, one plate of
spaghetti or other form of *pasta*. Few of the poor have ever even
tasted meat, which in Sicily is costly by any standards. The habit of
the poor of 'browsing', through sheer hunger, on odds and ends
such as herbs, snails, raw shell-fish and so on, is probably responsible for the—comparative—absence of obvious vitamin deficiency
symptoms.

The poverty of the people is reflected in curious small ways that
may strike a stranger before he is in a position to know the facts.
Early during my stays in Sicily I remember idly offering to a skinny
kitten a small piece of *mortadella*. The kitten was not a stray, it belonged to the household in whose single room I was sitting. It simply
paid no attention, and the more I chirrupped and stretched out my
hand the more indifferent it became. I recognised that human hands
had never fed it, had never had any spare food to give it; they were
things to be dodged. Food was to the kitten something found, something grabbed, not given. It was not that the animal was afraid of
human fingers, but that they were the last possible place to expect
food. I dropped the scrap of *mortadella* on the ground, and there was a
pounce and a gulp and it was gone.

The destitute do receive certain benefits, but they are utterly
inadequate, and a heavy political discrimination is discernable here as
in other State activities.

The town is, in fact, developing, but it is at present difficult to
say whether it is doing so along lines that will make any early or
appreciable difference to the bulk of its starvelings. There is now a small
but very luxurious hotel just outside the town's confines, but it is
staffed entirely by northern Italians, because, I was told quite openly,
the local people would not be considered trustworthy. Through the
efforts of one Bernardo Matarella, a Castellammarese until recently
holding the office of Postmaster-General in the Rome cabinet, some
eight hundred million lire (about half a million pounds) was granted

towards the construction of a new harbour, but the sight of this massive work in progress is of no direct comfort to those who have not enough to eat or room to sleep.

Castellammare has an evil reputation in Sicily; it vies successfully with Montelepre, the home town of Giuliano, as a place of blood and violence. While this is due partly to poverty, desperation, and traditionally Sicilian methods of vengeance, the chief cause is that the district is under the rule of the *mafia*. 'In Castellammare we can arrange anything, it is easy. Transport to Africa or out of Africa without papers, the silence of a man, his death if you wish it.' There used to be two great *capo* (chief) *mafia* families in Castellammare, whom we may call Abbate and Riccobono. The present holder of the title of *capo* is a nephew of the last, now an old man of eighty, who has been living for some time past in Algiers. He is said to have killed seventy of the Riccobono faction during his life, and the last Riccobono lived for fifteen years shut up in his house, afraid even to show his face in the street. They say of Abbate's house in the centre of the town that it is built of blood and bones. Many a Castellammaresi must have Abbate blood in his veins, for the old man had become a great landowner, and until thirty-five years ago the *jus prima noctis*, by which the feudal overlord had a right to the first night with every bride, was a regular practice in Western Sicilian life and came to an end only under the legislation of Mussolini.

Uncle Gaspare, who had arranged the runaway marriage of Andrea and Pietrina, had more than a nodding acquaintance with the *mafia* of Castellammare; indeed he might, on their account, never have been born. Some years before his birth they had made an abortive attempt to kidnap his father, who had been a man of considerable wealth. It was just after the railway had first come to Castellammare, and Uncle Gaspare's father was expected to arrive by the evening train from Palermo. By good fortune, however, he had missed this train, and when his reception committee saw this they grabbed the best-dressed young man on the platform as a substitute, paying no heed to his protestations that he was penniless. They took him to the cliff caves between Castellammare and Scopello and hid him there, and when they found out that he was in truth a student without wealthy relations they killed him in cold blood. Uncle Gaspare told me that the same thing would have happened to his father, for he was a proud man, who would never have stooped to pay the ransom.

The present Abbate, who is not personally an evil man, was concerned, as were all of the local *mafia*, in the doings of Giuliano, and Giuliano's 'representative' in Castellammare came directly under his protection. This was a man called Passatempo, for whom Giuliano had so deep a personal detestation, that, recognising his terrible efficiency and consequent indispensability, he set Passatempo in charge of the Castellammare area, the western limit of the band's territory, so that he should be as far as possible out of his leader's sight. Passatempo was typical of the minority element that has in some quarters earned Castellammare the reputation of the worst town in Sicily. He was so small as to be almost a dwarf, and his lack of physical stature produced an ultimate exaggeration of the compensating assertion to which many small men are prone. For most of his stay there he obtained shelter by threatening his unwilling hosts with assassination, and he obtained sexual favours by exactly the same means. Since he was a syphilitic he thus spread his disease rapidly. (Syphilis is very common in the town; it is rarely transmitted through the prostitutes, who were, until the brothels were closed under the Merlin Law in 1957, inspected twice weekly, but almost entirely through other infected individuals. It is compulsory to report the disease, but, like much else that is nominally compulsory in Sicily, it is seldom done.) Passatempo remained alive through the peoples' mixture of fear and admiration of the leader whom he represented.

I knew one man who had sheltered Passatempo, and it was a notable case of this curious ambivalence of attitude. My acquaintance, Vitale, had met Passatempo because Vitale's mother-in-law had learned that her son's putrified body had been discovered in the mountains, fed upon by a hoard of ravens and vultures. The *carabinieri* had called her to identify the body, but to them she said that she had never seen the man before. But vengeance she wanted, even if she was unwilling to ally herself with the *carabinieri* to exact it, and she sent word to Passatempo by her son-in-law Vitale. Passatempo did exact vengeance, killing the murderer (murdering the killer?—murdering the murderer?) in peculiarly unpleasant circumstances, but having done so he demanded indefinite hospitality from Vitale. At length, in desperation, Vitale appealed to Uncle Gaspare, who had arranged the runaway marriage of Andrea and Pietrina.

Uncle Gaspare pondered the matter; then he said: 'The man Passatempo must die; the town has travailed too long under the rule of that monster. Giuliano himself should have executed him, for he has an honest heart even if he is a foolish, but since he has not done so, I will do it myself.' Uncle Gaspare would have been certain of Abbate's protection after killing Passatempo, for his father had been a surgeon, and had saved the life of Abbate's uncle after a gun fight.

Passatempo came out only after dark, so that evening at dusk Uncle Gaspare took up his station with a sporting rifle on a roof overlooking Vitale's door, which was near to a lamp-post. As the time passed and the moon came up Uncle Gaspare felt as if he were a rich man again, a big-game hunter as he had been in Africa when Italy had colonies there; he felt as though he was waiting in a *machan* for a leopard to come to the kill.

It was three hours before the door began to open a crack, but as it did so Uncle Gaspare heard the tramp of a *carabiniere* patrol coming round the corner. He tried to line his sights on the chink of darkness formed by the inch-open door, but he could see nothing beyond it, and he was afraid it might be Vitale. Then the door opened a fraction wider, and for a single instant the light of the street lamp shone full on Passatempo's face. Uncle Gaspare settled himself and prepared to tighten his finger on the trigger, but just as he did so the *carabiniere* patrol passed squarely between the rifle and the target. At once the door closed silently, and when Passatempo left it was by a back entrance. Uncle Gaspare failed, but when Passatempo was killed at last it was as anonymously as he would have done it; the body was found by the roadside as full of bullets as a tin can be of peas.

Though the Passatempos of Castellammare are a small minority, they are not statistically distinguishable from those who are criminals because they have no choice but to be so. Some eighty per cent of all adult males in Castellammare have served prison sentences, and I believe that nearly one in three have killed—many of them when they were little more than children. Many women, too, are said to be handy with a knife and a gun—the latter, pistol or sub-machine gun, they learn to use in the country small-holdings where *carabinieri* are scarce.

Because the women lead a life of seclusion that is presumably a heritage of the days of Arab occupation and Islamic custom, it is very much more difficult to secure the life story of a woman than it is of a man. Women will not walk in the streets except on their way to church, and never in any circumstances alone. In the summer weather, when the women of the household carry their chairs and their work to sit outside, in front of their own doors, the unmarried females must sit with their backs to the street, and to show their profiles during daylight hours would be considered grossly immodest. Only after dark may they turn their chairs sideways, but even then they must never face the street, and they must at all times avoid looking at any man. It is a sight typical of these towns to see a group of women sitting together in the sun, sewing or embroidering or knitting; they talk and gossip and sing, a verse in solo and a reply in chorus.

All the women, whether they are honest and slaving housewives, prim spinsters, or pistol-packing mommas, present an appearance of the utmost decorum, and the vast majority are deeply religious.

Aunt Antonia, whom I would see day after day sitting demurely sewing with her back to the street, in a neighbouring town, turned out to be the perfect example of the religious spinster of whom there are many in every town, and she proved both able and willing to impart esoteric information.

AUNT ANTONIA [1]

'No, no . . . make yourself comfortable, it's better here inside—outside people hear us. Sit down—there's a seat here, it's made of olive wood, the kind of seat we poor people have.

'Ours is a poor house—see, this is the home of poor people; here we sleep, eat, do everything—we do the best we can.

'There's only us two, me and my mother, who is very old, and paralysed into the bargain—do you know how old she is? Ninety-five; in June she'll be ninety-six. With length of days comes a miserable old age.[2]

'Poverty means nothing to us, we were always poor, we were born poor, and by now we know a lot about poverty—if you only knew how much we know!

'We've always lived in this house, between these four walls. My father[3] was a peasant[4], but of the most unlucky ones. He was a peasant, but not a peasant with his own land—he used to go [5] daily to work for peasants richer than himself. What did my mother do? An ugly trade, a trade of poor people who are really wretched. I'm ashamed to say it—my mother was the "*cantarana*" of the town. A "*cantarana*" is a woman whose job it is to take away the chamber-pots and empty them into the river. A "*cantaru*" means a chamber-pot. They're given something for each chamber-pot, but not much, often a piece of bread or something to eat. Now there's no woman like that, because almost everyone has something indoors where they can relieve nature. But today the families nearest to the river still lead that sort of life, though they empty their own chamber-pots. They called her, and still call her, "'Ntonia the *cantarana*"—that's her "*nciuria*" [offensive or ironic nickname]. But when one works one shouldn't be ashamed of what one does. My mother didn't eat the chamber-pots and she didn't take them home—she did her duty and her work— the work of the destitute. It's hard work to get bread, but bread is sweet![6]

'What would you—I'm poor, and if I've never married, the main reason is this—I never had a dowry, and then I've always been a serving woman since I was a girl. For twenty years I served the family of Don Gallo, and then no more, because [blushing and embarrassed] . . . because there's many shameful people in the world . . . but I've always kept my honour . . . and . . . and they thought Ntonia was a cheat and that the hand of God should chastise her.[7] They didn't only want work from me—I worked like a dog—but they wanted dishonourable things. The rich marry and keep their wives[8] like tarts[9]—they marry for practical reasons but not for love, and then they try to ruin the poor daughters of honest mothers. So I stopped being a serving-woman, as I wasn't going to lose my honour so easily.[10]

'But people began gossip[11] about me—and think of it, a poor woman like me, gossiped about by everybody, a fine state I was in to get married! But I never think about these things—should I still be thinking about them at sixty-five? It was my destiny, each of us has his destiny, and mine was ill-starred.[12] Whoever doesn't carry his cross, that's the end of his soul.[13]

'And what could I do for a living? Ah, how I worked, how I struggled. I worked at a thousand trades—a laundry woman almost always, and I tried to earn something to live, and what I did earn was got with blood and sweat[14] for myself and my mother to live on, as my father died fifteen years before—and he too was old, and ill into the bargain, for it is the destiny of the poor to die in misery as they have lived in misery.

'Many trades my mother taught me, many things that are the gifts of God. I know how to give injections, and to heal wounds with certain herbs that I know well, and which are to be found in the mountains. Where?—Muntameddu, Sarsani, and other mountains. But do you think they give me money as they should? To a doctor they give 10,000 lire or perhaps more, for a single visit—but to me, who doesn't make them spend anything but does cure them, they give 50 or 100 lire. It's useless . . . we're destitute.

'On Sundays I get some 100 lire or less for singing in the church, and for a sung Mass which lasts two or three hours they give me 100 lire, and for short things nothing—but I go there to sing the praises[15] of the Saints of heaven.

'Everyone calls me "*'Ntonia a tabbuta*" [*tabbuta* is used in a derogatory sense, and means "wife of the priest", or is used of someone who is always in the church, praying] but I'm not offended by this. I'm not married, but I am dedicated to Jesus Christ, and whoever serves God and prays to him is near to me. These nicknames break no bones, and all of us must eventually go to that world.[16]

'Look at the nicknames there are in this town—practically all of us have them, especially the poorest. And if they ask after me do you think they'd say Miss so-and-so? No, "*Za 'Ntonia a tabbuta*", that's how it goes in the town. Who gives the nicknames? People who've got nothing to do, malicious backbiters without the fear of God, for the nicknames are traditional and pass on from father to son, from generation to generation—but thanks to God I've no-one to leave mine to!

'Yes, I'm a Catholic—I go to and fro between my home and the church—nothing keeps me away from the church, ever! It's true that when I'm very tired I don't go to church very often, but always I go there at least twice a day—in the morning for Holy Mass, and in the evening for Benediction and the Rosary.

'What does Father Pietro say? Holy words his are, and he knows of deep matters that we can't know—but how many don't hear his words, and play deaf—but it takes all sorts to make a world, and everyone must pull his own cart.[17]

'Among all the other trades I do[18] I'm also an interpreter of dreams[19]. There's a lot of us who do that here in Sicily, and in the South the interpreter also has to examine the dream, giving its meaning, and then drawing numbers to play at lottery, the national game. Everything that's dreamed corresponds to a number—see this book, written in Sicilian, where each object is represented by a number. For example, you see a girl is 81 and a wedding is 34. A donkey foal is 6. Yes, I'm a dream interpreter, that is to say I do interpretations of dreams by drawing numbers. We must believe in dreams, because in them we sometimes see our futures, or else things of the supernatural world, and luck can come from the dream sometimes, and sometimes souls in purgatory[20] who want to be remembered come and bring you good luck from heaven—and sometimes things that give you gooseflesh.[21]

'When one dreams a dream one mustn't talk to anyone about it— come to me and say "Donna 'Ntonia, I have dreamt this or that", and I can draw the numbers from the dream that is told to me.

'The numbers are from 1 to 90, and everything in the world corresponds to a number, so if someone dreams of a corpse—a corpse is 31— and the corpse speaks, then that makes 47. If one dreams of terror then it is 90, if someone dreams that he is mad, it is 22, and so on. I can get many numbers from a dream, but especially the essential numbers 3 and 4, and I have to work on a dream, because it can be interpreted in different ways. One has to understand the significance of the *gabbera* of the numbers. [*Gabbera* is a technical word of the trade, and means the "harmony" of the numbers.] Then the numbers go into lottery, and if two come out it is *"amo"* [that is, two numbers are called *amo*]; if three come out it is *terno* [three numbers which are winners in the game—*amo* has no relevant meaning in Italian]; if four come out it is *quarterno* [such as *amo* and *terno*—*quarterno* means winning with four numbers] and takes the money—especially when the game is *siccu*— that is, when the numbers are drawn for a single city, because each city gives out its own numbers every Saturday—that's the game. But fate is cruel, because I don't even get any money—I make other people win.

'In this book, you see, are all the numbers for the things one wants to look for, even the things it's not decent to talk about. It's written in Sicilian—it's old—it was my grandmother's,[22] then my mother's, now mine. Tomorrow perhaps it will be destroyed—I don't know.

'How much do they give me for an interpretation[23]? What do you think?—10 lire, 20 lire, not more. If someone wins he gives me a present, but all too often when people win they forget Donna 'Ntonia!

'I also do *raziuneddi*, which means the prayers some women like me know how to make to drive out demons, or cure illnesses and so on. I have a gift from God that no-one else in this town has, a gift that is a tradition in our family. I have the power to cure children of the evil eye, and other sicknesses of the devil—not only children but adults too.

'If someone has the evil eye or is sick then he comes to me, or if he can't go out they bring me his clothes and I say special prayers to drive out his devil, and then his soul is free.

'Do you want to see how?' She took a crucifix in her hands, crossed herself three times, and began:

> Jesus, Joseph and Mary,
> Come quickly to me.
> Michael, Gabriel, Isael,
> Run with your magic sword.
>
> Look upon this creature
> Who does not deserve nor wish to die:
> Satan has him chained,
> That demon of disaster.
>
> Saints of Paradise
> And angels, I have called upon you.
> Run with your magic sword—
> Open your great veils.
>
> Go away, demon, to hell;
> Give this soul to me.
> Go away, for all the angels
> Are coming to drive you out.[24]

She went on singing in a slow dirge, and after a few verses she began to grimace with her mouth, held one hand over her breast and produced a raucous sound in her throat as if she was going to be sick. Between one hiccup and another she said:

'I'm doing that to call my spirit, because each of us has a spirit inside, but it doesn't show itself to everyone. By doing this I feel inside me when my spirit is ready and then I speak with it, and say what I want or what I have need of. How do I perceive that my spirit is already inside me? Ah! that I can't tell you—it's a secret of my profession and a tradition of my family too, and it's not going to be me who betrays the family traditions, not me! It's very easy to feel the spirit; there's particular symptoms I can feel inside of me.

'And when babies have worms in the stomach I can kill them from outside with prayers and signs. The baby is stretched out on the bed, and I trace the sign of the cross upon its stomach, and say prayers, and a short while afterwards the worms die and the baby is safe. Yes, there are herbs for worms, but one takes those afterwards.

'For each *raziuneddu* they give me 50 or 100 lire, and for killing worms about the same, more or less—but sometimes I don't take anything, for this isn't a trade but a holy thing, and I only charge for it when I'm very hard up.

'Sometimes it happens that someone is possessed by another soul, and to set this man free—or woman, as the case may be—a great deal has to be done, and very powerful prayers said. I can't tell you them—they're secret. One has to burn the clothes of the deceased, with salt, and then invoke the Holy Ghost . . . and then . . . no matter what then.

'Where did I learn these thing? It seems you want to know a lot!

'Well, my grandmother did them, and my mother too, and now me. Is that enough for you?

'A lot of people call me "the witch", but I'm not a witch—I do nothing without the will of God. I've got plenty of nicknames, you see. If I was a witch, how could I go to Church? and sing?—and then would Father Pietro receive me? No, no, I'm no witch—I know a lot about religion; I've read church books and I know a lot.

'I make novenas too; one makes novenas for an Intention, and at certain times of year. There's the novena to the Infant Jesus, there's the novena to the Madonna, and so on. But the most beautiful are those made to Jesus Christ and to the Infant Jesus. When does one make novenas to Christ? There's no fixed dates, but it's always in the summer. When it doesn't rain for a long time, and the trees and crops go to ruin, one sings a novena to Jesus Christ for 9 days. We get together on a sidewalk about *vintumura* [*vintumura* is derived from the latin *Viginti et una ora*. The time now corresponds to 2 o'clock in the afternoon], almost all women, young and old, and we sing this song 33 times—33 times, because that was Christ's age at His death.

> O God give rain, give rain,
> Our lands are dead of thirst.
> Give kind rain
> Without lightning or thunder.[25]

'I sing the first verse solo, and the others sing the second in chorus. We do this for nine days, always at the same hour, and then after the novena God sends rain to ground that is parched. If it doesn't rain it means that God is angry with man and wants to punish us—famine comes, and those who suffer are always the poor.

'I don't often get paid for this novena, but they often give me grain or bread.

'But, as you've heard, we pray to God to send rain to the ground without thunder and without lightning, because those things are signs of the wrath of God, and are terrible.

'What does one do when there's thunder and lightning? One must do what our forefathers of old have taught us—one must pray to St. John,[26] because it is he who commands the tempests of heaven! One must turn to him! How? When lightning[27] enters the storm you must make the sign of the Cross at once, and repeat with a pleading voice "Oh, St. John, St. John the Baptist", and if one has in the house any salt that has been blessed one holds it in one's left hand and while there's lightning one throws it up as one makes the sign of the Cross, invoking the powerful Saint.[28]

'Often St. John takes pity on us, and the rain stops at once, but sometimes it goes on and our prayers make no difference—that happens when God is angry with us and wants to punish us. We old people understand that, because we've got more experience of life, but the youths, if they could get to heaven to do it, would blaspheme[29] St. John and all the other saints in paradise. When it rains hard on a Sunday or day of *festa* they raise their eyes to heaven not to pray but to curse and insult all the saints, beginning with God, and they blaspheme that poor St. John with foul words that are terrible to hear.

'But when the storm doesn't end,[30] St. John hears the voices of the good and of the wicked, and when he rewards the good the wicked rejoice too—but when he punishes the wicked we poor good people suffer as well. Often St. John doesn't hear the voices of either the good or the wicked.

'This story I'm going to tell you is the truth and no fairy tale.[31]

'Once some thieves wanted to rob St. John of his money, because he was very rich. Do you know what they did? They went to St. John's house and hid in the hay loft[32] and made a hole in the ceiling below them and lowered a rope to St. John, who was praying in the room below, and then they began to chant and sing:

St. John, St. John, Jesus wants you in Paradise,
Send up your treasure chest and then come up yourself.[33]

'And St. John thought they were angels, and that the moment had really come for him to ascend into Paradise. First he tied the treasure-chest to the rope and the thieves pulled it up, and then they lowered it again to lift St. John, but he'd hardly got hold of it and was lifted off the floor when the thieves cut the rope and he fell to the ground. Then he said to God:

> O dearest heart
> Of my sacred Jesus,
> For once you've let me down—
> Don't ever do it again.[34]

'And so when St. John remembers how he was tricked he gets very angry and the rain goes on and on.

'Then there's the novena to the Infant Jesus, which is made at Christmas. In every street there are little altar niches in the walls,[35] and I go about with three men who play musical instruments [bagpipes and brass wind] reciting prayers as lullabys to the Infant Jesus, and then I have to say some things in Latin that I've never understood, and perhaps I don't say them right.

> The angel of the Lord announced unto Mary,
> Our Father,
> Lamb of God that takest away the sins of the world,
> Have mercy upon us.[36]

'They give me offerings for the novena, but they give a lot to the men who play the instruments.

'But the most important of my trades is that of laundry woman—I've been that almost since I was a baby, I've always had my hands in the washtub. Washing can take a day or half a day, and I can earn 150 or 200 lire according to whether my client gives me something to eat—in which case the payment is less. Look at these bones of mine, sodden with water.

'But with all these trades of mine do you think I'm at one of them every day? Ah, that'd be wonderful—but there's times when I have work and times when I do nothing.

'Daily life at home is always the same, it never changes. You see these walls? I've always known them like this, and this *portale* [a kind of decorated curtain hung in front of the alcove, as an ornament] was always in this alcove. They say each family always has its own colour—this one is dark yellow and was always like that, the colour chosen by my family from the time of my ancestors. Then one should have a fringe of silk tassels but there's no fringe here—mine's a poor house and the things in it are poor men's things. Richer people have the *portale* with a fringe at the hem, and sometimes even embroidered in silk, but ours is like this, and we only have one. The rich have two, and change them, but we only have one, and we wash it every six years, according to the old tradition. [A common Rabelaisian joke in Sicily underlines the reverence accorded to the *portale*. It concerns a paterfamilias who returns home one evening to find a young man in bed with his daughter. After an hour of hysterical pleading by the girl her father agrees to spare her lover's life if he will marry her, but then suddenly changes his mind when he sees that they have stained the *portale*.]

'Above the alcove there's a loft.[37] It's handy—we put old odds and ends there, and firewood, and grain and so on—it's like a store cupboard, a poor man's store cupboard, because the richer people have rooms for these things, and roof-terraces.[38]

'The closet[39] is here behind the door—well, what would you, poor people's houses are like this—the closets[40] of the poor houses are always like this. It's just a hole behind the door without water. Often the closet gets blocked[41] and you have to wait for whole weeks, and go out of doors in the meanwhile.

'Rich people have "lavatories" as they call them, which work by running water, but as far as we're concerned we have to carry water in pitchers from the local pump.[42] Poor people haven't got the right to cleanliness inside the house—Jesus Christ created water only for the rich!

'Here's a *tannura* [cone-shaped oven] in the corner, one can cook in it with wood—or, if one wants less mess, with charcoal, but charcoal's dear—it's not made here, though it is in the nearby towns—and I hardly ever cook with it. Everyone has an oven of this sort, even the rich, but theirs aren't the same as this one—this is a peasant's oven.[43] The rich have steam cookers, too, and finally gas, which makes cooking a pleasure.[44] But of course I, who can't even afford to cook with charcoal, won't ever be able to cook with gas.

'The day goes by doing household work.[45] Thinking what to eat— when there is anything to eat. When there's not, I cook herbs that I get from the countryside, or stale bread crusts, or bran boiled with rice and tomato.[46] Otherwise one goes hungry—people who are used to suffering hunger aren't afraid of it; it doesn't even matter to them.

'Then there's sewing to think of, darning and so on, that one has to do every day. When the sun shines it gladdens my heart. Then I sit at the sidewalk with other cronies[47] and women neighbours. The oldest ones and the married ones sit facing the street, while the unmarried girls[48] sit facing the house, as they have to when they're not yet married. They must be looked at by everyone who can, but it would be a shameful thing if they sat facing the street—you know how it is in the town, they're strict about these things. When the sun's hot and high we put a black scarf over our heads to keep off the sun, but not the girls—they're younger and they can put up with the sun, and what kind of a sight would a girl be with a black thing on her head! A white handkerchief is enough for them.

'In the evening one goes to church, or rather I should say I go to church—and say the rosary, attend Benediction, and pray. One passes the long winter evenings by the hearth.[49] But one's always working at something—making fine stockings,[50] or while one's talking to the neighbours one shells beans.[51] One passes the evening hours like this and then goes to bed. But I can't lead that sort of life every evening—I have to look after my mother—you see, I do everything for her.

'I sleep with her in that bed where she's lying now. The bed's high, as it should be—all the beds of the peasants and poor people are like that. Beds ought to be high for dignity's sake—I don't say they ought to be soft, like richer folks' beds, but they ought to be at least half a metre high or more, like this one.

'This bed has seen the birth and death of so many of my family— here my grandparents died, here my mother will certainly die, here I hope to die myself too if God will grant me the favour.

'Those are pictures of the Saints on the walls, and photographs of my family dead—see, there's my grandmother, and this is a picture of St. Joseph, and that's Our Lady of Pompeii. I'm devoted to Our Lady of Pompeii—she's the most miraculous of all the Madonnas. Then that one with the white veil is Our Lady of Lourdes—she's miraculous too, but not as miraculous as Our Lady of Pompeii.

'This linen chest[52] is old and broken, sad to say. Here we put the oldest linen, and here in the bottom drawer we keep the newest, which we put on for Sundays and *festas*.

'I don't think the colour of the house is traditional. It's the man who paints the house[53]—he colours the walls with whatever he finds. These walls were always blue, and they'll be done the same way when we have to repaint them . . . if my mother could speak I could ask her.

'For everyday wear I dress the way I'm dressed now. The apron[54]— that's something we must always wear—almost all women wear it, so as not to dirty the dress. Look, that woman passing in the street's wearing one too. The apron's always black, for several reasons—first so as not to show the dirt, and then because it's not seemly for old women to wear coloured clothes—black's a more serious colour. The girls wear them too, but not black, not, that's to say, unless they're in mourning. The apron should be almost ground length—it's more moral to wear it anyway as long as the dress; young girls wear it shorter because the dress is shorter. But if you take a good and humble family who still lives in the old way, you'll see that even the youngest wear the apron almost ground length.

'When one goes out as one does daily one must wear a head shawl.[55] A shawl is indispensable—it hides much and covers the head, and it's unseemly and ill-bred to go out without one. My shawl was my mother's—it's an old one but still good, there's a fine fringe, and it's made of silk. Certainly the youngest girls don't wear the shawl— they go out with at most a small shawl[56]—but coloured, or with a coat that's got a hood, but it's all according to whether they're rich or poor. A rich woman doesn't wear an apron, and certainly she doesn't go out with a shawl, nor wear ground-length dresses—she likes to dress in bright colours and elegant clothes of the latest fashion. They dress for appearance, and if anything goes wrong with their clothes they're ruined. We who live in the poverty of these houses don't care about such things—we have enough to think about, and it's bread that interests us, and the rest can go hang.

'When one's in mourning, as I am, one must dress in black and wear a black handkerchief bound to the head—for seven years, or for all one's life if one really bears respect for the dead. Because they see, they see everything, and if they see, what then! But it's all according to custom—the richest women have another God and another law— they'd be ashamed to wear a black handkerchief on their heads—it would mean renouncing fashion, and that would be a hard thing! Many of the rich don't put mourning signs on the doors, or they only put a card there, but we put mourning on the doors—look outside here—a piece of black material—that means you love the dead!

'Here in this corner I keep the hens—I've got four of them and they lay eggs for me, but do you think I can sell the eggs? The hens lay two eggs a day and one goes to my mother—an egg costs 30 or 40 lire, and two eggs a day would bring me in something handy—but . . . Yes, I keep the hens inside—where else could I put them? People who've space put them in a separate room, but here there's only this one room and there's nowhere else to put them.

'It's not true that we women are afraid of dressing more elaborately—do you know why we don't?—for morality's sake. And morality isn't only a woman's affair, it's the affair of men too, and of everybody—it doesn't matter who they are. There's the rich—they haven't got any morals, morality for them means having enough money from sucking the blood of us poor.[57]

'What's a girl of good family doing going out alone, or going to the dressmaker[58] without a shawl or a white handkerchief in her hand? When a girl goes out it's a good thing for her to carry a white handkerchief in her hand . . . you want to know whether that's traditional—yes, it is, but whether traditional or not, it's far above any education. What's the reason for it? How should I know what to say about so many of these women's affairs—is it of any interest for you to know? And is there always a reason for these things? One does them—the people of old left us their education but they didn't leave the reasons—do you know who looks for the reasons?—the rich—they carry a purse, and rings, and bracelets, and dishonesty!

'When a girl is chaste everyone takes notice of her at once—the men look at everything, even these things. Nowadays there's a lot of modernity—"Look, look at so-and-so who's got some money," that's what one hears! Among the poor there's poverty, yes, but there's dignity and honour too. Until the destined day, that is the day of marriage, a girl must keep right away from men, because then the man will always feel proud when he looks at the bride-cloth.[59]

'Sweets?[60] I've never bought them in my life, but I know how to make them—many many different kinds. I make sweets for Christmas;[61] all families have them. Yes, I make them, not for myself, for the Gallo family, who are very rich—I make them every year, and they spend a lot of money on them. Even the poor make these

Christmas sweets—but how do they make them? There are degrees in everything, my good sir—"not all the Saints are near to God!"— as we say. How does one make these sweets? Ah, it's a very complicated thing, and you want skill too. Well, you want a good flour, a fine white flour—they call it Majorca flour—but it costs a lot, and the poor can't buy it. There are richer peasants who have *cuccitta* flour [*cuccitta* is a soft grain that is very costly], "but you know you can make the flour of hard grain fine. How? You rub the pastry board[62] with a few drops of oil, and the flour becomes very soft, but it's always a make-shift.[63] Then you knead it with the oil and eggs and sugar and vanilla and cinnamon and other spices until it's a very soft paste—and then comes the most important work. You prepare the filling,[64] from powdered dried figs and ground roast almonds and walnuts, roasted too, and then chocolate and fig syrup or honey—and all of these you mix together. It ought to be a beautiful dark-coloured paste. Then one puts a little of it into a strip of pastry dough, and works with a little knife, marking designs on the top. Lastly you put them in the oven, and when they're cooked one covers them with sugar—and then . . . and then . . . one eats them.

'But you see, we're different from the richer people in everything, as I've said so many times. Do you know for instance what religion is to the rich? It's the ornament market.[65] We go to Mass with the shawl and then we go barefoot to the procession to mortify the flesh, and because we also go to the procession to ask grace of a saint. What grace should the rich ask?—they're noble, and they lack nothing, and to go barefoot to a procession is lowering; for them there are elegant ways.[66] There are a lot of processions, more or less important. The finest of them? What a lot of things you want to know! The finest is the one of the 1st of August, the procession of the Assumption of the Madonna. One sings a beautiful song for fifteen days, from the 1st till the 15th of August:

> How beautiful are these two eyes,
> As beautiful as the sea.
> We want to shelter
> Under the mantle of charity.
> On the 15th of August
> There is a withered rose
> And Mary ascended
> And gone to Heaven.[67]

'It's a beautiful song, and one sings it for fifteen successive days, as I said, and the children sing it every evening. When August comes the children[68] make little decorated litters on small chairs and place effigies of the Madonna on them,[69] and candles, and tour the town singing that song, and collecting offerings which they take to the priest.[70] There are lots of effigies in every quarter of the town—they make several kinds of them, and the children vie with each other to make the most beautiful ones and to carry them. The little boys[71] carry them, and women go behind them singing.

'There's a similar custom for the Immaculate Conception in December. From the 1st to the 8th of December they carry through the streets of the town a much bigger litter with a statue of the Madonna, and then all the bigger boys [*picciutteddi*: boys from 6 to 13 or so; from *picciotto*, a name Garibaldi gave to the Sicilian soldiers when he came to Sicily in 1860] walk behind the litter with lit torches in their hands, singing and shouting:

> The lights in the sky,
> Happiness, Happiness,
> And long live Mary
> And her Creator,
> And without Mary
> One cannot live.[72]

'A torch procession is most beautiful, you know. The torches are made of *disa* [a herb that grows in the mountains] or of dry bamboo, and all the torch-bearers are peasant youths—as they're supposed to be the immaculate ones of the peasant people.

'I don't know why this is done—people of old taught it to us, and so we do it. There's some things it isn't necessary to know the reason for; we know that for the Corpus Christi we should hang our bedspreads from the balconies—is there any need to know why? Certainly one does these things to worship the saints and God, and then I don't know otherwise—a man who looks for reasons finds thorns as well as roses.'[73]

[A woman who has come in speaks: 'I don't know these reasons either—why ever should we know them? We know what we're doing, that's enough. God forgives us for that—and then we poor people don't put out our bedspreads because for the most part we live in single-storied houses—and away from the central streets where the procession passes, into the bargain. Rich people compete to put out the most beautiful ones.']

'My friend Mary's right—she's a poor woman too, and mother of five children, and soon will be mother of more. She's a baptismal relation of mine[74] and because of it we respect each other like sisters.[75]

'At Easter too there's a very beautiful procession, but that one's well known. It's not just one procession, there's several, and also several religious functions. For Good Friday they make sepulchres.[76] They decorate the church with *piatti*—bunches of white leaves which grow in the dark. There are big pews decorated with ribbons of every colour, and at the centre of the pew, or whatever else it may be, there will be a *piattu*, which is the leaf of grain, a white leaf because this grain grows in the dark, in lofts. One takes the grain a month before and mixes it with mud and water and leaves it lying in the dark, so that the leaf will grow to decorate the pews. The grain grows white for the virtue of Jesus Christ—what miracles God works! One takes the *piatti* to church and puts them round the sepulchre of Christ for ornament. I make *piatti* every year and take them to church— one earns merit in the eyes of God, and many indulgences.

'Then, after the function is over—the sepulchre remains one day decorated like this—each takes his own property and carries it home. If one has brought bread the bread is blessed; if one has brought wine the wine is blessed, and so on. They take the *piatti* out into the country where there's cornland, as it brings good luck to the crops.

'On Maundy Thursday there's the procession of the mysteries. All the men, women, boys, girls and little children take part in the mystery. The mystery consists of dressing oneself like the people of biblical times, for instance David or Samson, and touring the town in these clothes as a procession does. Everyone impersonates a figure from of old. After the whole procession of the mysteries there is Jesus Christ among the Jews and the weeping women. A very young man plays Christ, dressed in the clothes of the Jews, and women dressed in black with their hair over their faces play the Madonna and Mary Magdalen and the others.

'Christ carries a heavy cross, and He is covered with blood and wears a crown of thorns on His head, and the Jews spit upon Him and blaspheme Him as they did of old.

'The same man—or his son as he gets older—plays Christ every year—he doesn't do it for money, but for devotion. There are four

weeping women—I used to be one of them, but now I'm too old . . .
And Jesus Christ falls three times, and trembles and weeps, and when
they stop in the *piazza* the Madonna says to us, singing:

Madonna: Leave me to die,
Leave me to see,
Leave me to embrace, to weep and to kiss.
Ntu Ntu Ntu, open these bars.

Chorus of Jews: Oh who, oh who is there?

Madonna: I am your unhappy Mother.

Christ: O Mother, I cannot open to you
For I am in the midst of hatred and the Jews.

Madonna: Jews that hold you, Jesus Mine,
Leave him but for a moment, see
The Mother of sorrow and of sighs
Who weeps and implores your love and charity.[77]

'It's very sad—it makes you want to cry, doesn't it? You see what
the peasants can do—yes, because it's almost all us peasants who do
this. It's organised by Padre Pietro, who owns many garments, but
some others we have to procure ourselves. For taking part in a mystery
one gets paid 100 or 150 lire, according to the part one is playing.

'There's so many other things to tell—but do you want to know
still more? I have to think first . . . but then you know some of the
traditions as well as I do. Those are the most beautiful ones, but all
the things of God are beautiful.

'I'm not an educated woman—I've talked like an ignoramus and
none too well I expect, but what do you expect—among our other
trials we poor people are ignorant.[78] Ignorant, but I fear God, whereas
there's many who never go to church and go far from the things of
God. The poor and the peasants go Communist because the Party
protects them, but it tricks them too. I'm poor and I'm what I am, and
I want to die what I am too—but a Communist, never! Never, in
God's name.[79] Who carried the Cross? Was it not Jesus Christ—so
who should we vote for? The Cross bears us to heaven.[80] Who does
Padre Pietro tell us to vote for? Always for the Cross [the Christian
Democrat Party], for God knows how to reward us. My mother, too,

paralysed as she is—they carry her to vote, and I go into the room where you vote, and I put the sign for her, on the shield with the cross. I am not double-faced with God, I do not betray him.[81] Certainly all of us can make mistakes, and even in this Party there are men who make them, but God looks after them. High-ups promise us a lot of things, make us hope, deceive us, and then give us nothing—but that isn't to say that one shouldn't vote for God. There's many priests in the Christian Democrat Party, and there's the Pope himself, too, and how can these make mistakes? Look, I do my duty, and if they don't do theirs they must answer to God.

'Most of the time I'm forgotten by the authorities—the town council gives me 1,000 lire every two months, but what can I do with 1,000 lire—there's two of us who have to eat, and one of them ill into the bargain. With that money you can buy bread for 15 days—and then what? Then 'Ntonia has to look here and there for bread.[82] Should I put faith in prayers? Or in spells? or in interpreting dreams? You'd starve! Look at these arms—I've been keeping them in the water since I was born, I was born a washerwoman, and a washerwoman I'll die.[83] And I pay the family's taxes!—it's a fine thing that I who own nothing must pay the family's tax to the town council. I pay 2,500 lire a year—poverty's not taken into consideration, either I pay or they take it from my pension. We all ought to rebel and pay no-one—but who does? It's always the strongest who command. They give me 1,000 lire every two months—they give it with one hand and take it away with the other. And no-one gives us credit, as they're afraid we won't be able to pay—and where there's no money there's hunger. That doesn't matter to the town council or the authorities—they've got bread under their pillows.

'If I get ill who's going to cure me? What should I do? Who's going to give me medicine? The chemist says "Go to the town council", the town council says "Go to the Government", and so on, and I would die, and my death wouldn't matter a brass farthing to them. I know how to die without giving anyone trouble, because there's no-one who'd cry for me.

'This house doesn't belong to me, it belongs to the Church, and I have to pay for it, because you have to pay even the Church. Every month I pay Padre Pietro 300 lire, because if I didn't he'd chuck me out quick enough!

'Do you know when the big shots are prepared to know us? When do they make contact with the poor?—it's just for our votes! Then they take pity on us, bags of *pasta* arrive, and milk and flour, and promises and swearings, but then it's goodbye, and we stay in want and need and they become Members of Parliament.

'Help? Who from? From the rich? Sometimes we get on someone's conscience and he gives us alms—a little *pasta*, a loaf, something to eat for just one evening. Then there's American aid to the poor, because the Americans are rich and they're sorry for the poor. But often it doesn't come. The best part is divided between those in charge, and do you know what's left for us? Enough *pasta* or beans to last for one day.

'What can I do? My life's over already, my mother's going to die, and I'll follow behind her. I don't want to live that long—at least I've been here for my mother, and I'm here myself, but who'll be here for me?

'You've never been anyone's slave? And never been to bed hungry? Never eaten stale bread? No! You don't know what poverty is— what can you know of our sorrows?

'We poor are never believed. All the privileges and luxuries are for the rich—we are the poor, we have no right to live as men should. And the rich have reasons for everything, we are the ignorant, the common peasants, "there's things we can't understand". That's what it means to be poor!

'But that's enough for now—I've talked a lot and I'm tired, and you must be too! There's one thing I tell you, and don't forget it. It must have been we poor alone who drove the nails into the hands of Christ.'

CHAPTER FIVE

Two Old Men

IN one village that I knew well two men were nearing the end of their time; both of them died during the ensuing six months. Because their attitudes towards the approaching end were so utterly different in every respect, and their views of existence, too, so contrasting, I have put their stories in apposition.

UNCLE NICOLA THE CARTER[1]

'There was a time when everyone knew me—they knew me as Don Nicola the carter, and that name was respected and perhaps even feared. Now I'm 75 years old I've become Uncle Nicola the carter, sick and shoved to the bottom of the bed. I'm old, very old, but there's few who've seen, and learnt, and taught as much in their lives as I have. Old age is hard, no one knows how hard until they reach it and find out for themselves . . . and so when the engine breaks down[2] the end's near. There's only a matter of days left now.[3] I must think in terms of days—I don't know if I shall be in this bed tomorrow or if I'll be able to take a pinch of tobacco. First I used to smoke cigarettes, then cigars, then a pipe, and finally tobacco like snuff—but it's all the same thing. Old age doesn't ever pass off, and for someone like me it seems a century!

'I'm here with my daughter, who's ill too, and she isn't married. We stop here and eat what God gives us and some day or other we'll die. We've none of this world's goods.[4]

'As I said, first I was *Don* Nicola, and I made myself well known, and there are still people who remember me when I was young. I've never done harm to anyone, never—people who do harm get harm in return—but it wouldn't be easy for someone of 75 to do harm anyway!

'I started being a carter when I was eight, with my father, and I was a carter till I was 65. I've travelled half Sicily, I have. Corleone,[5] Partinico, Alcamo, San Giuseppe, Ballestrate, Favarotta, Terrasini,

San Cipirello[6] and so on. I've toured all those places, moving by night
and by day. Once, when I was nine, on the road to[7] San Giuseppe,
while I and my father were going to San Giuseppe to load flour at
night, we'd got a certain distance when two men appeared. They
were *amici*—that is to say bandits. My father was asleep with his cloak
over him. I wasn't scared; I kept on going, while one of them planted
himself in front of us and said "Stop where you are!" "How can I
help you, friends?" I said, and one of them replied that they were
looking for a smoke, because they'd been eight days without a cigarette,
and it would be the worse for me if I didn't give them something to
smoke. I didn't smoke in those days, because I was a child, but without
waking my father I got some pipe tobacco out of his pocket and gave
it to the two *amici*. "Anything else you want?" I said, and they replied
salutamu—and before making off they asked who I was. "I'm Nicola,
son of Don Nicola the carter; we are from Sangiuseppi Jatu."
"*Salutamu*" they said again, and cleared off. Pleased with my success
I began to sing the carter's song:

> O moon O moon O warrior moon
> Do you know what I should sing to you tonight?
> That a hundred battalions of fighting men
> Couldn't compete with my mule.[8]

'My father slept through it all—I told him about it when he looked
for his tobacco and couldn't find it.

'I married when I was 20, and had two children—the elder had
meningitis when she was eight and has been a bit soft in the head ever
since. She stays with me, and the other is married to someone from
Castellammare who lives at Palermo. But she's poor—she's got a lot
of children, and the whole family lives on her husband's miserable
earnings—he's a peasant.

'When I was 34 I was sent to Spain—and it's thanks to God that I'm
not dead. Sad days they were, like the stories of the plagues. I lost
my poor wife at that time—she was struck down with a fatal illness,
and left me with a daughter of twelve and another of eight. I didn't
want to marry again, I wanted to give my life to the future of my
daughters—to work so that they wouldn't go hungry and wouldn't
miss their mother.

'I've always been a carter, always! If you knew the guts I had in
those days! I used to get up at two or three in the morning, load up

the cart, and set off for some distant place. At that time I could hike a sack of 100 kilos as if it was a pebble. When I had to go to Palermo I used to leave at night, and get there after eight or ten hours on the road —according to how heavy the load was. When I was carrying *sommacco* [herb used for tanning] it took a long time to get to the city, because the *sommacco* is so heavy and bulky that there was always a danger of upsetting the cart.

'Those days are dead and gone now—no one knows what it's like to be up all night, or what it's like to walk twenty kilometres a day on your feet. Now life is modern, everything's modern—there's progress[9] —and hunger and unemployment and want go hand in hand with progress.

'In those days we worked—and how! Sometimes there were five or six of us carters and we formed a caravan. I don't want to boast, but I was always the leader—and at night we always met trouble on the roads. But Don Nicola was a friend of the bandits[10]—I protected them and they protected me! In a caravan where Don Nicola the carter was no harm came to anyone—never! You run up against a lot of difficulties in life, and I'm here because I knew how to cope with them. When you're on the road and the bandits show up, and want something to eat, or to smoke, or they want information, you have to do the best you can for them. And then "See no evil, hear no evil, speak no evil".[11] Then these *amici* will never do you any harm, but if you refuse them it'll be the worse for you, and that's never happened to me in 75 years.

'It was I who used to be the animal doctor—if there was a sick horse or ass or mule or cow they used to come calling to me at once. "Don Nicola, my horse can't shit . . . Don Nicola, my cow's gone dry . . . Don Nicola my mule won't eat . . ." and I used to cure all their animals. So many herbal medicines I knew, so many.

'Have I got a pension? Never a penny![12] I ought to have had one— and how!—because I've worked since the day I was born and I'm ignorant and illiterate, but the illiterate are always put on one side. I get some help from the town council, who sometimes give me 3,000 lire a month, sometimes 2,000, and sometimes nothing at all. One must eat; I don't work and I'm old and ill, and there's my daughter too—what can one do? One has to buy everything—I need medicine but I can't buy it, I've got piles that need ointment and injections, but where's the money? If I was in good health I'd get the medicines—my own medicines, the herbs. How many herbs do I know? Many, many—eucalyptus, for malaria, mare's-tail[13] against stomach trouble, *campanella* for piles—if only there was someone to get me the herbs I want! But not many people know them. I'm poor—once I could work and live, but now . . .

'Sometimes I get a coupon for a kilo of *pasta* or of bread or something else—the town council gives them at Christmas or Easter, but one eats it in a day or two days, and then one's back to the hard life. When there's elections and voting there's coupons for everyone—Signor X brings me *pasta*, and Father Pietro too. I'm always with them, but also I'm always with God, so I side with those who are with Him—the Christian Democrats. I vote for the Cross—the Cross comes first! Who makes us live? Who makes us talk? Isn't it God?—all right, who should one vote for? For those who are against God? Never, never, never—I am on the side of God.[14] The Communists come to me too, but do I vote for them?—for those accursed of God—no, never! Woe to those who set themselves against God! My father taught me that there is only one God, and that we must do what he tells us. And I do my work! In the last elections I voted from a stretcher—I went to vote in the Christian Democrat car, which came round the town and took all the sick people to the polls—and I made my vote from a stretcher.

'Do you see the Communists going to Mass on Sundays?—no, they don't go. I never missed Mass, never, the Holy Mass[15] came first of everything. Now I'm old and ill I can't go to Mass, but God sees me and pardons me. My time is counted in days now,[16] and today or tomorrow I shall turn my back on it[17]—and for my soul I've always thought "whoever leads a good life goes to heaven."[18] And I've already fixed up for the Gregorian masses to be celebrated after my death.[19] These masses are a comfort for the soul, they clean away the sins the soul has committed, and one goes quickly to Paradise. So the priests say, and they have studied, and they know these things. One must have faith in certain things—one does not live by bread alone, and woe to him who does not believe.

'Once, here in the town, a man died who had done much evil—he was a usurer. When he died a storm burst—what a storm![20]—and a raging wind and then flood! Ask anyone, ask them, anyone who saw that storm and is still alive! The man's name was Agostino, his sons are still alive.

'I believe in certain things—do you know anyone who doesn't believe in the soul?—the rich, the princes and barons don't believe in it—they think of riches and it seems to them that death will never come. We poor, on the other hand, believe in it, and our faith never changes—God never abandons us. Today I don't know what to do for food, but I have great faith in God—tomorrow I'm sure to eat something, whatever God wants me to. We must always do the will of God—His power is infinite.

'It's already evening—before eating some pieces of bread I shall recite the Holy Rosary and I shall take thought for the souls in purgatory, I shall recommend my soul to God, and then I shall lay myself in this bed and if God is willing I shall sleep well.'

He heaved a sigh, took a pinch of tobacco, and began to speak again. 'All the same, God has given us a fine time in this life—and the satisfaction of knowing that Death spares no one, not even kings and Popes.'

'DON PIETRO'

'I'm almost fifty-four years old now—I'm not really old as age goes, but ill, as you see. I've been living in this room for almost eight months—before that I think I've had twenty different ones in this town. I haven't got a house of my own—I live for a bit in one place and then for a bit in another and then they chase me out because they say I infect the room and the neighbourhood, and I have to look for somewhere else. The houses I've lived in have always been the poorest and meanest, always on a top floor, and cold, of course. This room, which is on the third floor, hasn't got water, and the lavatory's behind the door—it's a hole rather than a lavatory.

'I've got to quit this house because the landlord wants more rent— I'm paying 3,500 lire a month, but now he wants 5,000, which is half of my miserable monthly pension. I don't know where to go yet— there's plenty of houses, but they want a lot for them, and they want more still from someone like me. They've got no pity for me—for me everything's dear, even life—I pay dearly for it! But I'm fed up with living now—I've seen plenty and heard plenty and learnt plenty, and I think my end's coming quick now, and I'm waiting for it with open arms—because nothing but death can bring me peace; the grave's the only place where I'll find a permanent home, and there I won't have to pay a penny!

'Everything's in a mess here—you can't breath fresh air inside here; I'm waiting for the serving-woman, if she'll come. If not I'll have to stay this way.

'I've been in bed three weeks, since I had a bad heart attack, those worsening heart attacks that we T.B. sufferers get. With me they last a long time—sometimes a month—a month of suffering between four walls, suffering hunger and thirst, with only loneliness for company and sometimes despair too. No one hears my coughing and crying in the night when my pains come on. You see that picture of the Madonna?—that makes me cry sometimes. I look at her, I stare at her, but that steady, kind, motherly expression upsets me, I don't know why, and I cry sometimes, I cry like a baby, and if I'm sweating my bed gets wet with sweat and tears, bitter tears.

'Donna Caterina takes 100 lire a day from me for cooking for me and cleaning the pans, on the days when I'm in bed. She's old—she comes at nine in the morning and goes at midday, but sometimes she doesn't come, and I stay hungry and weak, without the strength to call for help—and if I did call no one'd hear me. After I've paid Donna Caterina and my rent I've only got 2,200 lire a month left for eating, and no one in the world could live on that.

'I was all right once, I had good health and I was strong, too, but fate was too much for me.

'How did I come to this? How and when? I don't want to think of those times—my story is as useless as my life is now.

'I was the second son of my family, and there was a sister older than me. My father died when I was a child, and I worked at his business from childhood, and things weren't so bad. When I was 28 I was called up—I wanted anyway to enrol in the Fascist Militia. They sent me to Africa with the IVth Artillery Company—against the Abyssinians. They sent us to conquer . . . the "Empire"! We sailed from Augusta, near Syracuse, and after a long voyage we disembarked at Massawa in Somaliland, and from there we began after a few days the exhausting struggle against the bands of rebel negroes. Asmara, Agordot, and then on the high plains, Chiedin, Decamerè, Decaiè, Semifè, Adegrat, Gimma, all of them conquered with blood and misery—by doing the impossible between sickness and fevers and burrowing lice and tropical sores. But I was young, and apart from that I'd become a *maresciallo* in two years of service in the Fascist Militia, as I was a Fascist then, although I didn't understand much about it. It's true that we of the Fascist Militia were privileged—we were much better paid, and treated with greater respect by the ordinary army.

'I became a full corporal, then *brigadiere*, and, after doing a short course I was promoted *maresciallo*.

'In the Fascist Militia everything was possible! We were specially chosen by That Man [*Mussolini*], we put on the black shirt, the cavalry boots and trousers, and the beret. We saluted with the Roman salute and we were the ones who gave orders—unjust ones, sometimes. During the war we waged in Africa against the negroes there was a graver and more terrible war, between the Fascist soldiers and the ordinary army—the first respected and better paid and the second maltreated and often despised.

'In 1937, after having wiped out the band of the negro leader Mangascià—gentleman, I ought to call him, and if his exploits were tragic and violent it was all our fault, the fault of those black-shirts, who maltreated the negro women, and quelled those poor people with force. I've seen a soldier of the militia kill a poor negro because the negro refused to clean the soldier's boots. If I'd wanted to punish that soldier I couldn't have done—because the *milizia* couldn't be punished, couldn't make a mistake, and were the living examples of the Roman legions—the glory of the "Empire"!

'I returned, after having understood everything, the injustices, the inequalities—I refused the rank of *maresciallo*. I came back and took up work again in my shop for almost eight years. I was going to get married when I was called up again for the great war [Second World War]. Without going into my long and useless story, I'll say that war was the end for me. Like many others I was sent to pine away in Russia. Cold, hunger, snow, exhaustion, and epidemics were the finish of me.

'I got ill in a short time. Little by little I got worse; I began to spit blood. By now I was a prisoner of the pain—it was hard for me—I had to think that by now my "I" was represented by a terrible abbreviation: T.B. I wasn't a *maresciallo* this time, and if they'd made me one I'd have refused it. I don't know how I didn't leave these bones among those snows. A long story—to cut it short I came back to Italy, and I knew then that I owed my life—if you call this life—to the Red Cross.

'In the town my Odyssey was crowned with thorns. My house had been sold, my sister was dead, and my fiancée had got married. They'd given me something at the Red Cross, 20,000 lire, and with that it was easy to live for a few weeks—then I had to go back to the authorities, to the town council, and to the same Red Cross, who turned me away, saying I ought to go to the Ministry of War. Meantime I had to pay for the house where I lived, and the town council gave me 1,000 lire a month as "assistance", so I shouldn't have to sleep in the open. I went to the parish priest and told him my story—he gave me 500 lire. "I'm sorry," he said, "I've got nothing for you." I went back to the War Ministry—I couldn't work, so I asked for a pension, but it wasn't granted. My illness made itself felt—I had hæmorrhages from the mouth, and someone told the authorities; there were some collections for me, but it didn't do me any good. The elections came, I talked with the Member of Parliament—"Yes, yes, yes, yes"—everyone said "yes" to me, but I never saw any of them again.

'Later I had an idea, a dangerous one at that time, but I had no other choice. I went to the *Camera del Lavoro*, and talked with Signor X, the Communist Secretary. I explained my case, it was considered, and I only had to wait a month before I was allowed a war pension, and a back payment of 80,000 lire.

'I saw that the best way to show my gratitude to that man was to enrol myself with him—to become Communist too, that is—I did so, faithfully, and I'm still one.

'That's how I became a Communist!

'I put the money at once into doctors, cures, and medicines, and now I live on the 10,000 lire a month, of which almost 5,000 goes to pay for the house.

'I can't get into a hospital—the cost's enormous, and if I wanted to get it free you need documents, the Ministry of Defence, and recommendations and they would receive me there when I'd already been dead a hundred times. But I don't lose heart altogether—I know how to suffer as much as I am able, and at last that poor heart of mine will get tired out, and then goodnight! So many thanks to the Ministry, and "sorry you've been troubled"!

'I haven't been to church for nearly eight years—I believe in God but not in the priests, bloodsuckers of the people, profaners of love and of the peace that Christ prophesied. Goodbye to that lot—no, not because I'm a Communist, but I hate them because they don't help the weak; they think of their own needs, and spread hatred between men.

'I've found a little understanding among the peasants of the *Camera del Lavoro*; what matter if they are poor people, what matter even if, as the priests say, they follow a mistaken ideology? What does it matter—what does "ideology" mean when there's understanding and love between men?

'Perhaps the Communists will be like this Government tomorrow if they come to power, but for the moment we should recognise how much they have done to push the Government into doing something in Southern Italy.

'The other parties are all the same—there's the new "fascists" who ought to be ashamed of themselves and at least think what they were and what they did. When I think that I was a fascist too I feel disgusted with myself.

'I have nothing to do but wait for this death that never comes. I have no one, and I think of nothing—not even of the threats of the Archpriest, because if I don't repent and come back to the Church he won't give me a funeral when I die and he won't bury me in a *congregazione* in a church, but under the ground.[21] So many thanks, dear Archpriest, excuse me for the trouble I'm causing—"I'm sorry, I've got nothing for you"—as you said to me nine years ago.

'I know how to read—I went to school, to a school that wasn't like the ones today.[22] I read when my head allows me—*Unità*, the Communist paper, but I don't miss reading *Giornale di Sicilia*, which boasts of being "Independent" in its own way. Sometimes I get hold of some books and read. But I don't want to give any more trouble to anyone. I'd like if I could to die outside this town—I'm so much without anyone any more. I hope they'll give me shelter in a hospital and death won't still be slow in coming—they've taken every right from me that they can, but not the right to die—that no!'

CHAPTER SIX

The Grain Harvest

SICILIAN peasant life revolves around the three annual harvests that give to the people the means of living: corn, grapes and olives, and these harvests play so central a part that no picture of the Western Sicilian outlook could be adequate without their description.

Of the three the corn is by far the most important. Whereas grain of one sort or another is a basic element of diet in most countries, it has for the Sicilian a deeper significance; it is the prop and mainstay of his whole life. Not one peasant who has the smallest piece of ground but sows his grain every year, always in the same way and always in the same spot; the idea of rotation of crops is quite unknown to him.

Bread is regarded as a tangible sign of the Divine Providence. Every morning he sets out to work carrying a big loaf of two pounds weight, just a loaf and nothing else, and he never forgets that it is his land, his grain, that has given him that loaf. Towards it he displays an almost religious reverence.

That is no exaggeration, for among the peasant families the children are made to kiss the bread before they eat. The mother of the family places it in the centre of the table, and during the saying of grace it is to the bread that the children are taught to look as the present symbol of divine reality.

The mother who has made the bread puts it, when it is not on the table, under lock and key; it is a precious thing, to be used sparingly—a sacred thing, too, for it is considered an unpardonable sin to throw out even a mouldy crust among the other household garbage. If stale or mouldy bread is ever found in a house—and that is seldom—it is put to immediate use, boiled in onion and tomato water to make what is called *pani cottu*, or added to soup. If the bread is treated with disrespect the harvest will be bad next year.

To the Sicilian peasant religion, or more precisely, a mystic approach, for it embraces much untaught superstition, is a matter of everyday life; he attributes a god-like power to anything which for him has an important biological function. The propitiation of the bread is based upon a belief in a life-force concealed within it, a belief that has been passed down the generations until it is at least as strong in them as their faith in the Madonna or the saints.

This is the main reason for the persistence of traditional forms in the sowing, working, and harvesting of the grain; if the people were to depart from the old usages the hidden power in the grain would become angry, and exact terrible vengeance.

For every other agricultural product there is a patron saint, but for the grain there is none but the Almighty Himself, and no intermediary.

Harvest-time in Sicily is June and July—very occasionally as late as the first days of August. The corn starts ripening in April and May; in May the ears have already begun to turn yellow and pale, and it is then that the peasants assess the probable abundance of the harvest. They use a method of their own for the calculation. They take a hundred ears of corn in one hand and strip off the grain; should the result be more than the same test gave last year the harvest will be better, but should it be less they say that the hand of God is chastising the earth.[1] The *metier* of assessor[2]—one who at this stage can forecast whether the harvest will be generous or meagre—is traditional, and those who carry it on are for the most part old men in whom the peasants have a blind faith.

As soon as the grain can be broken in the fingers the *contadini* begin to prepare for the harvest. They prepare cords[3] of *disa* to bind the sheaves; they sharpen their scythes, get out their old broad-brimmed hats, and wait for the word to start to be given by some wise elder. The next morning they set out at dawn, and even if the forecast has been pessimistic there is an atmosphere almost of *festa*.

The peasant paterfamilias who owns the ground organises the crew. If there is much grain to harvest he invites his relations, but in a bad season only the immediate family takes part, and the father assumes the position of foreman. Before they leave the town he lectures the party; in particular he threatens terrible penalties for smoking, or for leaving on the field so much as an ear of corn, for each one of these might go to make bread, and thus is holy in itself.

In the early dawn the gang passes through the streets of the town with an almost military tread; with their dark clothing and their wide hats, their haversacks on their shoulders and their sickles at their sides, they might, indeed, be mistaken for some guerilla band setting out for battle or a clash with rival partisans. Some member of the gang will whisper to his neighbour, or another, passing a friend's house, will call to him to make haste; the footsteps and voices are brittle and magnified in the silence of the dawn.

Sometimes two parties will meet, and there ensues a ritual for all the world like the exchange of passwords appropriate to the fantasy:

'Greetings! Today we harvest but tomorrow we shall eat,'[4] recites the leader of the first gang, with strange intensity, and the other replies:

'That is our life, as always.'[5]

When they reach the harvest field each man puts his haversack into the bamboo shelter; then with much bustle they shed their jackets and prepare for work. The old men are dressed, as befits their dignity and authority, in trousers and long-sleeved shirts, with a handkerchief at the throat and a red head-cloth as a symbol of their wisdom, but the young men and boys are stripped to the waist. Drawn up before the standing corn they watch their leader, silent and expectant. Suddenly he shouts: 'Let us go forward in the name of God, boys,'[6] and each goes down upon his knees to grasp an armful of stems with his left arm, bending his sickle to slice through the taughtened golden stems an inch or two above the ground.

They work silently and swiftly, while the sun is not yet scorching, laying their swathes[7] at their sides. An old man or a boy moving up and down the line gathers six or seven swathes together to form a sheaf,[8] and ties it with grass twine. Gradually, as the sun climbs and sweat begins to pour from the naked torsos, the pace slows and the songs begin by which the southern peasant supports almost intolerable labour. One man sings a ribald verse and another responds; their voices ring out across the pale sheets of grain motionless under the molten sun. Every now and again they are interrupted by the voice of the leader, who intones, rather than sings:

> Your hands and not your mouth's the thing,
> Today you sweat, tomorrow sing.[9]

Often there are other harvesting gangs nearby, who reply to the sung verses in an exchange that becomes ever more bawdy and blasphemous; paradoxically, as the labour becomes harder the atmosphere becomes lighter and lighter hearted. 'Long live St. Francis, boys,' shouts the leader of one gang, and another party hearing him from far off answers in chorus, 'Only if he'll stop this heat and give us some fresh air.'[10] The first leader tries again: 'What do we say to St. Cologero, boys?' and the reply comes drifting back through the shimmering heat, 'That we want corn and not hayseeds.'[11] Sometimes a third harvesting gang hears the interchange and joins in too.

'Our Lady of Pompeii said . . .'[12]

'You can't talk, you're f . . . d.'[13]

'The King said to the Queen . . .'[14]

'A f . . . every morning.'[15]

'And who was Uncle Andrea?'[16]

'He weighed his balls with a weighing machine.'[17]

'Shame to the tallest man here.'[18]

Each man tries to make himself look a dwarf.

'Shame to the shortest man here.'[19]

Each tries to appear a giant.

Their voices drift clear and melodious over the still, parched countryside; but for the distant braying of an ass, they are the only audible sound under the baking sun and sky. No breath of wind stirs the trees or the ears of corn. A boy goes round the kneeling ranks with a big earthenware jar of water, and as each man drinks he mutters 'Oh God be praised.'[20]

The hour allowed for eating is announced with another ritual shout from the leader. The men rise slowly, stretching aching backs and limbs, shaking the sweat off them as a dog shakes water from his coat. They leave their sickles where they lie and make for the little bamboo shelter that is the only oasis of shade in a desert of sun. Inside, they sit in a circle, and each takes from his haversack the hunk of dry bread[21] that is the habitual midday meal of the Sicilian peasant. He cuts pieces from it with a knife and eats with infinite relish; [something to eat with the bread is a rarity, and has a special word, *cumpanaggiu*, deriving from the Latin *cum pani*.] Between mouthfuls he drinks copiously from the big earthenware jar, holding it away from his mouth so that the water trickles in and the whole mouth is washed by it; Sicilians learn to make even water go a long way.

After the meal the heat is so intense as to make work almost impossible. The ground is burning under foot, the corn stems are like red-hot wires to the touch. Usually the leader allows his men to sleep for a while if they can; some cannot, for there are burnt shoulders and blistered hands, especially among the young boys who still have tender skins. These make for some olive tree at the edge of the field, and in its shade or high among its branches they sit and sing, slow monotonous tunes like dirges; some of the treble voices are as pure as nightingales', but the sound is as sad as a hunting horn in the deep woods.

When the leader gives the order to start again work begins with the same concentrated enthusiasm as at the beginning of the day, and to the accompaniment of songs and obscenities it goes on without pause until after the sun has set. The gang sets out for home in a body, as it left in the morning, but one man remains behind to stand guard over the harvested sheaves.

The harvest may last many days. They are not paid, these peasants who toil in the sun, for payment is unheard of between relations, and the work they do is thought no more than a fitting tribute to the head of their family.

After the harvest comes the threshing. This too is an affair of tradition, and the threshing-floors have been used for century after century. Each grain-producing district has its old traditional place, and to these each *contadino* brings his harvest to be threshed as his father did before him. The oldest of these threshing-floors are usually on some high knoll that catches whatever wind is blowing, and in a place where it blows from a constant direction. Very occasionally a peasant will make his own threshing-place, but never if he is within reach of one of the traditional *aie*.

The floor itself is a circular piece of ground some six or seven paces across, and its surface is constantly renewed with hard lime or with stones that fit one against another as snugly as bricks. It is kept in repair, and presided over at threshing time, by the owner of the ground. It is he, too, who arranges the order in which those who bring their grain may thresh it, for each must wait his turn, and at night he stands guard over the waiting piles of sheaves outside the circle. His duties at harvest-time are exhausting, and in recognition of his services each peasant donates a small percentage of the threshed grain from his own *timogna* or stack of sheaves.

The sheaves are spread on the threshing floor early in the morning, and from the moment when the sun is over the mountains the scene takes on all the characters of ritual. At the centre of the ring stands a young man dressed in a long white habit, with a kerchief knotted at his throat and a red band around his head. In his right hand he holds the joined reins of two mules, and in his left a long whip.[22] He raises the whip and brings the lash down upon the mules; as he does so he calls out to them in a great and musical voice: '*To the threshing, oh black ones.*'[23]

The mules begin to move, round and round the narrow ring, and as they circulate the young man sings to them. He sings to them only, exhorting them and encouraging them as though they were human and could understand the words of his song, a sad song, almost a threnody, to which the feet of the pacing mules keep time.

> To the threshing, oh black ones,
> Fine is the straw!
>
> Oh how willing they are
> These mules of my heart
> I only should tend them
> I only should tend them.
>
> Long live Santa Rosalia!
> The straw is for you, my mules,
> The grain shall be for me;
> You are happy and content
> For this work is nothing to you.
>
> This mule revolves and turns
> Like a girl from Piana degli Albanesi!
> We must grind while the sun is hot;
> Oh, St. Anthony, see how my mules go!
>
> Endure these torments oh my mules
> For the straw is yours and the grain is mine![24]

If the song should stop the mules become fractious and difficult; hour after hour it goes on, and sometimes within earshot is another *aia* where another young man with the reins and the whip is singing the same song to his mules, so that it becomes a chorus for two separated voices who keep exactly the same time, and sound as one.

With an occasional halt for man and mules to drink, and an occasional reversal of direction to avoid dizziness, the *pisatura*, or turning of the mules, goes on until the beating hooves send the bright grain dancing in the air and a hand thrust among the straw can feel it loose among the stems. The mules make their last lap, the young man invokes the saints to witness the splendour and valour of their work, and the *pisatura* is over.

The next stage is the *spagghiata*, or separation of the grain from the straw. This is a task calling for great skill and experience; indifferent work means that much grain will be lost. There must be some wind, even a gentle breeze,—which is the reason for placing the *aie* upon an eminence that will catch the faintest breath. Sometimes the *sirocco* is blowing, the hot wind that surges up out of Africa, and if it is not too strong the work is quick and easy.

First a tangent is drawn from the centre of the *aia*, a tangent of stones following the exact direction of the wind from centre to circumference, and along this line the *contadini* pile all the threshed straw and grain together. At each end of the line stands a man holding in his hand the *trarenta* or trident; they make the sign of the Cross and shout in chorus 'God's will be done'.[25] Then they thrust their tridents into the mixed grain and straw and toss it up into the air against the wind, so that the straw, being lighter, is blown backward and away from the falling grain.

The rise and fall of the tridents and the ragged wind-dance of the straw against the hard blue sky go on until all the grain lies clear; when the work has been done well the questing hand may hardly find a single ear of corn among the piled yellow stems. But here and there some conjoined ears remain among the loose grain, and to break these down[26] the *pala*, a wooden blade, takes the place of the trident. Finally all the grain is passed through a sieve,[27] and only when this has been done can the weight of the grain be estimated and compared with the prophecies of the 'assessors'. The straw is packed into big containers of basketwork bamboo,[28] and the grain into sacks, and the laden mules begin their long procession home in the twilight.

UNCLE IGNAZIO

'Sometimes we have *aie* in a town street too. Ah, how the children look forward to them, and what times we used to have—it's almost as good as a *festa*! There it's not the mules who do the *pisatura* but the

kids. It's funny to think of like that, but when you think that the *aia*
is in the street for three or four whole days from dawn till dusk, and
imagine all those kids running and dancing all the while you'll see
they really do do the work of the beasts. A hundred or more boys
and girls of all ages from four to fifteen—the evening was the best,
that was the time! They come from far away, in twos and threes
and groups and all together in the *aia* they do somersaults in the air
and sometimes all fall in one great heap from which some come
out crying and some with torn clothes, and some with almost nothing
on at all. That isn't always accidental—what can you expect with a
crowd of kids and the Sicilian sun overhead! Whatever they may say
kids are the same now as when I was a boy—after you're twelve or so
the blood starts boiling in your veins. In a scramble like that boys will
somehow manage to pull a girl's pants down and get an eyeful of what
they want to see—it's only human nature, and what harm does it do?
I remember it was half the fun of the *aia*; we boys used to get together
afterwards and compare notes, and I expect they still do. Those things
are one of the few pleasures the rich haven't got a monopoly in.

'But the evenings were grand too, and they have the same games
now as they did then. It would take too long to tell you all of them.
The old men take part too—in fact there's games in which the most
respected[29] elder has got to preside. Old men and old women of that
sort tell stories of the olden days, and all the neighbours with their
wives and daughters come and gather round and listen to a story[30]
they've heard many many times before—but this time, like every
other time, they'll find something new in it, something mysterious
and moving. The teller puts on a serious manner, and when he or
she comes to the ending "And they all lived happily ever after"[31]
everyone who's been listening answers "While we have to pick our
teeth with our fingers!"[32] In the late evening the peasants who've
organised the *aia* hold a party for their friends and give them what
their grandfathers and great-grandfathers gave before—a glass of
wine and boiled potatoes, or sometimes boiled beans. Someone gets
out a flute or a guitar, and the singing goes on far into the night.
Then one of the hosts goes to sleep on the grain in the *aia*, keeping
guard over it.

'In the morning the mules take a turn or two to finish the job, and
then they do the *spagghiatura* the same way as they do in the country.
The only difference is that the women sing instead of the men, so the

singing isn't as good—they sing religious songs almost always, and they sing in a low voice.

'They say there's many of us peasants in other parts of Sicily who take their corn to a machine for threshing. I've never seen one—they say the cost's terrible, and the old way is good enough for me and for most of us.

'We always use the same measures for our grain—it wouldn't make sense to talk about grain in any other measures. There's three: a *munneddu* is 4 kilograms, a *tumminu* is 4 *munneddi*, and a *sarina* is 16 *tummini*. The old ways are the best, no matter what they may say about progress.'

CHAPTER SEVEN

The Vine Harvest

'To us in Sicily the grape harvest is not so important as the grain harvest. The priority which nature has given to the ripening of the grain coincides with its greater importance in our eyes. To us grain is a manifestation of the Divine, the first thing in our lives, and so everything to do with the grain harvest is in a way holy: grain is bread; bread is life; life comes from God and the means He uses to keep us living is—bread.

'But the grape's got lesser sacred associations; grapes are a secondary product, and without them life would go on the same—if less cheerfully. Anyone in Sicily who owns a scrap of land always sows grain before anything else. If our land is big enough to yield enough grain for a whole year without sowing every yard of it, then we may think about cultivating something else in the rest. Or, if we own another small piece of ground apart from the corn field, we'll certainly plant something else, nearly always grapes. In fact if anyone owns a vineyard he certainly has a field, no matter how small, where he sows grain. It's a step up to own a vineyard, however wretched.

'But the grapes grown by the *contadini*, all put together, make up only a tiny fraction of the vineyards of Sicily. The large vineyards belong to the powerful landowners. The peasants who live in the plains hardly ever own any land at all; everything belongs to the landowners of noble birth; and they cover their lands with huge vineyards and often with citrus fruits, but those are grown only by the richest people.

'The wine trade has great possibilities, but as these good gentlemen control most of the vineyards, they pull commercial strings, and the small producers naturally suffer. Grain's different, it can be grown almost anywhere, in the mountains or by the sea, in the plains or on barren hillsides—but vines can only grow and bear fruit on flat ground, where there's both sun and some water. But the peasant's not going to be beaten, and so he tries to wring wine from the barren rocky soil

which is all he's got. He doesn't kid himself; all he hopes for is enough
wine to cheer his own table.

'Here in this district the contrast between the big producers and the
peasants has been the same for centuries and it shows no signs of
changing. Towns such as Termini Imerese, Bagheria, Monreale,
Carini and Partinico, are the centre of great vine-growing concerns, but
the mountain villages like Torretta, Borgetto, Montelepre, Corleone,
San Giuseppe, and many many others, as well as being kept out of
the wine trade, get exploited by the big concerns. Often one or two
big producers, owners of fertile plain-lands, round up the small
quantity of grapes grown by the peasants, and pay just as they see fit.
In the biggest villages this happens on a vast scale, because the produce
of the small peasants adds up to much more. There's a system of
protection among the great land-owners, looked after by the *mafia*,
which for the most part is made up of people who are land-owners
themselves. There's nothing left for the peasant but the hope of
salvaging just enough to pay his taxes and, if God grants it, a glass
of his own wine in the evening, that rough wine that seems to taste of
his own blood shed amongst the vines day after day.

'In Sicily the grape harvest is usually at the beginning of the autumn;
in the mountains it's two or three weeks later as the grapes don't
ripen so soon. The harvest generally lasts for the month of October,
but sometimes it goes on into November, particularly in the hill
districts. In big business the harvesting is all mechanised now, but the
peasants harvest the grapes and press the wine in the old traditional
ways.

'The first phase, the gathering of the grapes, that is, hasn't changed
even in the vineyards of rich landowners, for no machine has yet been
invented that can pluck the clusters from the vine; but all the same
there's a big difference between the way it's done by the big landowners and the peasants. The landowners pay the grape-gatherers and
they work only at gathering the grapes; they've no feeling for the vine
and the clusters they'll pick for days on end. With the peasants it's a
different story. There's a real and deep bond between them and the
clusters of grapes; the peasant knows every grape in his vineyard and
he's got a love for them almost like he has for his children. When
the great day comes the peasant, well satisfied with what little he's
managed to grow, never grumbling, creates round these vines which

have been so generous to him an atmosphere of *festa*, and he takes with him all his friends and relatives.

'The grape harvest's quite different from any other harvest; it gives the peasant a real delight; he's happy, and he makes a true family gathering out of it—gaiety's an absolute part of grape gathering. There's one, and only one, reason for this—the wine itself. Wine has always meant the same thing to everyone, right down the centuries; by some mysterious power it can give happiness even when our spirits are low, bring smiles to faces which didn't want to smile, and forgetfulness to people whose past is full of bitterness. And the peasant, who spends his whole life surrounded by bitterness, want, and disappointed hopes, feels almost pious towards the sap which can make him happy. What is this thing, wine? Why does it intoxicate him, make him smile? Anything with an element of mystery in it fascinates the peasants; they're grateful, and they express this even before they drink, at the very time when they gather the fruit to make the wine. The sad bitter expressions vanish at harvest time, and become joyful, gay and generous. It doesn't worry them if the grapes are scattered on the ground, or the work slowed down as the helpers sing and shout or actually dance over the grapes; gaiety's part of the tradition. Even the women help to gather the grapes, the youngest of them too, even the little girls, as if these few days were an exception to our laws of morality. The gatherers set off in large groups, and, though there are naturally more workers in the big vineyards, the small ones have an air of *festa* too.

'In the big wine centres there's an old old scene enacted, traditional and pathetic. The harvesters, young men most of them, come in from neighbouring villages. They arrive in groups of twenty or more; their destination is the main square of a town where there's a shortage of workers for the harvest. They carry a large basket and a good knife, and they go and sit down on the steps of the parish church in the square. The new arrivals join those who have got there before them and who are occupying the lower half of the steps. There's a queue which mustn't be broken; the lads who have just arrived take up their positions on the higher steps, while those in front of them move down, making it clear that they come first.

'They all wait until someone comes to offer them work in his vineyard. Often they'll stay there for days on end, especially if they're late arrivals, because they must wait until the ones in front of them have got work. At night they sleep on the steps and in the daytime they never go away. There's always a lot of them, often more than a hundred, and they all show one thing—desperation to find work. They pass the time playing cards, talking, reading—that is if there's anyone who can read—and often quarrelling over the first places in the queue. In Sicily it's customary for comrades in adversity to stand together, and these men are no exception; fights are frequent, and since they have knives they don't hesitate to flourish them at the least excuse.

'This is one of the most wretched things about Sicilian life—unemployment. If you look into the faces of these men you'll see sadness, discouragement, bitterness and accusation. As soon as these unshaven glowering men get taken on everything changes, and when they get to the vineyards they'll sing and shout at the tops of their voices as they work, happy as the day's long. The grape harvest fascinates them, just as it does everyone else.

'The conditions of work are traditional; the owner of the vineyard chooses the men in front of the church, takes them off with him in a car or lorry and leads them straight to the vineyard. Board and lodging is provided by the farmer—but what board and lodging! In the morning there's nothing for them to eat, and they have to start work straight away. At noon they get a piece of bread, two anchovies and a glass of wine, and in the evening vegetable or haricot soup. They sleep outside, or if there's a hut in the fields they doss down on the straw, or even on the pile of grapes gathered during the day. They're paid 800 lire a day.

'But these conditions are traditional, and so no one grumbles; they're satisfied with what they get, because they have no choice. They say: "You take it or leave it—it's this or nothing."[1] When the harvest is over each man is allowed to fill his basket with grapes to take home and hang on the wall until the winter.[2]

'In peasant families the grape harvest is really a family celebration. On the evening before the grape-gathering is to begin the family assembles and draws up a kind of rough-and-ready programme. What they'll take with them to eat, which relatives to invite and how many —these and lots of other questions take up the whole evening. The mother, the mistress of the household, must follow the custom of seeing that the macaroni is taken to the fields and cooked. The macaroni is home-made and only the mother of the family may knead the flour with salt, water and oil on a pastry-board[3] which is kept specially for this kind of work. It's a square block of wood on which dough is kneaded to make bread and spaghetti—every Sicilian family has at least one. When the flour has been kneaded into a solid lump of dough, the mother takes a knife and scores a cross on it with the words: "By the grace of God I see that you are now dough."[4] Then she divides the dough in four, on the sign of the cross which she has made; and only after that she allows her friends and her daughters to help her make the macaroni. They cut off tiny pieces of dough and roll them with their skilled fingers on the pastry-board until they're as thin as pieces of thread. When they have a thin strip of *pasta* about 18 inches long they roll it round a tough blade of grass called *busa*, so that they end up with a single length of *pasta* with the grass in the middle. Then, very carefully, they pull the grass out of the pipe of *pasta* so that it's left with a hole down the middle. They make thousands of these lengths of *pasta*, and at great speed; it only takes a few seconds to make a strip. Often they sing long dirges as they work.

'The macaroni is put into baskets and loaded on to mules in the morning, to be taken to the fields. The closest relatives are invited—how many depends on the richness of the vineyard and its peasant owner. Dawn's only just breaking when they leave in the morning; they all gather in the house of the owner, everyone, both men and women, with large baskets under their arms. The mules lead the way, loaded with provisions; macaroni, bread, wine, etc. They also pile on the mules' backs the canvas bags[5] into which they'll put the grapes when they bring them back to the village.

'So the happy party sets off for the vineyards, and it cheers you up just to look at them and hear them—the high-pitched shouts of the children, the laughter of the young girls, the songs of the men, and the carefree way in which they curse the mules, fill the morning air with joy. When they reach the vineyards the head of the family, that is, the owner, selects a foreman, the liveliest or the oldest, from amongst the men. The women tie brightly coloured scarves over their heads and then follow the men with the baskets, singing and smiling mischievously. Even the long rows of vines laden with grapes seem to exude happiness. The men gathered in front of the rows of vines wait for the old peasant to give his signal to start; behind them stand the women with the baskets. The foreman calls out: "In the name of the Holy Mother!"[6] and the men and women reply: "Let us make a start on the grapes!"[7] As the men kneel by the vines they cut off the bunches of grapes and drop them into their baskets rhythmically and happily. As soon as one of the women sees that a basket is full, she takes it away and puts an empty one in its place; the full one she carries on her head to where the grapes are being tipped out on to a canvas put ready for them. The older women stay and prepare the midday meal.

'The low voices of the men soon grow louder. The foreman begins to sing softly, and the others join in one after another until everyone is singing. The song gradually swells until it rings out over the fields. Infected by the men's song, the girls catch their eyes, and reply to their song. So the long choruses between the girls and the men begin, and the true song of the grape-harvest fills the air. The shouts and laughter of the children are loud above the never-ending songs, and they too make a melody, which is even more innocent and more sincere than their elders.

'The songs are sung with one verse by the men and the reply by the girls:

> Girls: These beautiful grapes
> Are like precious stones.
> I will make me a necklace of them
> For my wedding day.
>
> Men: Can you guess what I have in my mouth?
> A sweet, red grape.
> I want to put it into your mouth,
> A mouth of a thousand kisses.
>
> Girls: You should put the grape
> Only into my hand;
> You could burn yourself on my mouth,
> And that would be your own loss.
> etc. etc.[8]

'Often the men and the girls take up a chorus together: this is part of a song which is often sung here:

> You are as red as our blood, beautiful as the Infant
> Jesus, as sweet as honey.
> There can be no banquets in the halls of princes

Unless there is wine, great flagons of wine;
Oh, wine is the king of them all![9]

There are many verses of this song.

'The grapes are tipped out in heaps on to a canvas, and then other peasants load them into sacks and take them back to the village by mule, where they are pressed and their juice extracted.

'When it grows hot, with the sun at its height, everyone stops for a meal. The pastry-boards are laid out on rough benches and the women who have stopped behind to do the cooking have poured out on to them the macaroni tossed in tomato sauce and sprinkled with plenty of grated cheese. The men who've just stopped work, tired and hungry, feel a great rush of joy when they see the macaroni steaming on the boards; they feel almost as if they'd like to dive into the steaming coils. Hands and mouths plunge into the macaroni, so that from a distance it's difficult to make out their heads in the mêlée as they bob up and down like lots of little pigs, or their hands, which fly about wildly as if they were all struggling with someone they can't overcome. Bursts of laughter and shouts and cries ring out, all confused and mixed up with the sounds of chewing jaws. The hurried meal lasts only a few minutes before the heads are raised from boards wiped almost clean: the people are bursting with laughter and gaiety, and their lips are red with sauce, so that they look like circus clowns.

'Without bothering to wipe their lips—this makes them all laugh at each other and themselves—and with great lumps of bread and bunches of grapes in their hands, they go on eating more slowly, some standing up, some sitting, some stretched out on the ground, and between mouthfuls there's laughter and ribaldry.

'Afterwards they rest for a little while, though "rest" in this case has almost the opposite meaning. The grapes spread on the great canvases are a temptation to men who are overflowing with high spirits, and you can often see them pushing each other into the heaped-up grapes; when there are enough they even improvise dances on top of the piles of grapes. After an hour or two they go back to their work.

'These scenes go on year after year, with the same gay abandon. The old people remember the joyful grape-harvests of their youth and as they watch they're overcome with nostalgia for the past.

' "In our day everything was much better," they say, "we enjoyed ourselves more, there was more fun and high spirits than there are today; those were the days!" Partly because we all exaggerate the past and make it grander than the present, partly because they themselves were the chief actors in the scenes they remember, their tales of wilder festivities and funnier jokes than ours now, make one feel that things are really going down hill. Personally I do believe them up to a point, because our displays of joy at grape-harvest time are getting less, I think, specially in the districts which are much poorer than they used to be.

'During these outbreaks of joy the old peasants assume the rôle of great and wise masters; they suggest which songs to sing, and often lead the songs themselves; they supervise the work, tell the youths of comic happenings in the old days. They often think up jokes too, and get their companions to sing songs that are held together only because they rhyme.

'This is tradition: their fathers did the same with them, and now it's their turn to advise their children.

'"*Russu comu lu sangu nostru*," says the Sicilian song, "red as our blood," as the blood of the Sicilians. The wine springs from Sicilian blood and is bound up with our very existence; it's like a heritage handed down from our very earliest ancestors. There's no need to delve into ancient history, but I will say this; that it's not mere chance that anyone who sees the grape harvest in the poor country districts of Sicily finds himself thinking of festivities as they must have been thousands and thousands of years ago.

'Tradition here in Sicily is the same now as it's always been. Christianity has taken away from us only the names of the old gods; their spirits live on as strong as ever in our hearts.

'We Sicilians live by tradition, we give to tradition the devotion of sons to their mother. I call the powers of progress destructive—destructive in the sense that the Sicilian who is bound to the happiest and best in tradition must watch it being gradually swept away in the advance of progress. If progress will bring prosperity to the peasant, it is making him pay for it dearly—meanwhile it is taking away what he has and not yet giving him anything in return.

'The gathering of the grapes is over.

'The grapes are tipped into the canvas sacks and taken back to the village where the same peasants see to the extraction of the precious juice. As with the gathering of the grapes, this second stage has

undergone great changes, especially in the case of the large-scale producers and the richer peasants.

'The old ways still hold for the peasants of the mountain regions,
for those undeveloped areas couldn't have the new ways and means if
they wanted them. The rich wine-producers have huge warehouses[10]
where the wine is made. Modern machines, pumps and presses, are
used to squeeze out the juice, channel it into barrels, and do what's
necessary to keep it sweet. Among the small peasants all this is done
according to ancient tradition, by hard labour, so that the work which
a press could do in three or four hours takes the peasants several days.
This is the way they do it:

'When the grapes are brought from the fields they're tipped out
into a corner of the stable, which on this occasion serves as the ware-
house. In the corner of the stable there's a small vat, three or four
inches high, six feet long, and a bit more than three feet wide. This
isn't really a proper vat at all, but a kind of platform of cement or
limestone, on to which the grapes will be poured for pressing. The
vat—let's call it that all the same—slopes slightly, and at the bottom of
the slope there's a large opening into a pipe which leads to a tank in the
stable. The tank is generally cylindrical, about six feet in circumference and six to ten feet deep, and it will collect the juice which runs
down the platform. Three ropes—either more or less according to
family tradition—hang down vertically from the roof above the vat.
There are large skilfully made knots in the rope, or wooden rings
attached to it, so that the men will have something to hang on to. The
function of the vat is the same now as it was three or four thousand
years ago; nothing has changed—this is how the peasants of far-off
Crete, of Ancient Greece, and of Syracuse did it, they tell me.

'Some of the youngest and strongest of the men, wearing very heavy
shoes, roll their trousers up, bare themselves to the waist, and climb
up on to the vat, while others tip out some of the grapes under their
feet. The three men—there are generally three of them—grasp the
ropes. The oldest stands in the middle, the others wait for him to give
the signal. At last the man in the middle seizes his companions' two
ropes and with the cry "In the name of the Virgin Mary" pushes the
ropes forward. The other two rush forward after the ropes and so
begin a continuous moving backwards and forwards on the edge
of the vat, stamping their feet on the grapes all the time. The man in
the middle directs the work as he dances. Don't imagine that the

stampers dance on the grapes in any way that they please, for they most certainly do not—there are rules which must be followed, particularly the rules of their leader.

'Out of these steady whirling, stamping movements some sort of harmony takes shape, so that you'd think you were watching a real dance.

'For instance, every time the two others reach the edges of the vat the man in the middle shouts: "Turn round! Turn round!" They turn round while he dances backwards towards them; when he reaches the edge the other two stop in front of him, and he shouts again: "Turn!" This time the two men dance backwards as he turns and dances forwards. And so the rhythm goes on.

'The grapes underneath their feet are squeezed almost dry and the juice gradually runs down through the hole into the tank. Every so often a man will come in and stir the drying grape skins under their feet, and often someone shouts: "On with it, boys, on with it!"[11] Often as they stamp and turn, on and on, the dancers start up a song. The songs vary, they may be modern, or ancient; they sing in chorus— sad songs that are moving in spite of their untrained voices.

'Here's a verse of a well-known song they sing:

> Love is a fire which has no sparks,
> For it smoulders invisibly in the heart.
> More wayward than a child, it makes you impatient,
> It makes you laugh, it makes you suffer.
> The girl who will love you the best
> Can only be found in Sicily;
> She alone can console your heart
> Weighed down by the pangs of love.[12]

It's a long song, but I give you this verse because I love it.

'Often they sing a religious song about the miracle which Christ worked at the marriage at Cana when he changed the water into wine. This is the final verse:

> And the wine flowed sweet as honey in the land of Israel.
> And Christ He laughed, He laughed,
> And with Him laughed His beautiful mother, Mary.[13]

Everyone joins in the refrain:

> And Christ He laughed, He laughed,   etc. etc.

'After hours and hours of stamping, the three men, sweating and splashed with grape juice, climb down from the vat, and the others take the dried grapes out and put fresh ones in their place. Meanwhile the three men smoke a cigarette or wipe the sweat and grape juice from their bodies. *La trippiata*, as they call the work of stamping the grapes, begins again when the other peasants have refilled the vat, probably about half an hour later.

'Other peasants again pour the juice from the tank into the barrels, whilst outside the women are busy preparing the *cotto*. *U cottu* is the portion of grape juice which is boiled with special spices and then added to the juice in the barrels. Outside, in front of the stable, there's an enormous pot.[14] This great pot is filled with grape juice and put to boil on a large tripod. The women add special seasonings to the juice, and put it to boil with locust beans, peach leaves, sour quinces, honey or fig juice, ground almonds, and so on. Every peasant family has its own traditional recipes, so it's not possible to list everything that goes into the juice.

'This juice is put to boil for a whole day, from morning to evening, until it's thick, black and terribly sweet, like honey. Many people drink this liquid; the taste stays with you—it comes back on you as though you'd been drinking it for days. Yes, the boiled grape juice has got a familiar taste—a Sicilian taste. By cooling it for a long time you can make a sweet called *la mostarda*. You mix it with the flavourings and boil it in a small saucepan until it's hard. You let it cool on a marble slab and cut it into diamond-shaped pieces. The result is very difficult to chew, but it tastes good and it keeps for a long time, even right through the winter. To return to the *cotto*: you now add it in equal quantities to the juice in the barrels.

'The peasants take a lot of trouble over making their wines, for they think that it'll fetch a higher price if they sell it, or give greater pleasure to their guests, friends and relatives.

'Meanwhile the pressed grapes are not thrown away; they'll be treated yet again to extract the very last drop of juice from them. Almost every peasant family possesses a *strincituri*—a rough and ready press which is made so that it can squeeze the pressed grapes and extract the last few drops of juice. It's in the form of a circular cage about three feet in circumference and three feet high, placed on a round iron platform about twenty inches above the ground. Round the edge of the platform runs a channel which juts out at one point to allow the wine to run down. In the middle of the platform they set up an iron pole and fasten it with heavy screws. Then the grapes are spread out in the cage and covered with heavy round pieces of wood, which are screwed down with a large bolt. An iron bar is attached to the bolt, so that when the bar's pushed the grapes in the cage are compressed and the juice starts to run out. There are often two peasants to push the iron bar, or, if there is room in the stable, the bar is tied to the back of a mule, which is then made to walk round and round the press. So the last drops of juice are extracted, and the dregs are either sold to merchants or used as fuel.

'When the *vinazza* stage is reached, the people are beginning to get bored. *La vinazza* is the last stage, a mass of crushed flesh and of dried, squeezed dregs of a dark red colour; it's put into sacks and generally kept to feed the stove in winter.[15]

'The juice in the barrels is now given special treatment. With scrupulous care the peasant measures, scrutinizes, tastes, smells, touches, and with great caution and sense of importance he puts into practice instructions inherited from his father. He may add something of his own, something he has learned from experience and which he in his turn will pass on to his sons, for if he has a secret he feels proud of it.

'At last the work of harvesting and storing is finished, and now there's anxiety over the new wine and hope of a good vintage and some small profit.

'Often whatever wine isn't kept back for family consumption is sold to wine merchants who travel round the villages with their lorries. Others prefer to sell in small quantities, to their neighbours and to strangers who are passing through, though that's dangerous, because it's illegal.

'Without going into the whole problem—which is a terrible one for the Sicilian peasant—I'll just say that the outlook is always gloomy. Today, particularly in political circles, they talk about "the wine crisis", but not about the wine racket. The wine "crisis"—a fine word you'll hear from the lips of a thousand speakers at public meetings—is not a crisis at all; it's a crisis only for the wretches who produce the wine after enormous sacrifices. The "crisis" is discussed in Italian, good Italian, by men with enormous stomachs and bulging cheeks, it's discussed in luxurious lounges and by people who are too clever by half. The poor peasant watches this act year after year, and year after year he kids himself, while the large-scale cultivators and big

wholesale dealers are building up for themselves a solid monopoly.
It's not my place to say anything more about the real wine-growing
crisis; it's a big field, a field of politics and the political aims of well-
known political figures who grow fat on it. The wholesale wine
merchants act as bankers, lending the peasants money and in return
making them promise to sell their grapes to them only, so that the
price and the conditions of sale are in the merchants' hands. The
peasant obeys unless he wants to commit suicide.

'Just think of this: in a wine-shop wine costs 150 lire a litre, while
the peasant sells it at 15, 20 or 25 lire a litre. Incredible, yes—but it
happens to be true.

'What can the peasant do but resign himself to fate; he finds a little
comfort, in his despair, as he thinks of the harvest; of the songs of the
grape-gatherers; of the happiness of his children; of the smiles and
shouts and laughter. Even if he's got nothing but a piece of stale bread
he manages to smile—he's tough, and he has his ancestors on his side.'

CHAPTER EIGHT

The Olive Harvest

TOLD BY TOTO CASTELLO

'The olive tree is the third source of life in Sicily. As you look out over the Sicilian countryside spread out before you, your eye will constantly light on the big black clumps of olive trees, scattered here and there over the fields, still and beautiful.

> A life spent in digging
> is worth nothing
> if you plant no olive trees.[1]

'This proverb tells you a lot by itself; it shows just how important the olive is to the peasant. Like the corn and the grapes, it's something which the peasant's land must never be without. Even if the soil is poor, even if it lacks irrigation, even if it's mountain soil and full of rocks, the peasant will never, as long as he lives, tire of planting olive trees; with the tenacity inherited from his forefathers he'll go on trying to wrest from the miserly soil the mysterious power, as he calls it, which gives life to the olive trees. The olive tree is held to be "the third blessing",[2] that is, the third manifestation of divine goodness by which every Sicilian peasant feels he lives. To understand the really deep importance of the olive tree to the peasant you must have some idea of his conception of the produce and value of each tree.

'You may be surprised that a tree of everyday importance like the olive should be thought divine in the ordinary sense of the word, but this is also true of the corn and to a lesser extent of the grapes. The olive tree has its patron saint, often varying from one district to the next, and between the patron saint of the tree and the tree itself there's scarcely any distinction. The peasant prays to the saint to make the tree fruitful, but he also pays homage to the tree to turn away the anger of the saint. Ignoring pagan tradition, in a sense the olive tree is a sacred plant, and they say it had its part in the olden-day religions. In a song which is often sung when special prayers are offered to the patron saint, there's one verse which goes like this:

> Water covered the earth,
> Then a dove flew across the sky
> And from its beak hung
> A small branch of beautiful olives.[3]

This refers to the great flood, but, if you think of it you're always coming across olives in the Bible—Christ's prayers in the olive garden, the olive branches with which He was greeted at Jerusalem, and so on, which seem to show that it was some sort of sacred tree even then. Here the cult of the olive varies from district to district, so there are ceremonies and traditions in one area which are quite unknown in another. Where I come from they tie a sacred cord, handed down from one generation to the next, to the trunk of the olive tree as soon as it has finished flowering. They say this cord has the power to drive evil spirits away from the tree and propitiate the patron saint. When the olives are fully grown the cord's cut and the trunk of the tree anointed with holy oil. A snake, slaughtered and suspended from a branch of the tree, has the power to increase the harvest, and, like the cord, it drives away evil spirits. They hang other things on the tree too, horse-shoes, various animal horns, and, strangely enough, food-graters; I don't know why. Many peasants also hang up little wooden crosses, or images of the patron saint of the olive tree.

'In August, when they can already tell whether or not the crop is going to be good, the peasants carry out nine days' devotions to the patron saint of the olive tree. If the crop is poor they pray to the saint that there may be neither wind nor rain to ruin the handful of olives on the trees; if it's a good crop they sing thanksgiving hymns.

'The religious side of the olive tree is made stronger by the healing powers which the peasants believe it has. For a stomach-ache, for instance, they prescribe a broth made by boiling olive leaves. They treat a cut with crushed leaves mixed with oil, and a headache with poultices made of oil, breadcrumbs and boiled olive leaves. Then, too, there are old peasants, respected by the people for the wisdom that comes with great age, who can see in trees—and particularly olive trees —signs foretelling the future: what the weather will be like, the events that are going to happen. When the leaves of the olive tree tremble it's a sign of rain, when they are white on the under-side it's a sign that

—and her grandson

La nonna

" . . . a four-year-old daughter of a curious, simian beauty "

the tree will not bear much fruit; when the tree looks very black it's a sign that it will be loaded with olives, and it is also a forecast of a good year in general.

'It would take hours to tell you all the properties and powers they say the olive tree has; so I'll just talk about the most important thing of all—olive oil.

'For a peasant family it's a tragedy to be without oil. No matter how poor they may be, they always have, besides their little granary, their jar of oil. A poor peasant family is miserly in its use of oil, for when you're poor it's something precious. The trees don't always yield enough oil to last out the year. Often the peasants are forced to suffer year after year of shortage, and that's what's happening now— it's years since the trees gave a good yield of oil. In a hot climate like this the olive trees get periodic invasion of parasites, and sometimes there are real epidemics caused by microbes. Of the insects the olive-fly is far the worst—it leaves ruin behind it. But while the rich farmers succeed in destroying that terrible enemy with chemical preparations, peasants not only can't afford to, but have strong superstitions about it. They're terribly distrustful of the new medicines. Often they don't really believe that the trees have got a disease; they think it's a sign of the anger of this or that saint, or even the unleashing of evil spirits. So when a blight attacks their trees, they think it better to turn to the various divinities, rather than apply remedies, which they say would only increase the anger and the blight. They also think that if they use a modern remedy against a blight the fruit of the tree will be infected by the remedy and lose its natural flavour. You hear the peasants complaining of some ache or pain and declaring "those medicines they're spraying in the fields are poisoning every man jack of us". When the olive-fly destroys the crop, the peasants will pray to the various gods of the fields; they make vows and sacrifices, but they will not break the laws handed down to them by their fathers, they will not sully the virginity of their fields.

'Now the story that the atom bombs are poisoning the atmosphere is on every peasant's lips; they say that's why they haven't seen their trees heavy with olives for so many years. But that's not the only rumour in the air, only the latest one, and possibly the most likely to be true.

'Meanwhile the rich farmers have a yield every year which is far and away greater than that of the small peasant who is content with what chance, and chance alone, has in store for him—simply hoping for better things next year—which never comes.

'It's not their fault that the peasants still think in this way even in the face of the progress which is making such rapid strides everywhere —no, it's not their fault. So often poverty and wretchedness and ignorance are the real causes of ills they don't seem to have any connection with. With each day the peasant has less to cling on to, and all around him he sees nothing but injustice, injustice triumphant. There's nothing left to him but the comfort of tradition inherited from his ancestors; he doesn't realise that many of the laws he accepts blindly are so much nonsense. And no one tries to make him understand.

'The Sicilian peasant today is the slave of the big farmer. He doesn't want to sell the produce of his soil, because it's needed to feed his family, and he's burdened with taxes he can't possibly pay. So often he's got to sell some of what he needs to eat, although it means hunger for his family—but he can only sell to the large-scale farmer, who gives him the lowest possible price and then resells at twice the amount, or even more. There's no escape for the wretched people.

'The olive harvest hasn't got a happy atmosphere like the first two blessings, the corn and the grapes. It's a sad atmosphere like the autumn sky, an expression of a people worn down by their fate, and the grey November weather looks back at you with bitterness and discouragement from the peasants' faces.

'With the first rains of autumn the olives begin to fall from the trees. Often when the wind has been howling all night long the ground at the foot of the trees is covered with olives, and the peasants must start the salvaging of these still unripe fruit. One by one they must all be picked up from the ground; it depends on how carefully it's done whether or not there'll be some oil for the household.

'I remember my dreadful ill-humour, or as we Sicilians say, *lagnusia*—meaning a desire to do nothing at all—when many years ago after a night of wind and rain I used to have to get up when it was still dark and go to gather the fallen olives in the fields with the peasants' children. In the early hours of a dark autumn morning all you want is to curl up amongst the warm blankets and rock yourself drowsily to the tapping of the rain which is falling gently outside. I loathed those dawns; my mother would come up to my pillow and whisper in my ear, "Toto, get up, you must go out into the fields, the wind has littered the ground with olives. Come on, there's a good lad, do get up. I've made you a bun, your friends Pino and Ciccio are outside. Come on, up with you!" And she lifted me up in her arms. Only my mother's wheedling voice finally did the trick, and I got up, mumbling and grumbling at having to leave my warm bed. Outside, the peasants' children would be waiting for me. There were five or six of them sitting on the steps in front of our gate with their baskets. They were huddled up in old jackets, with their heads on their knees and their hands in their pockets, so that they were completely hidden from view. I used to hear them chattering as I went down the steps, and my heart lifted, for I'd always been fond of my friends. I was no better dressed than they were, and as soon as I opened the gate, they dived inside with shouts of greeting which pleased me, although they were insulting: "Come on, wake up, you idler! You lazy idiot, we must go, it's late, you slugabed!"[4] My mother gave me a bun seasoned with olive oil and salt, slung my basket over my shoulders, and said her final words of goodbye. I set off down the road chewing, while my friends whistled gaily. We put our big loose jackets over our heads, the baskets under our arms, our hands in our pockets and merrily whistled different tunes. In those dawn hours I was happy to be going off to work with the children of the peasants; I considered myself a peasant too, even if I now realise that I wasn't one. On the way we met dozens of other groups of children, peasants, women and old men, all with their baskets under their arms. They were all going to rescue the olives. We would start to sing with other boys we met; often we made merciless fun of some old peasant whose ass refused to go any further; often we started to scuffle with other boys we ran into along the way, as boys will, and after the fight we were the best of friends again. When we reached my fields we began work straight away. Here in the open the cold was more intense, and clouds of steam floated thickly round our faces with every breath; we managed to keep fairly warm by stamping our feet and rubbing our hands. Before starting work we made our usual bets: who would be the first to fill his basket with olives and who would have filled the most baskets by the end of the day. I never won.

'We knelt down round the tree, and at the cry, "One, two, three, go!" we began to pick up the olives as quickly as we could. I remember how the cold soaking-wet earth froze my hands, so that soon I was out of competition. This made me angry and ashamed; I wasn't a peasant, but I couldn't understand it.

'While we picked up the olives we would sing some song or other, generally obscene. The favourite was the one about the doctor and the beautiful girl. One of us would start:

> He touched her hand
> and the girl cried, "Oh, no."
> That's not where the pain is at all.

and we'd come in with the chorus:

> No, no, doctor,
> The pain isn't there,
> It's much lower down than that.
>
> And he touched her chest,
> And the girl cried, "Oh, no."

All: No, no, doctor,
     etc.

> And he touched her belly
> etc.

All: No, no, doctor,
     etc.

> And he touched her ————
> And the girl cried, "Oh, yes!"

All: Oh, yes, oh, yes, doctor,
     That's right where the pain is,
     That's right where the pain is, just there.[5]

But the song goes on for hours before the doctor finally touches the beautiful girl where she wants it. Often as we worked and sang it would start to rain. If it was only a shower we went on working, but if it was heavy we took shelter in a hut. And what pranks and experiments we used to get up to in those huts!

'We used to finish picking up the olives in the evening after sunset. They were all put into a sack which my companions took in turns to carry on their backs. I never carried it, because I was landlord. Coming home you saw the same scene everywhere; peasants coming back from the fields with sacks of olives on their backs; women sitting on carts with their hair soaking wet, and the marks of exhaustion and pain on their faces; mules walking slowly in Indian file; tired, breathless old men who trailed along behind everyone else. An atmosphere of melancholy hung over them all; they seldom spoke, and only the children would give raucous shouts which broke the evening silence. Today everything is just the same as it used to be then—nothing's changed.

'So the Sicilian olive harvest begins; not the real harvest, but its first phase: the harvest proper will take place in a few days, when the olives begin to fall more quickly. Those which have been picked up from the ground are put into large baskets and covered with plenty of salt, and left there until the harvest is over. There are more olives to salvage on windy or rainy days, and then everyone is mobilised; grown-ups, and children, women and old men.

'It's really as soon as the peasants have finished the grape harvest that they make a start on the olives. Here it takes place in November. In Sicily the olive harvest isn't at the same time of the year as elsewhere —each region is different. In Calabria it goes on into January, in Campania they even wait for the spring, while in Catania they often finish gathering the olives at the end of January. But in the west of Sicily, where the rule is poverty and destitution, the olives are harvested very early, because the peasants can't wait for them any longer. This is not traditional; many old people have told me that in the old days the olives were abundant even in this area, but that times have changed and the curse of God lies heavy upon them and their families.

'The olive harvest is a very complicated thing; above all it needs men who can do the various different jobs. There are four types of workers.

'First there are the *cutuliatura*. These are the men who shake the olives from the tree and are nearly always very strong and fearless young men who have gained a reputation for this work in their own village. They're entrusted with the most dangerous tasks; they have to climb up the highest branches of the trees in groups of two or three and shake the branches loaded with olives. Often they are provided with long sticks which they use to poke at the branches they can't reach.

'Then there are the *cugghitura*, those who pick up the olives from the ground; they're mostly women and children. Usually they're in groups of five, six, or seven, according to the size of the tree.

'Next are the *passulunara* [*passaluni* is the word for the olives which are kept under salt for eating], who are for the most part old men of experience; they separate the ordinary olives for crushing from those which will be preserved and then either sold or kept at home to eat with bread. They also select the olives for salting[6] which are green in colour and larger than the ordinary ones. They are preserved with salt and vinegar and will keep for a very long time.

'The *arrisciuppatura* are women and children who at the end of the day go over the ground under the olive trees a second time in search of olives overlooked by the *cugghitura*. The rich farmers take up most of these workers. There mustn't be one single olive left on the ground, or else there will be crowds of people under these trees later on looking for olives of any description which may have been left behind. There used to be *trappitara*, people who worked the mills which crush the olives, but today there are modern implements even in the tiny villages.

'The *cugghitura* are most important, particularly the children. Children work more quickly; they're given only small wages, and they give more in return for their money. Only the richer children go to school, but at the time of the olive harvest you won't see any children in the streets.

'The children rise at dawn, and go off to work, shivering with cold, and without breakfast; the farmer gives them nothing to eat in the morning. After half a day bent double over the ground they get a piece of bread and salted olives from the farmer. They go on working till late at night; often they sleep out in the fields on a bed of hay. Often they sing as they work; it's hard to keep a boy's spirits down. Here's a song they often sing:

> Oh master, we tremble,
> We want bread
> For we are children
> And we want to eat.
>
> If you will not give it to us
> God will be angry
> And will send you to hell,
> Where you will see Him no more.
>
> We cannot weep
> Because our eyes are cold.

We are children,
Please make us warm.

O St. Anthony,
You who make the olives
See, see
How they make us work.

Give us dried figs and locust beans
To eat.
We don't want
To be treated like animals.[7]

'It's a sad and moving song, with a lovely tune, and you often hear children singing it in the fields.

'They earn only 300 lire a day, a little less than the daily wage of the *cutuliatura*. But not every small peasant farmer can carry the cost of so many workers, and so he takes his whole family to harvest the olives.

'Often there will be a team of two small peasant families, consisting of four or more *cutuliatura*, about a dozen boys and girls and the women. At dawn they assemble at the house of the peasant who owns the trees and set off for the fields. The mules lead the way; tied on their backs are baskets, hampers, and long ladders which will be used to climb up the trees. They move along almost in silence among the many other groups of peasant families making their way to the fields. When they get there the *cugghitura* spread themselves out under the trees with their baskets in their hands. Then they all begin work in the autumn silence. The only sound to be heard over the fields is the rough voices of the *cutuliatura*: "Ready, steady—one, two, three— in the name of Mary! Have a swing at that branch."[8] They will curse almost musically whenever they have to make a great effort to shake the heavy branches. Under the trees the *cugghitura* stand in a circle, and their work gets faster and faster. Often the plaintive voices of the peasants begin, as they warm to their work, to sing, very slowly:

> The innkeeper's son
> Has taken a fancy to me:
> He has lots of money,
> He will make me rich.

Reply in chorus:

> A young man with a small moustache,
> A young mechanic,
> Has taken a fancy to me,
> And he has said he will marry me.

> Love is like a fire:
> It dies at the touch of water or wind.
> If you want to be rich,
> You must take this rich man.

Reply in chorus:

> All the water in the sea
> Cannot extinguish my love,
> Nor can you take love away from me
> With your money.[9]

'In the evening they finish work, load the mules, pick up everything and go back home. If they're going to have to come back next day they leave their tools in the fields.

'On the way back the cry is always the same, even if they've harvested quite a lot of olives—"This year we've got nothing—God is punishing us."[10]

'The olives are put in a corner of the house for several days under salt, and then taken to the mill.[11]

'At the mill the peasants put their olives in great baskets and sit down beside them waiting their turn at the mill. At night the work goes on just the same in the mills. In odd corners of the room old peasants, women too, doze as they rock to and fro to the monotonous noise of the machines. The millers whistle or hum popular songs and from time to time wake the peasants whose turn it is: "Eh, Uncle Turi, wake up! It's your turn, which are your olives?"[12] The old man grumbles away when he's woken up. Within a few minutes the olives are giving oil and the peasant follows each process of the manufacture closely. "Good God, the *nozzolo*!"—that's the oil which is given by the last milling—"Don't you want it?"[13] one of the millers shouts at the top of his voice. If it's left behind the cost of milling is smaller, and often the peasants will forfeit it rather than pay the higher price. As soon as the oil starts flowing from the centrifugal machine, the peasant dips his fingers in and tastes it and gives his verdict. On the wall round about him are hanging tin boxes containing images of various saints, and in each one of them he must place a small quantity of oil to pacify them. If you give to one of them you have to give to all, and there are more than ten of them. So he says good-bye to a litre or more of oil in this way. *"This is crucifying me!"*[14] .cries the peasant bitterly. But he's made all the saints friendly towards him and his conscience is at rest. A fair quantity of oil will be left for the mill owner if the peasant can't pay in money. The rest—if there is any rest —he takes home; it will be put in a jar and used with miserly care.

'Now I must tell you how those who've got no olive trees manage to get hold of oil. As soon as all the peasants have finished gathering the olives, they make a grand tour of the fields, carrying baskets, in search of olives which have been left behind. They're often women, mothers of families, who can't afford to buy oil for their family needs, so they must get some by hook or by crook. After a day of weary searching through the fields they can barely manage to fill their baskets—which can hold five kilos of olives—with enough fruit to yield 300 grammes of oil. They have to spend many days in this way, if they want even a drop of oil in the house. When it's all over they usually manage to make a few litres of oil, just enough to give their children pleasure.

'And so the olive harvest ends, a sad, dismal harvest. The oil is nearly always used for family needs—it's very rarely sold, except where there's enough to do both. It's the last of the three principal harvests of the year, and so the whole season ends on a note of pessimism which you can see in the eyes of every peasant. And they say once more:

> We poor must suffer
> If we want to live . . .'[15]

CHAPTER NINE

The Festa

DURING the time that I had been doing research into the life and death of Salvatore Giuliano—the bandit or rebel leader or gangster or Robin Hood according to whom you believe—I had come across an irrelevant but puzzling situation, one that had nagged at me and demanded future investigation.

At the time of which I had been trying to write, the towns and villages that are the background of this book had been under military occupation of an often brutally repressive character; externally, at least, there was a civil war being fought out in that corner of Sicily, though later there was great doubt cast upon the integrity of the leaders of the forces engaging Giuliano.

The local military authorities, however, had become absolute dictators, and they were both feared and hated. In Montelepre, the home of 'The King of the Mountains', there were curfews, mass arrests followed by torture—whole families were shipped into exile, but among the town people of Montelepre all these things produced only an intensification of the sullen silence that was as yet directed entirely at the occupying army.

This situation changed overnight as the result of an action, a minor repressive measure, it might seem to an outsider, quite insignificant by comparison with what the people had already undergone. The military authorities forbade them to hold their main annual *festa* in honour of the patron saint of the town.

This produced a reaction like none other that had preceded it; it appeared to them as if they had been robbed of their most prized possession, almost of their very right to live. There were no scenes nor riots, for the strength of the enemy in the town precluded any direct action, but the silent mutiny became something fierce and active, something to be felt almost physically; 'the eyes of the people,' as one soldier put it, 'spoke louder than rifle bullets, and it was more terrifying to be looked at by them than to be under fire.' Now, too, their hatred had for the first time widened to embrace not only the army of occupation but the civil and ecclesiastical authorities as well. All sections of the population reflected the same attitude, grown men and greybeards, old women and children, felt that something of immense preciousness, bequeathed by generation after generation of forebears, had been snatched from them. To them it was an outrage in a sense that no horror that had gone before had been.

At first the people sent deputations to the priests to demand an explanation, but the priests put the responsibility upon the civil authorities, who in turn placed it upon the military, and no one dared to approach them. A whole town felt dishonoured, insulted and betrayed, and groups of women formed at the street-corners screaming blasphemies and curses upon every power in heaven and on earth. Then they became a people in mourning.

The curious intensity of the reaction had, as I say, nagged at me; it was something that I knew I had failed completely to understand, and was clearly so essential a part of the Sicilian complex that the explanation was one I could not do without.

So in a later year I approached a certain retired doctor, by name Toto Castello, who was a member of the Festa Committee in a neighbouring town, and asked him if he would try to explain. Doctor Castello was a clever old man, not perhaps too well up in the latest developments of his profession, but shrewd and discerning, with a mildly cynical approach to both Divine and human nature, and he was by far the best read and educated man in the district.

'I see. You want to know how the simple fact of the people being forbidden to hold their *festa* produced all that fuss when they already had every indignity and distress that one can suffer. Yes, it's difficult, for a stranger to understand, and I don't think I could make it clear to you without getting you to realise how many different factors are at work. They're all important. I'll have to talk about three separate things—the attitude towards the *festa*, its preparation, and then the actual *festa* itself.

'Well, when one speaks of *festas* in a southern country like Sicily one-is approaching a vast field of history, ethnology, psychology and morals. A *festa* for the southern people is a whole world of ancient things which comes to being in a very short space of time. It's made up of so many many things that live deep in the soul of the whole people.

'You see, six whole months before a *festa* one begins to think about it and prepare oneself for it. People of every class and every trade begin to plan in their minds how they'll pass those few days, and what they'll have to do before it takes place.

'A whole world of promise begins to outline itself in the early preparation for the *festa*; everyone has something to promise to the patron saint of the town. For the sake of their crops and their livestock the peasants promise to offer a candle in the procession and give larger offertories; the cobbler, the carpenter, the painter promise something else for their health and for a better future; mothers of families promise to walk barefoot throughout the long procession for the well-being of their children and for the general good; the spinsters promise the same so that they may find a husband during the *festa* and set their lives in order; the old men, too, always have something to promise. It's hope that feeds the hearts of so many people. Everyone hopes, in the celebration of the *festa*, for a better world; the girl gets ready a new dress, with pleats and tucks at the side according to the latest fashion, and hopes and hopes that the new dress will bring her luck in love. The youths have new suits made, because they must compete with their friends and show themselves off, and at the same time try to find the girl of their dreams.

'The mothers think about their daughters' clothes too, and if they're engaged their mothers try to make them look worthily dressed at the side of their future husbands.

'The artisan works harder, because he hopes that with the *festa* more orders will come in and his earnings increase; the innkeeper, the butcher, the chemist, the sweet-maker, all hope to make a bit more during the *festa*, and that the *festa* will show off their district and bring new trade to it. Even the poorest people must appear, during the *festa*, if not well dressed at least decently dressed; they feel the right to take part in the general rejoicing. It's all a system of things that unfolds and repeats itself year after year, and for the people it's really a reason for living.

'Then there are the religious factors that dominate the atmosphere of the *festa* externally. The *festa* is held in honour of a saint, the patron saint of the town and of all in it, and everyone must show the saint his faithfulness and devotion. The people make of the saint whom they are fêting a human being, almost, by making him, as it were, share in their fun; he must be praised first in church, and then in the

town, by procession. All the amusements and entertainments are in
honour of that saint, who sees everything from above and would
surely love those who know how to amuse themselves in his honour—
each one, in short, should satisfy in himself the human desires of the
patron saint, because he can't do so himself, poor man.

'In the *festa*, too, there's the unchanging world of tradition. Every
year on that given day you *must* celebrate the *festa*, and that's interesting,
for it recalls an old popular legend handed down from father to son,
that on the saint's *festa* day something fantastic or incredible will
happen in the town, through the agency of that saint.

'The Divinity has, in the eyes of the people, the two eternal aspects
of nature, the good and the evil. In the popular mind God or the
saints can be either well-disposed or wicked, according to how you
behave towards them. If you neglect your patron saint you'll be
severely punished; if on the other hand you show attention to him
you'll be rewarded. This is no different from the idea the people
have of God; it's an idea carried on by tradition over thousands of
years. If we turn back we find people like the Romans, the Greeks and
others, where the idea of divinity was mythological, and where the
festa, which was part of their lives as it is of ours, had exactly the same
characteristics as a *festa* today. It seems that the modern idea of a
festa derives directly from the Greek and Roman games.

'In the *festa* today the world of two thousand years ago lives again;
there is an Olympus with all the gods, there's Minerva, kind and
charitable but terrible too, there's Diana, there's Pan, there's Mars—
they're all there, but in modern religious language they're called Saint
this and Saint that. Certain customs, too, have been absorbed entirely
into the *festa* of today, for example holding of games during the
ceremonies, bringing gifts to the patron saint, the supposed "purity"
of the youths, celebrating strange and obscure rites, and so on.

'So the *festa* is the world of a whole people who relive their
thousands-of-years-old history; it's something more than confusion
and swarms of people and noise—it is, in short, the fruit of the wisdom
of the people, and of their experience, a people who knows itself to
be so much in need of supernatural help. In it there remain the
indestructible roots of tradition—superstition, faith, fable, and ignorance; and in all that there's another thread, a strictly practical aspect,
for the people try to gain certain advantages from the exterior form
of the *festa*.

'So you see that when a people like that sees this world of its heritage violated, this common legacy threatened, it's capable of reacting in the most violent manner, with really bitter hatred, as if it were their own lives that were threatened. As I've said, the *festa* can even be called a reason for living.

'And now I'll tell you about the preparations for a *festa*, but you must understand that I'm referring to all *festas*, large and small, because the preparatory phases, the forethought, the concern, and the organisation go on in the same way for every *festa*. The *festa*, then, is held every year on a day fixed by tradition, and neither a day earlier nor a day later than that—only for reasons of a religious nature can you put off the date of the celebration.

'It is the people, above all, who hold the *festa*, but there's an organisation, a council, representing, acting, and working for them. There's the so-called "deputation" that consists of twenty or more members, from among whom is elected the Chief Deputy, Treasurer, and a Secretary. Those are the bigwigs of the deputation, and the others act as councillors. Every year the deputation is nominated and elected, but by whom? And how? They're certainly not elected in the ordinary way; it's the outgoing deputation that elects the new one—or to be more exact the outgoing Chief Deputy, Treasurer, Secretary, and a few other trusted members. Thus the new Chief Deputy elect is almost always an old man, someone with *savoir-faire*, a man in short that we call *ntisu*—*ntisu* means esteemed, but it can also mean *mafioso*, or one who knows how to make himself respected, or one who is well born, and so on—possibly a *mafioso* or someone who gets on with the *mafia*, because they too influence the happy outcome of the *festa*.

'As Treasurer they elect a man who is, probably, rich, and for Secretary one who is good at pen work. Often the whole deputation is made up of more or less well-off peasants, but peasants who are *ntisu*.

'The announcement of the nomination of the new deputation takes place in a characteristic and interesting way. To each member of the new deputation they send a candle, and carry it into his house. But to the new Chief Deputy they send a bigger candle, a torch, and it must be taken to him by the hand of the outgoing Chief Deputy himself. The other new deputies get an ordinary candle, and it's not necessarily brought to them by the outgoing deputies. No one can refuse the "candle of honour", as it's called, unless there are serious reasons such as ill health or mourning; if anyone did refuse he'd be just about ruined for life. They say he'd be cursed by God and by the people, and that misfortune would never leave him or his family. He'd certainly become the talk of the town, and certainly he would lose the respect of many—he'd become a complete outcast.

'This conferring of duties takes place on the last day of the *festa* in progress, so that the new deputies can follow, with the candles they have received, in the evening procession of the saint.

'I'm going to tell you now of the various concerns of this new deputation, which are the same as for all the past and future deputations, because these customs have never changed, and won't while there's *festas* held.

'A week after the *festa* that has just finished the new deputies assemble in one of the church buildings, to arrange the organisation and the collection of offerings for the funds of the next *festa*. The new Chief Deputy sits at the head of a table, with the Treasurer and Secretary at his sides, and the other deputies round the walls. The session begins with an examination of the situation left by the previous deputies, and with outlining the new programme for the next *festa*, that's almost a year ahead still.

'Most times the fund's empty when it's opened, the fund that in a year's time must contain so many hundreds of thousand-lire notes and other offertories for the *festa*. The work of the deputies begins at once; they are divided into groups of two or three people who on fixed days must tour the town asking offerings from the people. The days are fixed because they have to respect the turn of the other town deputations, deputations for other *festas* and other saints. The people contribute to all *festa* deputations, and give as much as they can, because it's considered an honour, even, apart from being a duty. What seems so strange to those who look upon the southern parts of Italy as poor and forsaken is that such a really poor people manages to get together such a really enormous sum for the sole purpose of fêting and propitiating a saint and holding a *festa*.

'The deputies who must collect these offerings begin their work in the morning and finish at dusk. Generally they ask for money, but in the towns where offerings "in kind" are more usual and more often brought by hand, they ask for all kinds of things as offerings. In May, for instance, the peasants are cutting hay in the country, and many of them give a greater or lesser quantity of hay, according to conditions. These things they give to the saint, almost as if to propitiate him.

'In June there's the grain harvest, and the deputies tour the country and the streets asking offerings for the *festa*; in August and September there's the grape harvest, and quantities of grapes or of unfermented wine, according to how the offering is made, pile up in the deputies' store. In November and December there's the olive harvest, and the offerings are either of oil already refined or of harvested olives. The deputies tour the olive-mills[1] and ask for oil for the *festa*; and there's other less common goods, such as, for example, almonds, lemons, flour, beans, locust beans, and so on. All these offerings of raw material are stored and sold. The proceeds are put into the bank under the care of the Treasurer, while the Secretary notes the transactions in the register.

'This work goes on throughout the year, but it's greatly intensified when the *festa* is approaching. Now the deputies no longer respect the turn of other deputations, and for 15 or 20 days before the *festa* all the deputies go out into the streets of the town at the same time, in search of new offerings, and now it must be in money. Not one of the people refuses this, which has become almost a duty—and no one escapes the deputies!

'A special collection, the most interesting and at the same time the most "official", is taken during the last three days before the *festa*. This is called the *questula* [meaning a collection, and stemming from the Latin word *quaero* meaning 'I seek', or 'I want' or 'I ask', etc.]. It consists of taxing every family in the town a certain sum according to its economic condition. The sum can be as much as 10,000 lire, with a minimum of 1,000 lire. This kind of final offering is the official payment for the *festa*; in fact, the *questula* is compulsory and those who pay it are inscribed in a register together with the sum they have given.

'Finally the Secretary must ask an offering from those who are not living in the country—from those who have emigrated to America. In those people the devotion to the patron saint still remains; a sense of nostalgia still binds them to their distant native land, and they feel it their duty to contribute. The offerings that come from America are noble, and sometimes make up two thirds of the whole sum that's collected in the town.

The storehouses of the *tonnara*

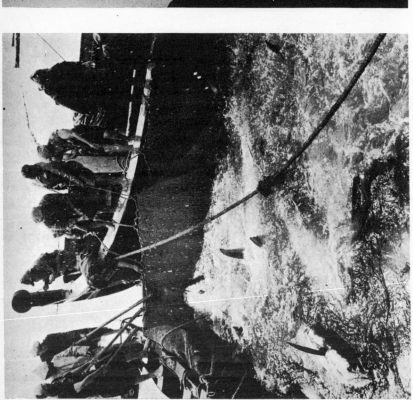

A corner of the 'chamber of death' before the

Mattanza at dawn

'They also ask sums from the town council [in the case of the main *festa*] and sometimes, especially if there's an election in the wind, they get money from the members of Parliament and other bigwigs; that happens when there are people of political importance among the deputies.

'So, in one way and another, the capital for the *festa* is raised, capital which varies with different *festas*, but which is always a good sum. If I had to guess I should say that it wouldn't be more than 5 million lire, or less at the least than 2 million, in a town of 6,000 inhabitants and most of them peasants.

'Now I'll tell you about how the deputies spend this money they've collected, and of the unwritten rules to which the deputies must traditionally conform in organising the *festa*.

'The sum collected, all in hard cash, is spent to the last penny; there's rarely anything left in the bank from the last *festa*, but if there is that gets spent too.

'In the deputation, as I've said, there's a directing body consisting of the Chief Deputy, the Treasurer, and the Secretary, and a working body of the rest of the deputies, but the real authority is in the hands of the first three. During the last period before the *festa* they get together to discuss the spending of the money, the organisation of the programme and what novelties they should include, bearing in mind that they have the heavy responsibility of the success of the *festa*. The three, then, having made a programme, must arrange the following:

'First, the decoration of the church in which the religious functions must take place. The decorated church[2] is of great importance to the people—the first thing they look at is how the church has been decorated, and whether the ornaments are beautiful, and these must satisfy certain tastes that are traditional. The decorator[3] is appointed by the Chief Deputy, and negotiations begin between these two to fix the price. It takes about fifteen days to decorate the church, and the skilled labourers at this work, besides being paid by the deputation, have the right to free board and lodging at its expense.

'How the church is decorated is not easy to describe; it's a long and complicated business, practised by only a few people in Sicily, and the art is handed down from father to son. The cost of decorating a church varies according to how it is done, but one can spend 100,000 lire or more.

'Next comes the question of the musical band. This is a difficult duty, because it's obvious that the music is the crux of the whole thing. If there isn't a band in the town, they must arrange to get one from a nearby town, or sometimes from far away. The Secretary has to see to writing to this and that band, finding out how much it charges, and informing the Chief Deputy, who will choose either the cheapest, or the most expensive, or the most distinguished, according to the advice of the Treasurer. Once the problem of the band and its price has been solved—and the price varies from a minimum of 300,000 lire to a maximum of half a million, the deputation has to arrange for the board and lodging of the musicians, from forty to sixty of them, who compose the band. The deputation has to meet all these expenses.

'Then there's the illumination of the main street, the square, and the façade of the church. This, too, is important; it gives the town a really festive air, and makes a beautiful effect in the evening. The cost of the illuminations varies according to the types chosen, but it's not usually less than that of the band.

'The horse-racing isn't an easy thing to arrange either; it needs a lot of experience and knowledge to deal with the horse-breeders. Along with many other items in a *festa*, great importance is attached to the horse-racing, and if the spectacle weren't presented to the people with all its traditional characteristics there would be a risk of ruining the whole *festa*. The deal with the horse-breeders consists either of paying a fixed price for a horse every time it runs, or paying a daily lump sum for it, whether it runs or not. But neither way is always cheap; in the first case the breeders ask a lot for each horse, and in the second the deputation risks paying for horses that don't run or put up a poor show in the race. It goes without saying that the cost of the horse-races is really enormous. On an average, for a *festa* lasting three days, you need twenty or more horses a day, and taken all together the expenses couldn't be less than 300,000 lire, nor more than 800,000.

'The fireworks, the so-called *iocu di focu* are another thorny question. They're presented to the people on the last day of the *festa*, and late at night, when the people are tired and the *festa* is closing. They constitute the last attraction of the *festa*, and great importance is attached to them—in them the people must see an almost super-natural majesty. The *iocu di focu* must make a noise, a noise that must be heard in heaven and the stars, almost as if to reach the patron saint himself and give him the last salute. In short, the fireworks must close the *festa*. If the people don't get what they want they turn their anger on the deputation, and don't hesitate to say that their money's been embezzled. The spectacle varies in length and magnificence, and so its price varies too—somewhere between 200,000 and a million lire.

'Above all there are the religious functions, but here there's no need for experience, nor exercise of choice by the deputies, for the prices are set and compulsory. The parish priest asks his "offertory" in advance for celebrating functions in the days prior to the *festa* and during it. The "offering" he asks is not small—often it's equal in amount to the sum required for decorating the church! Thus the priest presents his bill in advance—we needn't mention a sum, but I think it should be easy to imagine. The Treasurer pays that sum without argument. The deputation must arrange to get a preacher from some monastery, a preacher with a striking voice and if possible a beard—a man, in short, who will command attention. The preacher must speak to the people throughout the function, and for each sermon there's a fixed price! Then there's the final sermon, given on the last day of the *festa*; it's rather longer than the others, and it's paid for separately and at a higher price. To put it briefly, when the *festa's* over the good preaching father will take home to his monastery his hundred-thousand-lire notes.

'We've got a good story here in Sicily about one of the deputies engaging a preacher for this last sermon. The deputy had found a preacher, nice black beard and flashing eyes and all, and they got down to discussing terms.

' "May I ask, Father," said the deputy, "what remuneration you would require to preach this sermon?"

' "Well, my son," said the friar, "I've got a very nice sermon that everybody would understand, at 20,000 lire."

' "And have you any better than that one, Father?"

' "Well, there's one at 50,000 lire, which the educated people would understand."

' "And anything better still, Father?"

' "Yes, indeed; there's one at 75,000 lire which only the priest and the mayor and the deputies and I would understand."

' "Any *still* better, Father?"

' "Yes—for 100,000 lire I preach one that only the priest and I will understand."

' "We have money to spend this year, Father; is there yet another sermon?"

' "There is, my son—for 150,000 lire I preach a sermon which I don't understand a single word of myself!"

' "Then," said the deputy, "we will settle on that one, Father."

'At the time of the *festa* the deputies aim to give more work and earnings to the town shops and various artisans. A stand must be made for the band, a pallisade wherever there's a cross-roads on the course where the horses will be racing; this is builders' work, and the job will be given to whoever tenders the lowest figure. Then there is the saint's bier to be painted, and the altars and so on, and the same applies to these.

'The grocer, the sweet-maker, the butcher, the baker, and still others come in for their share. To feed so many musicians the deputies will need 30 kg. of pasta, 10 kg. of meat, so many kg. of bread, etc., and they buy the necessary quantity of each from the town shops. They will need cheese, oil and wine; they have to offer the musicians something to drink in the intervals of the public concerts, and sweets too, and all these things they buy in equal measure from the merchants.

'Finally, the deputation must give the people some novelty they've never had before; something ever more attractive and amusing. It may be a comedian, who'll clown about and make a fool of himself in public, or singers, or conjurers, or prize-fighters. Some of these people would come anyway, but if they are asked they want to be paid for it!

'These things I've been talking about aren't all; there are many I've left out, but they're of lesser importance. It's clear that to organise a *festa* needs energy, a good money sense and a business head, and a bit of cunning.

'Often the deputation finishes with an empty bank—sometimes even with a debit, which will have to be paid off by the new deputation.

'Well, by now the *festa* is organised. All this work takes place a week or two before the *festa*, and we must take off our hats to the deputies, because they put the interests of the *festa* before everything. Now they're waiting for the great days—what they call in a special voice "the great moment"—the *festa*. The deputies await the verdict of the people, who are the real jury of the *festa*—judgment that's often harsh rather than mild.

'At last the people come on the scene, the masters of everything; they've paid for their amusement, and now they've only to drink in what the organisers have prepared for them, and pass judgment on it, like some fine gentleman who reviews the work of his administrators. The people must enjoy these days as they've hoped to; it is *their festa*, and no one can deny it to them.

'And now the first day of the *festa*. It's still dark; the air is cool and not yet dried up by the sun, and in the sky is the dying light of the last stars. The town is passing, in this still silent world, its last moments of relaxation. Then, suddenly and without warning, an outburst of noisy fireworks shatters the last silence and with it the sleep of the people.

'Already it's almost dawn, a dawn that will be unlike others, a dawn filled with the heralding sounds of bells and explosions. Slowly at first, and then with ever-quickening tempo, all the doors of the houses begin to open; someone comes out and gives greeting to another, and in a short while the town is full of happy swarms of women and the excited voices of children. The first rays of the sun come over the mountains, and the first day of *festa* has properly begun.

'But it's not until the people begin to come on to the streets— mostly in groups, and all to the main street and to the *piazza*, that things really begin to move. The sound of the band fills all the main streets of the town, telling everyone that their promised days of joy are here, and a solid drove of children goes in front of them, miming with gestures the playing of the musicians, and laughing and dancing and shouting.

'Then the people begin to head towards the church for Mass. The square in front of the church is overflowing with people, all men, peasants most of them, showing off their new caps[4] and waistcoats,[5] gathered into groups, with their hands behind their backs, talking of the harvest, perhaps, or of country matters, or of things long ago. The part nearest to the church is occupied by elegantly dressed youths and young men, talking, smoking, and smiling, and every now and again lightly smoothing their hair.

'Many feet pass up the steps of the church; the heavy clumping of peasant men, the faltering steps of the old, the measured tread of the rich, and the light, musical footfalls of the girls. Every young man looks at the girls who go up the steps as if he had never seen them before

—the brunettes and the blondes, the tall and the short—all so beautiful and so elegant that one will have to fall in love before the *festa* is over. The women are well aware of so many male eyes directed at them, and play their part gracefully; they know how to blush, how to meet a glance and turn away from it, how to smile, how to incline their bodies sweetly, and how to show off as far as they are able their elegance and their curves. It's a story that's repeated at every *festa*, but which never grows stale—each time it seems a complete novelty. Among the youths who are already secretly engaged,[6] and who are now admiring their fiancées proudly and lovingly, there are others who have still to find one, and those who haven't yet made up their minds. A continuous chatter comes from the group of youths; the phrases you hear most are things like: "What a sexy piece!"[7] or "Look what breasts!"[8]

'The Mass finishes about midday. The men come out of church first and form groups as before and take up their discussions where they left off, and there's a lot of handshaking and exchanging of greetings. Little by little the people move out of the square; only the youngest remain, near to the church steps or its pavement, and the scene before the Mass is repeated—the smiles and the looks and so on.

'Now you begin to hear the voices of the pedlars above the music and the general confusion. The people begin to promenade the street, looking at the most attractive novelties of the *festa*, and taking in a general panorama of it. Soon the shouts of the various pedlars completely fill the air; groups of youths begin the festivities with target shooting[9] and betting and challenging each other to matches. The nougat sellers,[10] the peanut sellers,[11] and the ice-cream sellers[12] are among the first to get custom. Groups of people gather round the various wide boys—sellers of perfume, combs, alarm-clocks, shaving-bowls, etc.; they know how to attract customers by a game of prestige or by off-the-cuff clowning on the side-walk. There's a fortune teller dressed in weird clothes who goes round among the people, carrying mysterious equipment—a little house full of white mice—and telling the fortune of anyone who consults him—and there's a lot who do!

'But what I've described lasts only a short time, because the people have to go home to lunch—the real *festa* takes place in the afternoon and evening.

'At table today there's a completely new atmosphere—there are relations and intimate friends, and the fare is very different from every-

day food. The peasants make a real event of this, it's seldom they're
at table in the daytime, as they have to work all day in the country.
But today all the meals are carefully prepared. Even the poorest
families find some form of flesh—they kill a turkey, or a rabbit, or a
cockerel, or a pigeon, and prepare it with the greatest care; there'll
be plenty of wine, and no table will lack a white tablecloth and
embroidered napkins, and the best cutlery, sometimes even of silver.
Every household has possessions that are never used except on *festa*
days, because they give a new look to familiar surroundings.

'Every family will buy or make some kind of sweet; among the
peasants it's usual to prepare a tart of buttermilk cream, and *i sfinci*
—a sweet that's made in many different ways, but only for *festa* days.

'Lunch is over by about one o'clock, and then the men go back to
the streets, and the women set about putting the kitchen straight.
Then the real *festa* begins, which will not end until late at night.

'Later on, towards evening, the women come out too, and whole
families promenade the streets for hour after hour. They go into a
sweet shop and eat their fill, and come out again some holding in their
hands a big poke of peanuts and watermelon seeds or fistfuls of peanuts to chew. The families move in a certain definite order, the father
at the centre beside his wife, and the children either at the sides or
moving ahead of their parents.

'The shouting of the stall-keepers becomes more and more deafening.
"Come to the targets!"[13] shouts one voice; "Taste what I've got!" yells
another; "Come and eat my nougat!"[14]—these are the commonest
cries, and they really fetch the people, who move in response to these
voices as if they were gusts of wind.

'A small bazaar is improvised in a side street close to the main street,
where oxen, mules, horses, goats and lambs, brought in from the
country, are ranged along the street. The middlemen [15] have a great
time, praising the beasts and fixing the prices; the peasants look, ask
lower prices, drive bargains with the middlemen in exchange for
other goods, and each one is convinced that he's done good business.

'At length one hears the bangs announcing that the horse-racing
comes next. The swarming crowd becomes denser, everyone's filled
with expectation, and the balconies along the main street become
suddenly packed with people—particularly with women. The great
moment has arrived. The people crowd in behind the barricades, and

all eyes are turned towards the starting-point. The street itself is completely empty of people, blank; for a few instants the noise and dust of the crowd stop; there's almost a moment of silence when *Boom*—and the horses are off, ridden unshod up the street. Everyone's on tip-toe, their eyes glued to the point where the horses will come into sight. Perhaps no one sees anything, but that's of no importance—the mere fact of this atmosphere is satisfaction in itself.

'Imagine the scene. The square's all trimmed up; the façade of the church is decorated with multi-coloured hangings, the windows adorned with flags, the balconies round the square hung with trailing palm-leaves, the pavements boardered with fences painted with gay designs. On the steps of the church itself, or at the side of the steps, stands a little wooden platform, completely covered in coloured draperies, flags and palm-leaves. Leaning against the wall in the middle is the image of the saint whose *festa* is being celebrated; facing the onlookers is a row of very aristocratic-looking chairs, with a larger and more monumental one in the middle, which has above it the coat-of-arms of the local municipality. It's on this chair that the mayor will sit, and on the others will be the local authorities and most important councillors.

'The balconies along the street are crowded with women sparkling in new clothes, and all of them beautiful when you first look at them; the men and children stand crushed together on the pavements behind the fences. Some of the councillors and the policemen are seeing that the street is kept clear during the races. Many of these councillors wear a red sash slung across their chests or round their hips or their arms, according to village custom. By now the crowd is ready and waiting, crammed together and hemmed in behind the fences, whilst from time to time a policeman or a councillor with his red sash can be seen crossing the almost empty street.

'The people wait impatiently for the horses to be led out along the street so that everyone can admire them and weigh up their qualities. The children make up the first rows behind the fences; you can see long lines of their faces in the foreground. For them the horses are something more than a mere entertainment; in these wild stampeding races they live out the fantasies of their imaginations, and in the intensest moments of the race they're seeing the heroes and knights of their dreams.

'As soon as all the people are ready and everything has been settled, the councillors send for the *abbaniaturi*—heralds who inform the people of the councillors' orders. These heralds still exist and make their living in this way in many Sicilian villages. The *abbaniaturi* come to warn the people that the races are about to start, to ask them to be careful while they are taking place and to keep a particularly close eye on the children, and then they wish everyone a good time. These characters are traditionally well loved by the people; often a man who does this for his living, or who lends himself to the occasion, will dress almost like a clown in order to win laughs, or he beats on a great drum and shouts out his proclamations in a sing-song fashion. He stops at every corner, takes up the most comical posture possible and chants:

' "Ladies and gentlemen, your attention if you please. The council will not pay for any damages. No one may leave his place. Anyone who dies, dies on his own responsibility. Shout as much as you like but don't look skywards."[16]

'That's directed at the boys because they would see the legs of the women on the balconies. Usually he'll chant this as a verse.

'All the people greet the *abbaniaturi* with gales of laughter, and the children get madly excited, so that their yells and shrieks rise above the general confusion.

'After the herald's announcement comes the march past of the horses: all the horses hired for the races move down the street. Their manes are decorated with plumes, they have magnificent saddle-cloths on their backs, strips of different coloured materials in their tails, and often ribbons hanging from their ears. The jockeys are dressed in brightly-coloured clothes like your jockeys in England, but often they don't fit so well. The horses and jockeys are cheered by the crowd and followed by the band playing a triumphal march. The fitness of the horses, the magnificence of their finery, and the multi-coloured clothes of the jockeys have a tremendous fascination for the crowd; in these few moments the people get the feeling of being present at the departure on some grand mission of knights and heroes of the past. The onlookers comment on each horse as he passes, and one gains the impression that the favourite must be an awe-inspiring thunderbolt, and his jockey no less than a hero.

'The horses are drawn up in the square in front of the platform, where the mayor and all the military, religious, and municipal authorities, as well as the most important councillors, are seated. As soon as the horses are paraded the mayor stands up and rings a bell as a signal that the races can begin. Then the report of a gun warns the people gathered along the race-course, and in the distance another report answers from the winning-post.

'After the first shot there's a sudden silence from the crowd. Among the people squashed together behind the barricades and along the balconies, all plunged suddenly into silence, expectation grows tenser with every moment. The shouts of the vendors, the laughter of the women, the hoarse voices of the men, the noise of the children— all are quiet now.

'Every eye turns towards the square, waiting in an almost unbearable suspense for the sound of galloping hooves. Often, in the full intensity of this moment, while everyone's on tiptoe and craning his neck, a dog, all unaware of what's going on, will cross the white empty street with sublime indifference. You should see what happens then!

'All this tremendous solemnity has just been upset by a filthy little animal like that; all this tensed-up nervous expectation has been distracted by a mere dog. The yelling and booing starts.

'"Oh Oh Oh Oh Oh!!!"

'"B . . . . off! Get the hell out of it!"

'"Someone twist his balls off!"

'"Jesus wept, a *dog*!"

'"Slaughter the bloody thing!"

'"A stone, a stone, my kingdom for a stone!"

'The silence is over; the news reaches the square that there's a dog on the road. The dog has to find a way out. The unfortunate animal runs hopelessly here and there and finds no exit. Terrified, it runs to one side of the street, only to be driven back by shouts and waving arms; turns back, turns round, and round again, whining pitifully all the while. At last it is either hit by a massive stone or runs right into the horses, amid the shouts of the crowd. Such incidents are common during the races and often have a sad ending; the horses run down the dog and crush him, or the dog will be killed by stones. He has to be lucky to escape. Everyone finds these things a heaven-sent opportunity for shouting and swearing.

'While the people have been going through these agonies of expectation let's see what's happening in the square, at the starting point.

'Don't forget that the majority of the spectators are passionately fond of horse-racing, and there's also the connoisseurs, "*afficionados*" as they are called. In every village there are always people who are expert on the subject of animals—in this case, of horses. As I've said, there are connoisseurs of music, of conjuring, and of horse-racing too. For the most part they are middle-aged or old men, all more or less *ntisu* (respected) as far as horse-racing is concerned, and generally at least one of them will play a prominent part in any dispute about it. Tradition, or perhaps respect, demands that these men stand in the front rows round the square. They wear their *coppula* (Sicilian cap) turned up in front, carter-fashion[17] as they say, as a sign that they are connoisseurs. They are, indeed, for the most part carters, or ex-carters, horse trainers or former horse trainers, men who have spent their lives with horses and so have learned to know them, to appraise and value them for what they are worth. The opinion of these experts is decisive; in fact one could say that it depends on them whether a horse wins a good name in the races, and whether many of the races themselves are successful.

'The number of horses to each race is generally three, occasionally four. The start is very complicated. First of all, the horses are listed on the paper which the mayor holds in his hand, and then divided into groups of three or four. Each horse has a name followed by the place from where it comes; for example "Boiardo di Carini", "Folgore di Palermo", "Morello di Balestrate", "Freccia di Alcamo" and so on. The mayor stands up and reads out the names of the horses who are to run, and their jockeys mount as the trainers hold the reins. The horses move restlessly from side to side, pawing the ground with graceful steps as if they were dancing, and the eyes of the connoisseurs take in every inch. They have a special terminology which they use to describe the merits or defects of the animals.

'There are two different kinds of start: *alla pari* or *a vuci*.

'*Alla pari*, or "the scratch start", means gathering the horses behind a rope stretched horizontally in front of them and then waiting for the mayor to ring his bell as the starting signal. This scratch start is used when the horses *sa runanu*—that is when they are all equally good runners. If one horse is much better than the rest the race is started *a vuci*; that is "by voice".

'As I've said, there's always some expert on horses amongst the councillors, so from the platform he decides whether the race should begin with a scratch or "voice" start, according to whether the horses, in his opinion, are of equal or unequal merit. Often the opinion of the "*afficionados*" also carries weight.

'If the decision is that the horses are to run *a vuci* the rope is taken away and we wait until the horses are ready. The "voice", the word to start, is given by the rider of the best horse, that is to say its owner is given the privilege of being starter, but he's handicapped a few yards behind the rest.

'It will be quite some time before the man holding the reins of the last horse—the best—begins the race! Obviously each of the men holding the reins of the respective horses, realising as they do the importance of the moment, tries to give his own horse a better position than the rest; the last one in his turn tries his best to distract the attention of the men in front of him, so that at the crucial moment he can drop his horse's rein and get away to a better start. Disputes flare up between the trainers holding the horses' reins, disputes whose continuous flood of oaths, blasphemies, obscenites and insult make them as good entertainment as the race itself. The best man turns to someone in front of him: "Hey! Do you want to move or not, you son of a bitch?"[18] A man in front: "Do you think I'm a bloody idiot, getting yourself ready like that?" Another: "Pig of a ——, go on, move! You're scared, that's what you are, scared!" The best man: "Son of an unlicensed prostitute—I'll make you eat dirt!" Yet another: "Eh, you! I'm not budging an inch to let you get in front of me!"

'Between oaths the best man makes as if he is going to loose his horse: "He's off! Who's off? They're off. Everybody's off! No, they're not—yes—no."

'The horses stir restlessly, the onlookers laugh, but nonetheless follow with the closest attention everything that is going on, for the horses may really be off any moment now. In a bedlam of threats and curses the last man seizes the opportune moment, screams at the top of his voice: "Eeeeeeh eeeh!" and the horses gallop off, followed immediately by a gunshot.

'As the horses race down the street the yells of the crowd fill the air. The instant the horses have passed the crowd streams across the road like a river in full spate.

'In the interval between one race and another the people can stroll on the street, discussing the race and the courage of the jockeys; they buy and offer things to eat, and those who have families on the balconies hurry to send them a poke of nuts, or peanuts or watermelon seeds, and so on.

'The youths look skywards—there are so many balconies full of women and of girls! They all walk close to the pavement in single file, so as to be able to look up vertically; their glances have a certain precision, and they are rewarded by the sight of so many white female legs—and sometimes, when a girl's underclothing is disarranged, by even more *piquant* sights. They would never drop their gaze if the bangs of the cardboard bombs didn't announce the start of the second race.

'In the square some of the experts have been making bets, and everyone is talking about the kind of start it was and waiting for the result. At the winning-post a jury made up of councillors checks the order in which the horses arrive. The jockeys go back along the race-course by car, balanced on the running-board and hanging on to the door with one hand. The winner holds his whip aloft as a sign of victory, the runner-up stands on the other side of the car, the third comes along on foot leading his horse. The people applaud the winner and settle down for the next race. When the car reaches the square it drops the jockeys and goes back to the winning-post; there's a rattle of gunshot and the mayor gets up and reads out the names of the horses in the next race.

'Generally the races last for four or five hours, and there are often ten or more of them. After the first three or four races there is the colts' race.[19] The colts run without jockeys; they're inexperienced, and often one of them will stop for a rest on the way, although they've got small fireworks tied to their tails to frighten them. Their race is accompanied by shouts and peals of laughter, especially from the children.

'After the first day of racing the people have already formed their own ideas about the horses and the courage of the jockeys. During the course of the evening the greater part of the conversation will be taken up with criticism of this or that horse, excitement over the courage of such and such a jockey, and the forecasting of tomorrow's races.

'On the first day's racing the favourite jockey, who is often a boy, stands out from the others and the horses most likely to be picked for "The Banner Race"[20] can be guessed at. The ambitious names of the horses exercise a powerful influence on the minds of the people: "Thunderbolt from . . .", "Fearless from . . .", "Young Eagle from . . .", "The Executioner from . . ." There are plenty of names like "Mad Orlando", "Roger of the Castle" and, in the case of a mare, "Brada-mante", showing the influence of the puppets which are still popular in Sicily and tell the story of the French paladins.

'During the *festa* a few words can start a real craze for this or that horse and for this or that jockey.

'All this may seem to you just a vulgar display, an event for the rabble, as they say; but don't forget that this horse-racing is a real example of the time-honoured tradition that the people feel to be their only true religion, their veritable "book of the law". It was dictated by distant ancestors, so it is venerable and inviolable. It's true to say that when the horse-races are over, everyone, besides having been entertained, feels his conscience at ease because he has fulfilled what is a traditional duty: going to the races.

'In the evening the promenading people crowd the bar, the nougat counters, the ice-cream bars, and the amusement stalls such as the target ranges are surrounded by swarms of people.

'Anyone who's officially engaged must do his duty according to custom—he must invite the family of his fiancée to walk with him, and you see long files of people strolling leisurely down the street. The fiancée stays with her betrothed's mother, and he with her mother, and between them walk the brothers-in-law, mothers-in-law and other relations. It's no fun to find yourself in the shoes of that unfortunate fiancé!

'All this coming and going continues incessantly through the brightly-lit evening of the *festa*. Later in the evening the people assemble round the bandstand, and the musicians begin to play the music of Verdi, Bellini, Mascagni, etc. There are *afficionados* at the musical concerts, old men these, for the most part, who stand very close to the bandstand and try to introduce a more serious atmos-phere, really savouring the music, and these are the only ones who applaud. The others stay further off; they hang about for a time and then go away indifferently.

'Among the pedlars present at the *festa* the luckiest is certainly the peanut-seller,[21] followed by the nougat-sellers—and that's because everyone must buy for 100 lire, or at least 70 lire, his poke of peanuts, and carry home a reasonable quantity of nougat.

'Often there's some novelty at a *festa*, for example a lunar park, or horse rings, where lovely young ladies provide *piquant* spectacles; it's at this time in the evening that the public look for novelties, and the flow of people becomes greater and greater. But the traditional things mustn't be left out, and no one misses the *o bianco e nivuru* [black and white] which is a kind of touring roulette table.

'Very often competitions are organised with prizes for the winners. *La ntinna* consists of a long pole stuck upright in the ground and covered with something slippery, soap for instance, or oil or wax, and a special substance obtained from the plant of prickly pears. Prizes are fastened to the top of the pole, often a flag and some money, and whoever can reach it gets the prize. It's a difficult task, but there's no lack of the brave and the daring to provide a comic spectacle, and a dangerous one too. When the unfortunate climber has reached a certain height he suddenly comes hurtling down, clinging tightly to the pole amid the laughter of the spectators.

'Often the competition only lasts a short time, but it can go on for hours when no one manages to reach the top. The public love it and go off full of praise for those who've taken the risk.

'There's another fine comedy for people who like their amusement raw. This is the game of earthenware pots.[22] It consists of hanging a number of earthenware pots along a wire; in one of them there is every sort of filth, urine, dung, and mud, and in others there are prizes, usually of money. The competitor has to break a pot with his own head. You can imagine what happens when he breaks the wrong one—he gets that filth on his head and the hoots and jeers of the crowd about his ears.

'There are other competitions, which take place in the street, sack races,[23] blindfold races,[24] and so on. They're all traditional, but the coarser ones are becoming less and less crude, largely because the authorities oppose them.

'The bedlam and confusion of the *festa* begin to die down during the late hours of the night, and the people drift off home, exhausted and sleepy. Only a few youths remain on the street, hoping to prolong their amusements through the night.

'The first day of the *festa* is over, and during the night a shot announces the fact. Tomorrow there will be another day of *festa*, as good as today, or even more exciting.

'The second day gets off the mark slower than the first; again there's the explosions and chiming of the bells, but the people are slower to get up. At daybreak the band goes out on the street, preceded as before by a swarm of children, but the atmosphere is not the same as the first day. In the morning the *festa* life goes on as before, but now the families think only about the lunch, for those who were guests yesterday must return hospitality. After lunch the people go back to the street[25] prepared for the second day of the *festa*—the promenading crowds, the shouting of the pedlars, the babel of voices from the loud-mouthed, the din of the target-booths. The pedlars are lined up along the pavement; they have staked their claims a long time before the *festa*. At the more central points the obstruction caused by their stalls is chaotic, their voices deafening, but nobody minds, because this is part of the atmosphere the people enjoy, it is the *festa*.

'Meanwhile no one's bothering about the patron saint. Not that he's completely forgotten, but for the people the simple fact that they're enjoying themselves shows their honour and their respect for the blessed saint who is in paradise. The southern mentality as you see is complicated and contradictory.

'From what I've said already you'll have understood that at a *festa* a common interest binds the youths, and there's a specially important aspect of this interest in the opposite sex. Especially in the mountain towns, there's no brothel where they can go to satisfy their physiological needs; but during the *festa* a brothel of a sort is formed. Many prostitutes flow into the town, and for the most part these tour the streets; they find clients readily, and some place or other to do their work. But very often someone gets hold of a house for the tarts, possibly just outside the town, and so a real brothel is set up, although a temporary and unlicensed one. The youths and men spread the good news, and everyone streams to this house of delight—it's nothing unusual to see long queues forming in front of its door, like you see outside cinemas.

'So here we are at last on the third day of the *festa*, the last, and the most important and the most intense. The last day has a special atmosphere; the people are closing the *festa*, entering into the spirit of it with abandon, letting themselves be drawn further into the maelstrom of confusion.

'On the third day there are the finals of all the competitions and games; there is the procession, the fireworks and the banner race;[26] it's almost always in the evening, because the number of races is greater than on any preceding day.

' "The Banner Race" is the most eagerly awaited race of the lot, the most exciting of them all. It takes place in the early evening after the other ten or more races. Twilight has already fallen over the square, and the almost silent expectancy of the onlookers grows tenser and tenser as the start of the final race approaches. The first lamps are lighted on the pedlars' stalls, the façade of the church is gradually illuminated, and the string of bulbs along the race-track light up one after the other. Both the people along the track and the people in the square become almost jittery in their nervousness and excitement; there is anticipation written on every face.

'The horses who take part in "The Banner Race" are the ones which have won the most races, the fastest and wildest, and they can't help but arouse this general tension: in a few minutes they will be runners in the race to end the races.

'The mayor rings his bell and gets up from his chair, steps up to the wooden rail round the platform, and reads out the names of the horses which are to take part. He says this is to be a scratch or "voice" start. As soon as the mayor announces the horses' names, the packed crowds round the square shout and yell their applause. There are three or four horses taking part in "The Banner Race" and the winner gets a banner; on which is written: "Council of Saint Rosalia, 1958 chief councillor, Don Pasquale Frollo". Pinned to it are anything from five to ten thousand-lire notes which are the winner's prize. Often there is a small banner for the runner-up and some smaller prize-money, but that depends on how prosperous the Council is.

'If they decide to give the horses a "voice" start "The Banner race" takes place very late, because the rigmarole of insults, oaths and obscenities seems never-ending. The people crowd even more thickly into the square for this race, so as not to miss a word of the abuse. It may seem odd, very odd perhaps, that while the trainers are cursing wildly, and even curse the patron saint of the festival with obscenities, the parish priest should laugh as happily as anyone else; even he finds the oaths and the filthy language just something to laugh at.

'And now here come the horses: amid deafening applause the man who has been awarded the starting "voice" leads his horse round the square, swelling with pride. The same old arguments begin; first the other horses are too far from the favourite, then he is too close to them: it would take at least half an hour to reach an agreement, but such an agreement has never been reached within living memory.

'The man who has been awarded the starting "voice" exclaims: "At this rate we'll never get started before tomorrow morning!"[27] One of those in front, turning to the back-marker: "Don't shoot your mouth off so loud—I'll give way if the others do."[28]

'Another, also addressing the last man: "You watch yourself! I bet my balls are bigger than yours!"[29]

'The last man: "None of you swine are going to pinch my banner—the honour is mine and I'm going to hold on to it!"[30]

'One of the jockeys in front turns to the man at his side: "Watch the old bastard, Don Toto; as soon as you look the other way he'll give his horse a dig and be off. Look out, look out, he's off, he's off!"[31]

'The last one: "I'll do for you, you sod, once we get going!"[32]

'It often happens that the man who's supposed to give the word to start pretends to loose his horse and so begin the race; then all at once he'll change his mind and make everyone look a fool. Then he shouts: "Stop, stop, you morons!" and the jockeys in front stare at him fixedly, ready to loose the horses' reins at any moment. But "Hey, hey!" he says. "Hey, hey! That's not the start, that's not the start!"[33]

'The front ranks streak off and they've covered almost half the course before they're halted and brought back to the square. This move on the part of the starter is about the most cunning he could make, for in making the other horses run to no purpose he wears them out and makes his own chances better. The owners and trainers who he's tricked in this way call him every name under the sun, but he takes it all with hoots of coarse laughter.

"Swine!"[34]

"Bastard!"[35]

"That banner will stick in your gullet!"[36]

"Haha haha, I had the laugh on you! You can't make a fool of Peppino from Palermo!"[37]

'One replies: "You said it, baby!" "You swine . . . you ponce . . . we'll move back, all right—but if you start then you'll see what you'll get!"[38]

'The horses take a step or two back, the hands of their trainers trembling with the fear of being taken by surprise by the last horse, and their barely controlled desire to drop the reins and shout the start of the race is written all over their faces. The spectators realise that the climax is near, and a moment's silence falls over the square. The back-marker is still busy trying to distract those in front of him:

' "Just wait while I light a cigarette—don't be afraid, I'm not going to start. Hey, what's this—you're scared? You're as red as a lot of cocks!" He doesn't actually finish the word, but everyone laughs.

'At last it seems to him that the right moment has come, and covering up as far as possible, seizing on any excuse to do so, he edges his horse up a few steps and then shrieks: "AH AH AH AH AH! Away, away!"'

'The others shout back:

' "EH EH EH EH EEE! Let's get hold of that banner!"[39] The horses streak off like lightning in a thunderstorm, and the pent-up enthusiasm of the spectators explodes as they go by. Everyone rushes into the square; the balconies empty one after the other; confusion and the shouting of the pedlars reigns where there was silence a moment ago. Meanwhile everyone waits for the result of the race. The band moves from the square to the finishing-post so as to acclaim the winning horse and jockey, and many of the spectators go with them to pay homage to the hero. He, on his own horse, goes back up the street to the applause of the crowd. He is followed by the band, which strikes up a victorious anthem, and by a great crowd of people. The march past is headed by the children, all gleeful and shouting at the tops of their voices. The jockey holds the banner with the money, the owner of the horse walks beside him holding the reins, bursting with pride and satisfaction. In the square the procession breaks up, the crowd go off to enjoy themselves, the horses go to the stables, and the trainers and jockeys to drink in the pub. Often the money won in "The Banner Race" all goes on drink, for after all the trainers are still good friends. They meet in a pub, order something to eat and spend the whole evening right away from the uproar of the *festa*, drinking and talking. Often they get drunk, but they don't mingle in the general hubbub; instead they wander through the side streets with a bottle of wine under their arms. They're the first to leave, before the dawn breaks. In the hush of the small hours, when everyone else has only just gone to bed, they leave the village, whistling or humming some mournful song. They make their way off to some other village where more crowds await them.

'But to return to where we were—after the racing is over the procession follows, in which a large part of the people take part, mostly women. Two long parallel single files walk ahead of the saint's bier, each individual carrying a candle. In front of these two long files goes the drummer, behind him the children and then the girls, and behind them, all in single file, a great number of the townspeople, many of the women barefoot in honour of the saint. Behind these again come the religious orders, monks and nuns, and then the congregation of the town, and lastly the priests with the bier. Often the first files, after having marched the whole route, have got back to the church before the bier has yet emerged!

'A few yards from the bier you see the senior priest, dressed with great pomp and splendour, and escorted by other priests less finely robed than he. At the left and right of the bier stand guards, and behind it the new deputation—because they're already thinking about the next *festa*, though it's a year away—with their lit candles, the mayor of the town and the civil and military authorities. Behind them again comes the band, and then a dense mass of people, mainly black-shawled women. There's a continuous rustling of voices, and everywhere you hear the mutter and murmur of the Pater Noster, the Hail Mary and the Salve Regina; you see pushing and jostling to right and to left—an utter confusion. At the very last come many peasants with their beasts—mules, asses, oxen, goats and sheep.

'The bier is carried by from thirty to forty men dressed in traditional costume, which in most cases consists of a sash tied round the head, like a pirate, and a red cummerbund whose end hangs down at the side. The bier-bearers' function is traditional and the post is handed down from father to son, so that it becomes a special duty and devotion.

'Above the bier stands the image of the saint, a statue or painting, ornamented with flowers and candles and long ribbons to which are pinned the offerings received along the street. The bier is covered, too, with gifts such as bread, sweets, fruit, wine, and so on. Very often babies are placed on the bier, often sick ones, to be cured miraculously —this is done to show the devotion of their fathers to the saint.

'There is a man who carries in his hand a little bell, which announces

a halt when the bier bearers are tired. These halting-places are traditional, and never vary. All along the procession the people show
their devotion; a sweet-maker will throw towards the bier whole
pounds of caramels or chocolates; the peanut-seller will throw many
handfuls of peanuts; the drug-store keeper offers drinks to all the
bearers, and so on. From time to time, when there's a momentary
silence in the immediate vicinity of the bier, one of the bearers shouts
out *"As we are all dumb long live SAINT JOHN, lads!"*[40]—or St.
Joseph, or whatever other saint is the business of the day.

'The procession lasts a long time—often it finishes in the church
towards midnight. A fiery sermon by the visiting preacher—paid for
separately as I told you before—closes the religious side of the *festa*,
driving home to the people their right and proper devotion toward
their patron saint and the faith, and wishing everybody a happy
time.

'Then the music begins, and goes on far into the night; the people
go on enjoying themselves, and some families organise their own
festas with their relations, usually dances.

'The promenading continues as before, noisy even between the yelling and shouting of the pedlars and the strident voices of the loud-
mouthed.

'Many hopes have been fulfilled, though there's always someone
who hasn't benefited by the *festa*—but as the Sicilian proverb says,
"Luck may come tomorrow."[41]

'The night wears thin and the first dawn light appears in the sky.
The music stops, and the bars and ice-cream bars and shops close and
the lights are put out, and there comes the last spectacle of the *festa*, the
fireworks. Everyone is present at these; their majesty and fantastic
beauty create in the minds of the people an almost dream-like state of
wonder. A great roar of applause ends the show, and the dreams become sad reality.

'The people are tired, and sad because the *festa* is over so soon—it
seemed as if it could never finish.

'In the dawn hours the pedlars, who've had to work while others
amused themselves, hold their own *festa*; they get together and eat, and
often get drunk, and get into mischief generally. They take down their
stalls and go away to some other *festa* in some other town, bringing
fleeting happiness to other people. No *festa* could do without them—a
festa without pedlars would be like a church without a priest.

'On the day after the *festa* the people don't work, but go into the country to pass the day in peace and quiet.

'It's all over now, but it's nothing to wonder at if a few days later the new deputation start to present themselves at the door asking for offerings, inspired by new hope for the next *festa*. And so they begin to weave the new tapestry, so long and laborious, all to be destroyed in a few hours.'

CHAPTER TEN

The Pedlar and the Prostitute

PINO THE PEDLAR

'Yes, I'm a pedlar. How old am I? Eighteen? No, I'm sixteen—soon I'll be seventeen, but everyone gets it wrong, because they see me so big and even a bit overblown perhaps, but I'm still sixteen. In the same way sometimes someone who's twenty looks fifteen, and someone like me who's sixteen looks twenty. I'm sixteen, but it's all the same to me, because I lead and always have led the life of an eighteen-year-old.

'My mother died the day after I was born—died because of me, because of my birth. I never knew my father. A lot of people say he's dead[1]—he went to the war and never came back—and lots say he's a prisoner in Russia, but I think he must be dead by now. I never knew anything about him. From the first day I came into the world I started suffering—think of coming into the world and not knowing your parents. Even children of unknown parents know broadly that their parents must have been shits, and often don't want to know them—but I . . . I . . . well, what wouldn't I pay to see my father, because my mother's dead.

'Perhaps if I'd had parents I wouldn't be like I am, and wouldn't have led the life I've led; I wouldn't have lived so ignorantly, and certainly at sixteen I wouldn't look eighteen! I was born unlucky.

'I was taken and adopted by a relation of mine, and I've lived there since I was a suckling—my uncle had no children then. I'd hardly begun to understand, when—I was only six—they told me I hadn't got a father or mother, and I suddenly wanted them when my aunt had a baby. From that day I became an intruder in the family, and it was obvious that if I wanted to stay with my uncle I was going to have to pay a bread tax—that is work for my keep.

'Luckily, they didn't drive me out—I started working. For me there was no childhood, no games, no presents, no mother's kisses, no thinking like a child. At seven I began to tour with my uncle's cart—

157

I used to go with him to the towns selling roast peanuts, salted water-melon seeds, nuts, and other things of that sort. My uncle's a pedlar, a peanut-seller,[2] and I was always with him, and a great help to him too. There were no mornings in my life, because at dawn, when you could still see the stars, I used to get up, at four or five o'clock. I've been the early bird since I was a baby. They give me a piece of bread, and we have to set off at once in the cart full of our wares. When I was a kid I remember I used to cry, and sometimes fall asleep on top of the cart. We would go to some town I didn't know and that I could hardly see till we got there—that's what a pedlar's life is. I always sold peanuts and water-melon seeds, sometimes toys, balloons, combs, buttons and so on, according to the place and time. Now, for instance, as there's "the dead" ['The Feast of the Dead' is a feature of Sicily—the children are told that on November 2nd the dead come back to bring them presents, which their mothers buy for them. The same thing is customary at Epiphany, but the Feast of the Dead exists only in Sicily, and is unknown elsewhere], we go from town to town selling toys, dolls, balloons, etc., which we exchange for old iron and copper to be sold later in Palermo. You cry your wares in the streets where there's most children, and you sing this song:

> See what the dead have sent you
> A doll with twisted sides
> The mouse that used to dance
> And the cat that played the trumpet.[3]

'And the children laugh and want to buy the toys from you. There's always work for "the dead", but it doesn't last long, a week or two, and then woe betide us, because the winter comes and in the winter business is very bad. Our work starts in April and finishes now, with "the dead", in November. In April the *festas* begin—each town has a *festa* for its own saint. There's small *festas* and big *festas*—the biggest *festas* are when you have horse-racing and lit streets, like you have in this town for instance. You have to leave for that town two or three days before, to stake a claim where you can set up your stall. You have to have your wits about you—you have to put the stall where there's most coming and going, where there's a church close by. If you don't you sell less. During a *festa* everything's in a muddle and whoever's got the loudest voice sells most. My uncle stays with the stall, while I go among the crowd on the street—I have a basket full of peanuts and water-melon seeds and walk about yelling "Peanuts! Peanuts! I've got hot peanuts, salted seeds and nuts!"[4]—or "Taste how sweet!"[5] You have to shout because if you don't no one hears you and you sell nothing. And you've got to be cunning and know where the biggest bustle is, because that's where you've got the best chance of selling.

'You stop shouting at night—at two or three in the morning, and your throat hurts and your mouth's dry. Then you eat something, a bit of bread and something, and when I'm hungry I eat half a kilo of bread! When the *festa's* over we set off to look for another one—it's the same thing with every *festa*, we're the same pedlars, the same peanut-sellers!

'I've led that life since I was seven, and I'm used to it now—but it's not a trade. Today you eat—you don't know anything about to-morrow. If it rains you can't go out and sell peanuts and water-melon seeds, and for five months you have to stay in the town because in the winter the chance of selling anything isn't much. We go whichever way the wind blows, and if there's no wind you have to stay still. In winter we try to sell balloons and combs and buttons, in exchange for old iron and copper, and to sell American clothes which we buy in Palermo—but you don't get much for the clothes—you don't even make the little you need to eat.

'You have to be cunning in selling things—for instance, if I've got to sell something worth 50 lire, I say it costs 100, and when the buyer says 50, I say it might be worked for 75—so he's saved himself 25 lire and I've earned 25 lire and everyone's happy! If you don't do that you earn nothing; and if you haven't got the knack you shut up shop and you're left with the cock up your arse.[6]

'Some days you can earn 1,000 lire, some days or weeks nothing, and so—what you lose on the swings you make up on the round-abouts, and you keep alive.

'I owe a lot to my uncle—he gives me a roof over my head, and I ought to do everything he tells me. Anyway—where could I go? I can't read or write, and all doors are closed against me. Anyone who knows how to read and write is lucky. Last year I was going to evening school, but I wasn't always able to be there and I had to stop going. Now I'd like at least to learn to understand something, but I'm afraid it's not possible—if you don't work you don't have bread to eat! There are boys like me who still go to school and are still "mother's boys"—they get up in the morning at eight and have milk, they go to church, and know prayers and so on. But what do they know about work. If I don't work I don't eat. The Church?—I don't know anything about the Church. I've never been to church, and no one ever sent me! I know there are saints, and Jesus Christ and the Madonna, and one prays to them to go to paradise, but I've never prayed to them because I don't know how to pray. I only know the Hail Mary. As far as I'm concerned it's enough to make the sign of the cross before I start work in the morning—I begin the day with it, and I end with it when I go to sleep. I hardly ever go to Mass—I go occasionally when I'm in the town and free. I go there because all the girls go to Mass on Sundays, and there you can see them better. There's one girl who really is a dish, and when I see her I get so excited I have to go and (masturbate).

'Women like that make us men lose our heads—it's the lower head that makes us lose the upper head! But if there were no women what would one have instead—cows?

'I started (masturbating) when I was eleven—other pedlars' boys taught me. I was in Cinisi when I tried it the first time—it's funny, in a way, that I started later than most people. Afterwards, I used to do it in the evening when I was in bed and again in the morning before getting up. I still do—the priests say it kills you, but I'm fine thanks—they've got their reasons for inventing things, just like the politicians have. I'd say on the other hand, that it would kill me not to—I feel ill if I don't, though a woman's better if you can get one. I started going to tarts when I was thirteen, and now I'm an old hand at that game. Working at a trade where people aren't very clean, I was only just thirteen when I first had a tart. The first time was at Partinico—the other pedlars took me there, and I remember the woman laughed at me because I was so small, but she soon found out size wasn't everything. As time went on I got a taste for tarts, and went very often. You have to be eighteen before you can go with tarts legally, so I always went secretly. At the time of the *festas* a lot of tarts come into the towns, so five and six of us pedlar boys of the same age would get together and each of us turn in 500 lire, which would make up to 3,000 or 3,500. We give the lot to a tart and she stays with us three or four hours. The place is either a house in the country or a house in the town, which the tart pays for. Birds of a feather flock together—we are wandering pedlars and so naturally we go to wandering tarts. There are lots of odd things you can do with women, but I won't do them with tarts because tarts are filthy. When there's a lot of us we mess about with each other while waiting our go; and some, when we haven't got any money for a tart, (have) each other in turn—but I don't like that—it doesn't seem to me natural between men. In a year and a half I'll be allowed to go to the brothel, but that won't be anything to write home about—I've been "eighteen" for three years! And in any case they say the brothels will all be closed by then—some new law. I don't know what we'll do then—perhaps God will take away our (manhood).[7]

'Politics and the government have never interested me, first because I've got no time for politics, and then because I don't understand them. But everyone who's in politics makes money for themselves, that's the truth of the matter—everyone says so. When I'm unemployed I have dealings with politics, because if they've got no work for me at the labour exchange I have a try with the Christian Democrats or the Communists, but neither gives me work because I don't vote and I don't matter to them. In the government there are big-shots who eat everything and everyone, while we have to work for a whole day to earn a piece of stale bread. That's not fair.

'I shall go on being a pedlar until I find some steady work, because being a pedlar is no life—you earn almost nothing and you lose your health. If I don't work my uncle chucks me out—I've no parents or other relations to take an interest in me and I have to look after myself in everything—that means I'll always have to suffer. That's what it means to have no father or mother.[8] There's other boys like me, orphans, but don't they work under a roof and know they're going to get paid every day and live happily? There's no place of work in my business—when you're on the road one place is as good as another. You sleep where you can, by the roadside—or if you're in a town you may be lucky enough to find a stable to sleep in. You can't call that life. Now the winter's coming and it gets my spirits down.[9] My uncle doesn't pay me every day—he gives from 300-500 lire a week when we're working, and nothing when we're not.

'With that I've got to dress myself, buy shirts and so on, and buy bread. I have to buy everything, and as you see I'm dressed in second-hand American clothes because they don't cost a lot. I don't smoke except at *festas*—if I did I really would have had it. But you understand that with want like mine I couldn't even live with what my uncle gives me, so I have to do something for myself—I keep a little of the money from the stuff I sell. I sell fewer things at a higher price, and so without robbing my uncle I get something for myself—enough to pay for a tart!'

THE PROSTITUTE

'This is a house of pigs. You'll excuse me, won't you, because I'm not the owner here nor my companions either. He's not here; he only comes in the evenings to collect the money—and to have a woman if he wants one.

'We can talk here, but it's better to shut the door, or someone'll come for (trade) and then I shan't be able to tell you anything.

'I know already what you want me to tell you—you want to know how old I am, why I'm a prostitute, when I started it, where I was born, what my name is, and all the rest of it. And then you'll get all worked up and heave a long sigh and say "Poor wretch! A life sold for money!"—at least you'll pretend to get all worked up, and you'll leave after your curiosity's been satisfied.

'But what does my life matter to you? Better think about your own, as I think about mine!

'Yes, I know what you want—they come and ask me what my name is, how old I am, whether I've got children and so on. But I assure you no one really gets worked up—they have [the usual thing] and go away. You look like one of those to me. Do you think us tarts are here to get worked up about, or to satisfy people's curiosity? Ours is a trade—aren't there many different ways of earning a living? Ours is one of them—we earn our livings with our (bodies). It's a trade, and I can't understand why anyone finds it odd. Don't we work too?[10]

'I see you're taking notes already, and you're not yet in tears— all right—what do you want to know? The things I expected? But I hope you're going to be a gentleman and not say afterwards, "Such and such a tart told me all these things", because I should be despised for it.

'There's a lot of things I shan't tell you, because there's things I don't care to remember, and also because we can't be a long time about it or I'll lose too much trade, as you see.

'I'm not a Sicilian, as you'll have noticed from my accent—I was born in Acerra, a country town near Naples, 29 years ago. My family doesn't exist any more—my mother's dead, and my father too, I

think, but I'm not sure. My brother—I had a brother too—has been
in prison for some years, but I don't know anything definite about
him.

'My father was a carpenter—or rather he had two trades, woodcutter and carpenter. He got the timber himself and worked it in his
own shop, which was house and shop in one, and he made doors and
gates and things of that sort. He earned money, but he didn't give
anything to the family—we were starving. He was a drunkard, and
whatever he earned he went and drank in the *trattorie*, and my mother
had to cope with everything. My mother was a washerwoman, and
also a chair-maker, but she turned her hand to anything so as to be
able to feed her children.

'Our house was a hovel. We never cooked inside. Every day there
were scenes between my father and mother; often they came to blows,
and when I was a child my brother and I were present when those
things were going on.

'Time passed, and when I got a bit older I was put to work as a maid
with one of the richer families of the town. My brother went to
work in the country, and my mother went on being a washerwoman.
My father was given up entirely to his base life, until one day he had a
really bad quarrel with my mother, and threw her out in the street.
I could look after myself, doing washing and scrubbing dishes and
working like a slave; my mother slept here or there wherever she
could, until one day she was found dead in a hut in the country.

'My father pretended to be sorry for everything he'd done. He
wanted me to live with him and my brother, but after a bit he went
back to his drunken life again, and I took the place in our home that
my mother had had.

'I was between thirteen and fourteen years old then. I managed to
make just enough to live; I slept in my father's house, and every evening
there was the usual grumbling.

'They were sad times. I grew older and didn't want to be a maid
any more. I wanted to get married to someone or other, just in the
hope of getting away from that awful house and that drunkard.

'I had to face everything—hunger, and grief, and pain, and squalor,
and lice. In the end, too, I lost my "honour"—yes, my "honour".

'The time came when my father wouldn't work any more, and
my brother was away from home. Who knows where he was, because
he'd taken to stealing. I was in danger of being thrown out into the

street and dying of starvation. My father didn't understand that I was a woman by then, and he treated me very badly. He wanted me to work for his living as well, and he forced me to become a prostitute.

'At first he took me to the most important people in the town. He made me be friendly to a certain lawyer, and then he made me [go to bed] with the man, giving his own approval. It was he himself who got me the clients—every evening there were some fifteen of them—and think, I was only seventeen! I was the disgrace of the town, and everyone's gossip was about me. Then I was registered publicly as a prostitute. I didn't understand what was happening, and I felt highly flattered.

'But I understood when I found myself pregnant—I could have died of shame. Where was I going to give birth to my child, and what would the people say?

'I couldn't really know whose my child was, but I've always had a terrible suspicion that it was the parish priest's. My father used to bring the priests to me, and it was Father X who encouraged me, who told me that it was nothing and that it could happen to any girl, a thing God pardons—and then that it wasn't a sin if he, the priest, encouraged me.

'I had no other choice but to flee that town—my existence in those surroundings had become impossible. But where could I go? I was completely lost, I was pregnant, and those were hard times, because the war was on. At last I found a way of running away, but I paid dearly for it. A certain Signor X had found me work with a family in Naples, and arranged for me to give birth in a hospital—but the condition was that I would remain his private tart and sleep with him in the evenings.

'I decided to run away with this man, and I did so in 1946. I arrived in Naples with a little money, 25,000 lire, and my baby inside me.

'After a month I gave birth in a clinic, but luckily the child was stillborn, and if I grieved for it it was still a good thing for me, as it took a weight off my shoulders. But my man was nothing but a scoundrel—I only saw him in the evenings, when he came to the house to spend the night with me. I lived in a very dirty quarter of Naples, full of hovels like the one he'd put me in—hovels of lath and plaster, and during the nights it used to rain inside as well as out.

'That was the red light quarter—each hovel had its tart, and a *ruffianu*, a pimp that is, got clients outside and brought them to the tart that he was working for. He earned something for each client he brought. I had a pimp too, an old man of sixty, but he didn't get me many clients, and whatever I did earn had to be a livelihood for two parasites, myself and the old man who got me the clients.

'The luckiest time was when the Americans arrived—men of all colours, dirty men, sick men, infected men, English and American and negroes, dockers and thieves, and all sorts, and there was room for all of them in my flesh. Several times I caught some inflammation, then I got gonorrhoea,[11] and I ran a serious risk of getting syphilis.

'I became [bruised and lacerated], too, and I saw myself the victim of a terrible fate.

'After a few years of that life I was arrested, because in Naples I was an unregistered prostitute, and, charged with offences against decency and various other things, I was sent to prison for eight months.

'During my time in prison I knew a lot of other prostitutes—there were a hundred or more of them in the prison, and among them there were girls of fourteen and fifteen. I was now twenty-three.

'My destiny was sealed by then—I would always be a prostitute, but I wanted to be in a brothel, somewhere where there would be more security against diseases and better earning possibilities. When I came out of prison I joined with some of my friends, prostitutes too, to get ourselves organised and taken on in a brothel. But the things that were required before you could get in!—personal documents, medical visits, digital examinations, and so on and so forth. We were three days in hospital for medical inspection to get the permission from the health authorities. Doctors took our blood and analysed it, and if the test was negative it was O.K. and you could be a tart, and if not and you were ill you had to cure yourself and give up hope at the same time.

'After all that, if you're all right, they give you a card at the police station, on which it's registered that you're a prostitute. On the card are all the particulars and a photograph of yourself, and you have to carry it with you always and show it when required to.

'We were taken on in a house, an important one. It was a brothel, but a first-class one, where the richer people went, and it paid well.

'It was at that time that I fell in love again, and I became pregnant a second time. You want to know that story too?[12]

'Well, he was a mechanic, very young and very *sympathique*—I liked him, you know. He had a fine body, and he was able—I'm not joking—to do it ten times running. We began a relationship, but I was always a prostitute and he a mechanic. It was a real pleasure, (physically)—I gave myself to him heart and soul.

'When I told him that I was pregnant and that he was the father, he took it badly, and said to me "Hey—don't you forget you're a tart—I want children by an honest woman."

'A daughter was born, who was the living image of her father. I kept her with me two years, but it broke my heart to see her in surroundings like those, and I entrusted her to a convent of nuns at Naples. She's seven years old now, but I haven't seen her for four years—I held her in my arms for the last time when she left for Naples.

'At that time, when I was going to leave Naples, I had the last news from my home—that my father was ill and that if he went on drinking he hadn't much longer to live, and that my brother had been arrested and then freed and then arrested again. I washed my hands of it— what pity could I feel for that "home"? "Get on with your own life,"[13] I said to myself, "who's had pity on you so far?"

'I didn't even have any pity for my child—I left her with the sisters, in the hope that she would never know anything about her mother, and that some family or other would take her in. If she ever finds out what her mother was she will certainly curse me, but what can I do— that's the hardest suffering Christ can give me!

'I'm here, but I come from so many different places—I've been at Taranto, Reggio Calabria, Messina, Catania, and many many other places. I'm here today, but tomorrow I don't know where I shall finish up. I've been at Palermo for about 8 months, in a second-class brothel, because I'm no longer suitable for the first-class ones. Do you know who is, now? Women teachers, and students who need money, and chamber-maids, "honest" people from the respectable world—those aren't tarts, but I am!

'I don't know how long I'll be staying here—it's a week since I arrived, and I'm seeing how things go—but the set-up doesn't suit me. How does one get oneself transferred? It's certainly not the Eternal Father who sends us from one town to another—it's us, with our feet! It's not easy. When we've already been a fortnight in one brothel we ourselves begin to think about a transfer to another. We take one or two photographs, either nude or clothed, and we send them to some brothel or other where we want to go. If the owner likes them he

Mattanza—the struggle to lift the fish aboard

The moment of danger, which can result in broken heads or hands

gives us permission to go there, and we stay in that brothel for so many days more.

'This is a small brothel. There's three of us, and each of us has her own room—as you see there's a wardrobe, a bed, a mirror, a wash-basin and pedestal, and that jug of hot water for washing ourselves after each client.

'We open at nine in the morning here, and we close at midday to eat, and then reopen at three in the afternoon to close at ten on ordinary days or at midnight on *festa* days.

'The days here are always the same. People of all ages come, adolescents, married men and old men too, but it's obvious that our clients are really the youths. There's a lower age limit before a boy can come here—eighteen. A boy of less than eighteen isn't supposed to be able to do it, but when they get a chance they do—haven't they got the right to?

'Do you know a boy of thirteen or fourteen arouses me in a way that a youth of twenty-five can't? You should know that at that age one is capable, and it's not true that it harms them—on the contrary, I'm telling you it does them good. But they're too quick and they've hardly finished before they start again—they're really passionate. Often when I've been amusing myself with a young boy[14]— I'm not joking—I get as excited as him.

'Certainly the little ones can't get too much of it, even at their age, but to let them taste it every now and then doesn't do them any harm.

'But you see how it is ordinarily—the client comes in, does what he's come for and goes away; five minutes is quite enough. If someone wants two in succession it's more, or if they want a quarter of an hour or half an hour it's more again—you pay according to what you want.

'If someone asks for something special there's a tariff, and why shouldn't they agree to it? According to what they want to do they pay more—my God, we might even hurt ourselves sometimes.

'There are "specials", for example—the *pecorina*, the *sponza di letto*, the *micciusa*, almost the same as *pecorina*; *la spagnola*, and many others at a special price. But, as I've said, it's all a question of time and whim. But I don't always allow these demands—it's according to what kind of mood I'm in and whether the man pleases me.

'After each client we wash ourselves and him and wait to see if another will come. Man is made for woman, isn't he?—I'm firmly convinced of it by now. There's no man living who's never tasted it —that's quite certain.

'I'm a woman before I'm a prostitute. Many don't know that— they think of a prostitute as something to abuse, a being that doesn't count in society. Isn't a prostitute flesh and blood like anyone else? And hasn't she got a heart like the others? And so I get a kind of horror when someone comes here and I feel afraid just to look at him— when I have to serve dirty and diseased people I get that horror. Many of them think a prostitute ought to do everything with her eyes shut and just serve—that's what they think!

'Certainly there are things one pretends not to see so as to earn one's living, and one sets one's personal feelings aside and works—but you must realise that this is my trade, which gives me my daily bread and the means of living. For example, I lack nothing. Just because I'm a prostitute shouldn't even I enjoy life and amuse myself? Rather I amuse myself *because* I'm a prostitute, and when I'm able, at the expense of some "parrot". My silken flesh is my dear and ever-lasting friend, and good clients are never wanting!

'Do you know what our worst misfortune is? It's when one of us ends up by falling in love with a man—that's ruin for us, because it's he that becomes the "prostitute" and never the client, and *we* have to pay *him* [laughs and blasphemes].

'If I have one of these "prostitutes"—and certainly I have, though not always the same one and not in all the different places—it's because every now and again one needs one.

'Sleeping with a *ricottaro* [prostitute's lover] is quite a different thing, because you know who you're sleeping with, and don't worry about anything. You enjoy the happiness that you expect, and then to have a *ricottaro* is often a good thing, because he becomes someone you trust; you can say so many things to him; you can go out together, as I know; he gives you the feeling of having a husband, a different kind of husband, but a real one.

'There are cheats, too, those who drink a girl's blood, many, many of them, and many of them I know!

'When you have a lover you're ruined, because you give him every-thing you earn, and you run the risk of being left like a dog! But a lover can help you, too, according to whether he's a man of honour or not. For instance, if one of us is being hunted by the police he sees to it, and helps us to remain hidden. In short, he helps, and brings us money too.

'But our business, as I've told you again and again, is to earn a living, and to do that we risk everything, even the loss of our health. Here there's entry for everyone, and not everyone is healthy. One contracts diseases, as I've said, and very easily, and if you catch a good dose you're ruined—you lose your health, you're chucked to the bottom of the bed to die. They don't use contraceptives here—the priests give penalties for using them. Certainly I try and take care— I examine a client and see whether or not he's got a disease, but often you can't see the disease outside—it's only in the blood you can see it, and if you catch it there's nothing to do. We're inspected every day or every two days, and they see if there's any external signs of infection—if you want a complete examination you pay more.

'Payment here is a complicated thing. It's good when one works a lot—that is has more men. It's always like that. For each time one gets a tip[15] in the evening, or on Saturdays, they give the tip to the boss and he pays us in cash.

'For each time they pay 350 lire, but here in this brothel they go half and half, that is half to me and half to the boss. I never have less than ten or fifteen men a day, and so I get at least 1,000 lire a day. In some city brothels it's different, specially in the luxurious ones, as they work on a percentage basis, and according to the *clientele* and the profit to the brothel the prostitute has a percentage of each go. In some brothels it's as high as 70 per cent, in others less, down to 40 per cent, but most go fifty-fifty. The owner has to pay a certain tax, but he makes money too.

'We never have to worry about eating. We all eat together, and so we spend together; in the morning when we've decided what to eat one of us goes out and does the shopping and then the cooking. If anyone fancies some particular food it's that one who cooks it. We eat well because we work hard, and what we eat is the sweat of our bodies—don't you agree? Should the rich and the big-shots eat well? No matter who envies us, we too, thank God, eat what the good-livers do.

'We earn our bread outside the brothel as well as inside it. Sometimes someone wants us for an evening or for a whole night, and they have to pay plenty for it. Or again, specially during *festas*, a lot of youths come to me in their own town and find me a room and feed me, and in return I give them a moment's pleasure—a moment or two is enough. That sort of thing suits me, as I get a lot for a little, but if I'm caught I'm ruined—they'd take my licence away and arrest me at once.

'There's prostitutes in every town—there's prostitutes everywhere—we have a proverb in Sicilian which says "Where there's a church-bell there's tarts",[16] because when you show an "honest" woman money and presents she forgets her "honesty". There's another proverb that says "At the sound of money the pillars tremble and judges and honest women are corrupted." But it's we prostitutes who are in the public eye—we're prostitutes and that's that.

'Do I ever go to church? Whatever would I be doing in church! I know well enough that I'm not worthy to go to church, but I also know that the people who are in command in the Church are even more corrupt than I am—that I do know. But I believe in God and in the Madonna—I believe in them, but I say they're happy enough looking after their own business, and what do I matter to them? We have to pray to them because we've been taught to, but in the end to believe that God takes care of us is a cracked idea. I believe in Him, as I've said, but I don't believe in the priests. They talk of religion, and of brotherly love and of chastity, and say they don't marry because they want to make a sacrifice—what a joke! They deflower the most honest girls of the town, they put horns on the most faithful Catholic husbands they know, they sleep with the most devout and religious women. You go to a priest to be confessed and he starts talking right away about hell and purgatory and sins and miracles—certainly I never go to confession, because I know it's all a buffoonery. And then if I went to confession I'd have to promise to become an honest woman, or at least to sleep only with the priest and not be in brothels any more—and would I go and eat at his house? You don't know those priests—they're real Turks;[17] they have wives by the dozen.

'I don't believe in popes or bishops or cardinals. Do they know me? No, and I don't know them, so that's fine.

'I'm not a Communist or anything else—I'm a prostitute and that's that. These political parties don't interest me—all of them think of themselves and the poor remain poor. I don't vote, I've never voted—those things don't interest me, and I'm talking about them to you for the first time. What interests me is earning my living, and that's enough. There's one law in the world, that each thinks for himself and God for all.

'At the moment I do just know about politics because of the Merlin

Law. Merlin[18] is a prostitute, and perhaps she caught a good dose of syph. and said "Enough of the brothels". The brothels won't be easily closed, my son, and they won't finish, and prostitutes won't disappear from the face of the earth. Close the brothels and you'll see there'll be all the more prostitutes. I mind and I don't mind that they're closing the brothels—I mind at losing the security of work, and I don't mind because I'm sure I'll always be able to get a crust of bread.

'You see, if they close the brothels where are all these youths going to go for a woman? Or are they supposed to use their hands? So if now they pay 350 lire for a woman, tomorrow they'll be willing to pay 1,000 lire or 2,000 or even more, and the prostitutes who work in their own houses will be more and more, because everyone likes money. And then the diseases'll come!—because while now they're cured somehow or other who's going to cure you tomorrow? And when? And how many times? There won't be any more control, and there'll be chaos.[19]

'Things'll go badly for us prostitutes, perhaps, but we certainly won't die of starvation. Merlin says she'll give us a pension and make us all "honest women". Where? What with? Shall we all make ourselves nuns?—then we shouldn't be prostitutes any more because we'd do it with the priests!

'They say we'll have work—but where? and what work can we do? If you had a shop would you take a prostitute to work there? Certainly not—well, who's going to give us work? But don't think we're going to have men in the streets and under the trees like the French do.

'But all this Merlin Law is a put-up job—man is made of blood, and blood needs some fun. Who can get along without women—who? Down here in the south we can see what the consequences of the Merlin Law will be—in Italy the men are colder, but in Sicily where the sun makes the blood boil in the veins it won't be so easy!

'But not everyone thinks as I do—there's some who are optimistic, and think the closing of the brothels is a good thing for us. They think society's going to welcome them again, that they can find work, or that in a jiffy they'll find a man to love them and keep them. They also hope to find a blessing in the houses of correction that they'll have to set up now—but I can't really believe they're so simple as to hope to wash out their whole lives and the name of "prostitute"—I can't believe it!

'But let's leave these things alone—leave them to time; I've got great faith in time. I've got one big worry in life, and that's the fate of my daughter, because I haven't forgotten her yet.

'I don't know yet what I'll do—I've earned enough by my work to set my life in order, but I don't know yet how or where. Will I buy myself a house? stay inside it?—and how would I eat then? Get my daughter back and keep her with me?—but will I ever find her again? I've so many things to think about—above all because I know I can't go on being a prostitute for ever. I don't know exactly what I'll do. I haven't decided yet and I can't tell you anything. In September they'll close the brothels and then I'll have to make a decision. Now I only think about working—"I think about today and God thinks about tomorrow".'[20]

CHAPTER ELEVEN

The Nun

'MARCELLA is the name the bishop gave me, when I was consecrated to God. I can't use my real name any more; none of us must use the real names we were born with—they're forgotten.

'I'm forty years old, and I've been a nun for eighteen years. I've been in several convents; at Trapani, Palermo, Agrigento, Sciacca, and now here. Tomorrow Divine Providence may assign me to another convent, and, as we must always obey the Divine Will, we are always ready to do so.

'Oh, how great is Divine Providence! When I was young I used to live in a town in the province of Bari. We were a big family, three sons and four daughters, and I was the third child. All my brothers are still living; one of my sisters died many years ago, and my parents are dead too. My mother died two years ago—she used to live with my brother, who is a chemist at Bari.

'No one told me that I should become a servant of God, a bride of Christ, but the Divine Voice called me, and I was ready to dedicate myself for my whole life to the holy mission.

'I was twenty-two when I entered the convent of the Sisters of Misericordia. My family forbade me and obstructed me in every way, but I was convinced of what I wanted to do, and I ran away and took refuge in a convent of nuns. Why did I become a nun? Because life outside was full of sin for me, because I understood that the worldly life was too dangerous and hard, while if I gave myself to God I should be happier and have a heart of grace for the rest of my life.

'My family wanted to marry me to a rich man whom I did not love. I had had a relationship with another man, but we won't talk of those things—they're over and done with.

'It was the parish priest who convinced me. I was a member of Catholic Action and I was his right hand; he convinced me that I should become a nun to understand the Divine Will. "Sylvia," he said, "why don't you become a nun? You'll live happily, you'll lack for nothing, you will always be near to God, you will espouse Christ,

and He will give you eternal life." He gave me these talks every time
he confessed me, when I was alone with him at his house. I was convinced by his words; I knew many nuns, and all told me that they
were happy in that life. I began to see an ideal world in the life of a
convent, and slowly I made up my mind.

'I had one grief in my heart, leaving my family—parents, brothers
and sisters. But the priest told me I should overcome these feelings—
that it was a noble sacrifice, pleasing to Christ. I should be able to
pray for my loved ones more easily, as I should be nearer to God.

'I told my family, but they were all against me—my father made a
scene with the priest, and I was kept at home for some months, forbidden to go to church.

'One night, by arrangement with the priest, I ran away from home
and went to his house. He welcomed me like a father, and I remained
hidden secretly in his house for five days. Then from his house I was
taken to a convent in Bari, and there I was welcomed with great
affection and given shelter.

'They cried for me at home, and said they had lost a daughter, but
when they came to see me they all embraced me, and none of them
said anything about it.

'I stayed at that convent for two years. I was dressed in the clothes
of a novice, a black habit and a white veil. During those two years I
had to prepare myself to become a nun, to pray, to study, to learn the
rules of the order—in short to prove myself worthy of consecration.

'The day of consecration came at last. There were ten of us novices
to be consecrated; there was the bishop of the diocese and many
religious authorities, the Mother General, and many other people,
including my intimate friends. It must have been the most wonderful
day of my life, or perhaps the most decisive.

'The ceremony when a nun is consecrated is very beautiful, and
whoever understands it is deeply moved. We are dressed in white
habits with a white veil on our heads to symbolise our virginity.
Before the bishop we pronounce the vows of perpetual virginity,
and the vows of obedience to the rules, and then he takes off our veils
and cuts off our hair, which is the symbol of vanity, and puts a dark
veil on our heads and pronounces his benediction, consecrating us for
all our lives.

'The ceremony is long and complicated, but in general that's how
it takes place.

'After the ceremony there was a wonderful party, like a *festa*, and the bishop and the Mother General and my family were there.

'I was consecrated to God for ever; I'd taken the vows—if I broke them I'd be damned and excommunicated.

'I was twenty-four years old, one of the youngest nuns in the convent, and all the other nuns showed great kindness to me, even the Mother Superior, who treated me like a daughter.

'My order is the Sisters of Misericordia, an order founded by Sister Zaugara, in . . . in . . . 1893, if I remember rightly, and many of the rules were laid down by her. We venerate her as a saint in the convent; we keep a portrait of her in the big room, as she's certainly in paradise.

'We dress as you see me now—a full maroon skirt, with a crown at the side of the belt, which represents the devotion to the Blessed Virgin, and on the chest two strips of white linen with a crucifix between them; we wear it on the breast to symbolise that it's always within us. We wear a black veil on the head, and below that a white one which covers our hair. All our clothes show our life of penitence, far from worldly things.

'There are many convents of our order in Sicily, and all of them are governed by the Mother General, who is the highest nun of all our convents. She lives in Palermo, but she visits the convents and she can stay at them if she wants to. Last year she came to our convent and even slept there.

'For us she is a real mother and we are her beloved daughters. She's very kind and understanding and affectionate—she really seems like a madonna. You ought to see her when she's sitting by the side of the bishop at big functions, how well the two look together, the Mother with her daughters and the Father with his sons.

'The Mother General is nominated by the bishop; she rules over all the convents and decides where to send us; she's responsible for our maintenance; she protects and helps us. There's the Mother Superior of the convent, too, who is chosen from the eldest, or the most beloved and able, by the Mother General. The Mother Superior is our second mother ; she looks after the whole convent ; she alone sees to everything, and to everyone's soul. She dresses like us, but she's distinguished by a big cross, bigger than the ones we wear, to show her authority, and she wears at her side all the keys of the convent. She decides what we eat, and allots the duties to the nuns, arranges the

work of the girls, and sees to the needs of the convent. Ours is a
family, and in it are love, order, obedience, charity and prayer.

'We take in orphans at the convent—there's forty of them with us,
and they come from all sorts of towns. We adopt them after making
the necessary enquiries, because we never take in children of Communists, for example, as they're excommunicated.

'Our orphans must be without parents, or at least they must be
children of extremely poor people whose obedience to the Church is
well known. Before adopting an orphan we require a recommendation from some priest. We keep them till they're sixteen or eighteen,
and then either their families come and take them away again, or they
consecrate themselves for life, like us. We welcome orphans of any
age, from the new born up to girlhood, and unfortunately we also
welcome grown-up girls whom life has deceived—people who've
put their trust in someone's affection and have been betrayed by it.

'There can be anything from ten to a maximum of fifty nuns in a
convent; here we've only twelve, as it's a small convent, and forty
orphans.

'The Mother Superior chooses some trusted Sister to help her in her
arduous work, and each of the others has her duty. I am the Mother
Superior's help, and when she's away from the convent it's me who's
in command, and I make myself heard, because I know how to command.

'Each sister takes her turn to go out and beg for alms—she goes out
with two orphans and tours the streets asking the people for alms.
There are also sisters who are in charge of cleanliness, and those who
teach the orphan girls women's crafts, and those who pray, and so on.

'The convent is very well-off for rooms—it's a little paradise for us.
In a big room upstairs is the orphan girls' dormitory, and below it is
our room; there's a large room for daily work, rooms for receptions,
and the refectory, with long tables in rows.

'How does an ordinary day pass?

'In the morning the little bell rings at five o'clock, or six o'clock,
according to whether it's summer or winter. The orphan girls go and
wash in their washing-room—each of us nuns has a small bath in our
room. The girls take turns to go and sound the church bell, as the
church is joined on to the convent, to announce Mass. They all go in
silence to the church, where the priest is waiting to celebrate Mass.
We don't hear Mass from the body of the church but from a place

specially made for us, and well apart from each other, so as to be able to pray better.

'Every morning almost all the orphans take Communion, and all the nuns must do so compulsorily. Then we go back in single file to the convent, to eat. The girls who've been detailed by the Mother Superior prepare the milk—concentrated milk and flour—put the bowls on the table, and serve it as soon as the orphans have got back. In the morning each orphan gets a bowl of the milk and a slice of bread. We nuns eat at a separate table—there are two orphans who serve us with the milk that the cowherd brings in the morning and the coffee that's ordered from the bar the evening before.

'Then we go to work. Some of the girls, under the charge of one of the nuns, look after cleaning the rooms, others do the kitchen, and still others go to work with the nuns; they embroider bridal clothes and make trousseaux, or sew shirts or knit woollen stockings and things of that sort which are ordered by our benefactors and paid for. In other rooms is the infant school for the town children, which we also charge for.

'At midday we go to eat. For each orphan there's a plate of *pasta* and a slice of bread. The *pasta* we cook every day is with soup—sometimes with beans, sometimes potatoes, sometimes marrow, but always with soup, because it fills up the bowls, and if you don't have it you need so much *pasta*. For second course there's a sauce to eat on the bread, often the same sauce as there was with the *pasta*—that is to say if it was potato it will be potato and bread for second course, and if it was beans it will be beans.

'Before the orphans begin eating, the Mother Superior makes them recite grace; then she leaves her little daughters and goes to eat.

'As I've said, we nuns eat separately, and by the good will of God we eat well. Our table is well furnished, partly for prestige; there's usually meat for us for a second course, and wine and fruit, and something else nice—whatever Providence sends.

'After we've eaten we go back to work; each one of us has her work assigned. The afternoon is the time of prayer, and most, but not all, of us go to church to pray; prayer is to us work too, because we earn money praying. We also give lessons to the smallest of the orphans—the priest instructs the older ones.

'Towards the evening all the orphans come together to us in the church for Holy Benediction that the priest celebrates, and the rosary to the Madonna. After that each one of us goes to be confessed by the priest, for the Communion of the morning after. There's a room where he can hear our confessions in the convent and then remain alone with us afterwards to give us all the spiritual comfort we need. Having received the grace of God we think about supper. The orphans get a piece of bread with a little American jam or cheese—we nuns can eat what we like, because we have everything in the storerooms. And at last about nine o'clock in the evening we go to bed, when the slow tolling of our bell tells us it's time. We nuns can stay awake for a long time; we pass the time reading or listening to the radio or watching the television—yes, we've even got a television here, which the Christian Democrat Member of Parliament, the Onorevole Aldisio, gave us. Often the priest comes to keep us company and stays a long time with us discussing church and convent matters.

'And all our days are more or less like that—there's small and exceptional differences, but with us the days pass with the same rhythm.

'As you see, our lives are for God, for good, and for charity; we have a high calling like that of the priests—for them doctrine, and for us the teaching of love and charity to the small and the needy. We are the Brides of Christ, we bear towards Him the burning love of Mary Magdalen at His feet when he was on the Cross.

'What do we do for a living? Who looks after us? Divine Providence, my son—we are the beloved daughters of God, and He looks after us, He protects us and shelters us under the great mantle of His compassion.

'We live by alms. Every day one of the nuns goes through the streets of the town begging alms for the orphans. In a town like this they don't give much, and she brings home little or nothing.

The Mother General helps her daughters—every two or three months—or sometimes every month—she sends us a lorry with *pasta* and flour, or stuff for the orphans to make dresses. But the convent has property of its own too—we have lots of land that the faithful who were devoted to the nuns left to the convent—good land that produces grain and hay and olives and lemons and other fruits. These lands are looked after by the peasants free of charge—good peasants who are devoted to the Divine Compassion, because Divine Compassion is the strongest of all God's powers—it's better to pray for compassion than the Holy Ghost or the Sacred Heart of Jesus.

'Everything we reap from our lands goes into our store-rooms; we keep enough for ourselves for a year, and we sell the rest to get money.

'And then we have the help of the Holy Father—so much help! The P.O.A.[1] sends us many things, special subsidies in money, and various goods too—such as clothes, shoes, *pasta*, cheese, and things of that sort.

'There's the Government to look after us too, the Christian Democrat Government—and what we owe them! The benefits of the Christian Democrat Government are very precious to us, specially at election time. How much help they give us—they protect us, and we protect them too; the bishop writes that we should, and tells us so whenever he comes to the convent. Just to ask a Member of Parliament for a sum of money is enough to get it—Aldisio is a good and charitable man and he's really helped us. Besides sending us lorry-loads of *pasta* and flour and so on, he left us, the time he came to our convent, a blessed sum of money, two hundred thousand lire—surely God will give him all paradise, because that's what we pray for him.

'And American aid!—we get so much, so very much of that! That comes to us from far-off, from America, and you can see that the Americans are both rich and charitable; above all they're not Communists—they believe in God and they're all Catholics. It's from America that we get the most valuable help of all. The Pope, America, and the Christian Democrat Government, those are the three great benefactors of us Sisters of Divine Compassion.

'But there's also the people; they think of us too. At the times of their harvests they give something to us too—each peasant gives us a little grain or oil, or hay to assist the orphans, and it all gets sold, as we can't put everything in the store-rooms. There's townspeople of ours in America who send us offerings in dollars for the *festas*. Everyone helps us except the Communists, who are excommunicated by the Pope, and do not have the grace of God.

'One day it will all be rewarded by God, because what's given to priests and nuns and what's given to God are the same thing.

'Our parish priest gives us a lot of help; he gets us help from everyone he knows—he knows such a lot of people—and over and above what we get there's a small sum for him—he has so much need of it! We are women, and you know how it is—we can't do everything for ourselves, and we must have a man to help us, and God gives us our parish priest.

'As I've said we work too, running the infant school for fees. Children from three to seven years of age can come to us, and for each child there's a small charge of 2,000 lire a month. We have fifty children. There are two nuns who look after them and teach them prayers and small odds and ends of religion.

'Our whole existence depends upon alms.

'We receive alms for prayers too, for reciting prayers for the people; and we get paid according to the importance of the prayer. For example there's one family who wants a rosary recited to the Madonna every evening, for a soul who has passed away—a rosary costs 100 lire, and that makes 3,000 lire a month. There's prayers for which we're much more generously rewarded—at religious functions, funerals and weddings; the families concerned ask us to pray, and we say whatever prayers they like. If our orphans sing at a wedding we get a bigger sum than we would if we only had to pray. Our prayers are acceptable to God, because the voices of the needy and the afflicted touch His heart.

'But there's many who fight against us—there's the Communists, who say that we're rich and that the beneficences we receive are shameful, and that we live in the luxury of the convents, and many other accusations. But it's not true—those atheists are liars; you've seen how we live, by alms alone.

'They want to come to power to destroy the Church and the convents, but Divine Providence will never allow those people to come to power.

'How good the Christian Democrat Members of Parliament are— you can see it just to look at them, all of them rich men who have no need of alms—but it's enough to look at the Communists to know that they're wretched people who have nothing and want to live without working, on the alms of the poor nuns. We pray to God that He will make all the Communists die and that He will destroy them for ever. But the Cross will never fail—it's the Church that rules on earth, and for ever.

'We nuns live by alms, but we give alms too—we have many girls in our convent, and we bring them up in the teachings of God, deliver them from the perils of this world, teach them to work and to pray. Some of them become nuns. We are the strongest, and we are always increasing—when we die there will be others, and always more and more of them.

'There are insinuators and idle gossips who go about saying that there's luxury and corruption in the convents, but they know there's nothing but holiness and dignity. The well-being that God gives us makes them jealous, and they would like us to die of hunger or beg for alms at their dirty feet. We have drawing rooms, and radio and television, we keep our rooms neat, we are honoured and respected— those things are the reward of our prayers, and jealousy can't take them away.

'We can't take thought for all the poor—they give us alms, and so we can't give them alms. For the poor there are those whose job it is—we shelter the orphans, and that's a lot by itself. They say we shelter orphans to exploit them, to make them work and take their earnings, and even that we force them to become nuns, preventing them getting married or bettering themselves socially.

'What they say is true, but they don't know how to say it. We bring up the orphans in the religious way of life; we don't say to the girls "You've got to become nuns", but it's they themselves who are attracted to the sweetness of monastic life and they themselves who express the desire to become nuns.

'I'm already old in this life, I'm well practised in the ways of convents, and by now I know much. There are many duties that weigh on us nuns; it takes a lot of care to rule a convent, we have so many responsibilities, and everything falls on our shoulders, especially on the older nuns. We have to feed and clothe so many girls, prepare for visits from the bishop, or some Member of Parliament, or for the Mother Superior's birthday, or there'll be a *festa* in the convent, and it pleases the girls just to look on.

'I'm a nun, but I feel I have the quality to be a Mother Superior—I know very well I have! Our Mother Superior is getting rather old, and she's not really suited to the work. Perhaps it'll be me who takes her place, or perhaps some other nun, depending on where the Mother General's sympathies lie. Everything's a question of the Party and of recommendation—I know a lot of important people, even the bishop himself, and one day, God willing, I too shall be able to glory in being a Mother Superior.

'For the moment I'm a nun—tomorrow, I don't know, perhaps I shall be in command, for the ways of Providence are infinite.'

CHAPTER TWELVE

The Priest

'MUCH of this you don't know, my son,' he said to me, because I
had asked him what the Church was in itself, 'but the Church has been
for nearly two thousand years the fountain head of human wisdom,
justice, brotherhood, peace and compassion. She is the refuge of mankind, especially for those to whom life and its passions has brought
only ruin and despair and sometimes loathing. She is the mother who
wraps her children in her cloak, showing them the half of heaven.
She is the guide of humanity who runs blindly hither and thither in
search of an illusion; she is the light by which one may find one's path
in the dark; she is the comfort of whoever suffers. She is . . . but there
are some ideas that it isn't easy to understand, one must study in order
to understand. I will try to be simple. Then the Church is also the
teacher of the holy rights of mankind, and the exhorter of the duties
which God has imposed upon His children; she is the mother of
philosophy, of St. Augustine, St. Thomas Aquinas, St. Jerome; she
is the cradle of reason.

'You see, there would not have been two thousand years of life on
earth for her if it had not been the will of God, two thousand years
governed by His true representative, the Holy Father. Whoever
understands this mission that God has given to the Church cannot be
other than awed, cannot do other than rejoice in such greatness:
greatness both spiritual and political. The Church has always commanded the world, she has always made her voice heard above all
others.

'Often one does not understand the mission of the Church, it is
uncomprehended, and for this her enemies have tried to overthrow
her, but be sure their struggles will be in vain—the Church was born
from the blood of the martyrs, she was born to conquer, and by
now she is accustomed to conquer all, for the hand of God is over
her.

'I am proud to serve the Church and God, however miserable my
work may be. For the welfare of souls I have put aside everything,

The close of the season—
the massive nets are
carried ashore

The grape harvest is the height of employment—the autumn and winter months following it are the depths. Grapes are brought in the open barrel (upper, at right) and the juice is extracted by a horse-operated press (below)

even the things most dear to me, even life itself, for life does not belong
to us but to God.

'We priests are the ministers of God; we have a task in society both
high and grave—the task that Jesus Christ entrusted to us: "And I
will make you fishers of men—go forth and preach to the world—I
send to you your Father who is in heaven."

'That is what Christ said to the Apostles, and we accomplish His
words in our holy duty, for we are nothing but fishers of men.

'I was ordained a priest at the age of 25, at Palermo Seminary, in
1946, immediately after the war. I entered the seminary when I was
eleven, and left when I was 25. Fourteen years of study and of pure
sacrifice, the hardest of all studies, perhaps, but also the most beautiful.

'Perhaps when I was a child I did not fully know the duties of becoming a minister of God; but I shut myself in a seminary and there
inside it I studied. Certainly I knew that I must become a priest, but
on some distant day, perhaps, a day I used to think of often, but which
I used to be afraid would never come. Between those walls one
learned many things, one learned above all to listen to the voice of
God, one learned to know God and to taste Him, to defend the
Catholic faith, to have contact with all men, saints and sinners. And
little by little we learned the duty that must rule us for all our lives.
If we made sacrifices, and many of them, what a wonderful satisfaction
it is when one is a priest—one is no longer a man like all the others,
one has become an authority, respected—and feared.

'I've been a priest now for twelve years. I can't claim to have had
a long experience, but I am certain that I have already proved the
things I dreamed of from a child, and what I learned in the seminary,
and what my superiors told me—it is all pure reality.

'The care of souls demands much, it demands a quality which often
we have not got—it demands surrender, care, authority, patience
which often we lack, or which deserts us.

'Our mission is not only a spiritual one—at least formerly it was so,
but now, today, it is different. Our activities and duties extend into
social life too, and specially into political attitudes—questions with
which we are very much concerned. In the small communities,
especially, to whom can the faithful turn? There is no one who can
help them more than the parish priest; they all come to us, and to each
we must give an answer.

' "Father, this or that has happened."

' "Father, can I do such and such?"

' "Father, can I marry that girl?"

' "Father, I have committed impure acts."[1]

' "Father, I have lost . . ."[2]

' "Father, I've done this or that."

' "Father, I'm angry with so and so; shall I make it up?"[3]

' "Father, they've insulted me."

' "Father, is it true that . . .?"

' "Father, who ought I to vote for?"

' "Father, is this a sin?"

and so on and so forth.

'And I have to answer all these questions, and sometimes I'm at a loss, but if I didn't answer I'd cut a sorry figure—for better or worse I've got to answer.

'We have to look after the religious and social education of little children and of boys and girls—the men and mothers of tomorrow. I have to guide them all along the right road, the road to which the Church directs us.

'In the parish there is a Catholic Action centre—two rooms for men and another two for women. In these rooms they have to learn the teachings of the Church, form their outlook on religious and political ideas and social life—questions of the greatest importance. The Catholic Action centre is also a rendezvous for youths in the evenings. When do I give them religious teaching? Well—every Sunday about four in the afternoon I get the girls together and give them a catechism lesson for almost two hours, then in the evening the same with the boys. Then there are lessons during the week of an evening, but certainly the most important is the Sunday one.

'The youth of today is a delicate problem—it follows too easily at the heels of the vulgar instincts of this age. Modern youth wants to live the life which seems to them splendid, if fleeting, and thinks to find in material and fleshly things the fountain of happiness. Today there is corruption everywhere, and the sources of corruption are the cinema, the newspapers, vulgar books, filthy pictures and obscene entertainments—obscene and splendid into the bargain.[4]

'I've heard talk these days of Rock and Roll, a kind of dance— and, as I've heard, a phrenetic one, that leads a youth to shameful depths of lust. Now everywhere they're talking about strip-tease— yes, even that! You see the secret immorality that's about today. One can put up with a house of immorality provided it's shut away and under surveillance, but strip-tease! So many youths dream of seeing nude women like that—very often actresses—and then from those dreams are born shameful actions.

'Everyone nowadays follows the lives of film actors and actresses, everyone admires them as the ideal way of life to strive for. You hear boys and grown men on the streets saying "How sexy!"[5] talking about some actress with practically nothing on. Youth is in danger, both in the towns and among the traditionally humble and ignorant people of the country—the ignorant too are all too ready to be lured into this evil.

'I know about these things because I am a priest, and I feel ashamed when I realise that between this world and higher things stands another world—the world of sex. But this conception of that part of life is something we have created ourselves—there is no sexual world, for God would not have been able to give to man anything so tormenting and so filthy. It is we who have created it—remember that the soul of man is more prone to evil than to good.

'Do you know what some say to me?

' "But, Father, we're men, we're made to live, to love, we have blood in our veins—what we do is natural! Life needs some outlet . . ."

'If these people knew how great is the value of a human soul they wouldn't talk like that. How many souls are lost forever in the performing of certain actions? With what guilt do those stain themselves who for a moment of "pleasure" have thrown away the seed of a human life? It is a serious question!

'It is with sadness that I have learned in the confessional and from the relationships between boys and girls that their sexual activity occupies a central and basic position in their lives and their mentalities. I can state that there is not one boy above the age of seven who does not masturbate—not one. And the girls too are given to this swinishness. Any girl who is fifteen I would not call a virgin any more, because to be a virgin is a thing that carries great responsibility, and judgment too—but when even a girl already commits certain acts by herself, then she stains her virginity and tricks whoever marries her believing her to be pure.

'The youths and grown-up men, shame to say, are completely blind, and given up to this activity. Whoever hasn't got a sexual life doesn't count—to be a man means something quite different nowadays from

what it used to. When the youths haven't got any money in their
pockets they set about it alone, and justify their activity, saying to
themselves "If I had any money I wouldn't do this, but go to the
brothel." As if having money just meant frequenting brothels.

'Often they fall into the mire of the flesh, and when they see the
terrible consequences they try to come back, but then it's too late.

'Once when I was confessing a youth of almost twenty I realised
that he was very ill. I saw this from his eyes, and from his face, which
was pale and fleshless. I wanted to ask him what was wrong, and I
did so while he was telling me, under seal of the confessional, his
detestable carnal activities. I asked him if he was sick, and of what
illness.

' "Father, I have been ill for many months, and I'm afraid it's all
up with me. I have wasted my youth quickly, and all that's left to me
is to hope to save my soul." My God! And after some months it was
I myself who gave the Last Sacraments at his death-bed. That poor
boy was dead, victim of a terrible venereal disease. That's what the
results of the "splendid" life are—and sometimes its filthiness knows no
limits. They don't know that this act brings loss of vital energy, that
each time they are losing fluid from the spinal column, they don't
know that to abuse these organs means the encouraging of terrible
diseases—cancer, tuberculosis, syphilis, pneumonia—diseases which
spring above all from these acts. All youths and women, babies and
men, are victims of this instinct. The Church has absolutely forbidden,
and will always forbid, giving in to this baseness—she will always
prohibit these things, and show the true light to the minds of men.
Apart from the religious point of view, the Church protects by her
very attitude towards these things the health and morals of mankind,
and his dignity too! Many marry with only one object from the out-
set—for them matrimony is no more than a game of carnal pleasure.
Conjugal happiness is highly prized, and is understood in a strictly
sexual sense. "Father, if I didn't find anyone to keep me company in
the evenings, if I didn't forget a hard day's work, if I couldn't give my
affection to my wife, if I had to sleep in a cold and empty bed—father,
what use would life be to me?" A man said that to me in confession
once. According to them a man loves his wife because she knows how
to give him company in the evenings, she knows well how to embrace
her husband and make him forget a hard day's work. That's what
they think a woman is for a man. And again some say to me:

' "Father, we can't always provide for the children, they want too much looking after, and too much spending; it's a good thing to have children, but not too many of them. Which is better, to put them in the world and not be able to feed them or not to put them into the world at all? So what sin are we committing if we avoid their coming into the world, by the means which exist nowadays?—like that it's easy." And they reach this point—they waste the medium that generates life for carnal and, I would say, brutal pleasures.

'But if we priests were not a firm authority to these people, if we did not give a ruling to them, if we did not reproach them, what would happen?

'For them everything is human, is natural, and some say to me "But, father, you're human too, you too have blood in your veins", and think they've won the point in that way, because they think I wouldn't know how to reply.

'It's true that one is a man—everyone has blood in his veins, but that blood is not meant to be uselessly squandered. Man is disposed to evil by nature, but God has given a brain to man, a brain able to bridle the bestial forces of his blood. What would be our function on earth if we priests yielded to this power of the blood—our mission would be finished. We priests can make mistakes too, because we're men too, but in making mistakes we don't exhort others to follow us—a fine thing that would be!

'And then there's homosexuality—it's not a new thing. There are those who sleep with their brothers, those who carry on with a cousin, those who love a fair boy, those who pay him. There are those who buy and those who sell. This department of sexuality may appear sporadic and rare, but in fact it exists everywhere, even here, as I know well. There are mature men who, with money and other things, corrupt little boys still of tender age, but for these there is a famous verse from the Bible. "Whosoever offends one of these little ones, it would be better for him if a millstone were hanged about his neck and he were cast into the sea."

'There is no place for these men in society—they are against nature and against the dignity of man.

'Sexuality, dear son, is a world by itself; it is not a mystery, as many believe—it is only one aspect of life, perhaps the dirtiest of them all.

'That there is corruption, and that it is spread everywhere, is very evident, but as long as there is still fear of God and as long as there are us ministers and the bulwarks of the Church, one may hope for the salvation of so many lost souls who are deluded and deceived.

'How many calamities corruption brings with it! Corruption, that child of modernity, that achievement of two thousand years! Understand one thing clearly—when there is modernity there cannot be honour or marital fidelity. It is clear that adultery is commoner in corrupted circles. I know some things—perhaps I know too many!

'Here in this town there are only two parishes. My parish is very small—it's about a third of the whole town, and the rest is part of the parish of the mother church. And naturally mine is the poorer parish. The faithful who regularly attend all the functions of the Church are few, and those who contribute are fewer still. Mine is a parish of peasants, all peasants, and the poorest of them into the bargain. A church is rich not if its parishioners are faithful but if they are rich, but a priest does well where his parishioners are poor and humble—for the poor turn to the priest because they are in more need, while the rich do not seek him often. They think they're in direct touch with God— that's my experience, however funny it may seem.

'However, a church must be kept up, and that takes money, a lot of money. I myself have to live on the offertory of my parishioners— myself and my family. How do I manage to live? You might well ask whether mine is a profession at all,[6] and unfortunately it's not one. However, as far as society's concerned it is—the reason is that ours is a human activity and so is often confused with others, by those who don't know any better.

'One draws a daily earning from religious functions, above all from Mass. Mass is celebrated every morning, and without doubt that's the most certain earning of the day. There's no tariff for religious functions, they're paid for from the offertory, and of course some people give more and some give less. So for the sake of convenience we make a reference table, that is to say we put a basic price on every function, and the faithful can go above this sum if they like but they can't give less.

'For example, a Mass usually costs 700 lire—naturally anyone who wants to give more is free to do so, but one cannot cut anything from this basic price established by the priest. Yes, we do make a sort of tariff—a false tariff, because the real tariff is alms. But you understand that some people give more than others, and so in order not to create injustice we fix a minimum and leave the maximum open.

'Sometimes there are people who can't pay that amount, and then one closes an eye and accepts 600 lire or 500 lire—but never less.

'Anyone who wants a Mass celebrated comes to order it the day before, tells me who it is for or for what he wants it celebrated, and then on the arranged day the Mass is celebrated. An ordinary Mass costs 700 lire, but then the price goes up with the number of prayers, and with the ornaments. A Mass with the altar lit costs more; if the altar is decorated with flowers it costs more still; if someone wants a Mass with special prayers then the "offering" goes up again accordingly. Sometimes it happens that no one comes wanting a Mass celebrated, and then one celebrates it alone and receives no offertory.

'Less often I celebrate a sung Mass for the faithful, with the organ and so on—that's expensive, and they pay from 2,500 lire upward. The faithful dedicate Masses to their dead above all, but sometimes to give thanks, and so on.

'But more than the daily Masses, the richest source of income for us are the *festas*. Here in the town many *festas* are held during the year, some of them important and some less so. There are three more important *festas*, but there are others too. We priests take part in each *festa*, and naturally if the *festa* takes place in my church it is I who have the biggest earnings, and the same with the other priests. *Festas* are almost a necessity for the people—it's a strange thing, but those who favour the *festas* most are the poor rather than the rich.

'When there's a parish *festa* everyone contributes, either with an offering in money or in kind. There's a committee constituted every year, who sell the offerings in kind and form a bank account.

'The cost? If it is a small *festa*, or only a religious one, the cost varies between 100 and 150 thousand lire, and half of that sum goes to the priest. On the average there's one of these *festas* every month throughout the year, but they're most frequent in the summer.

'For example there's the *festa* of St. Joseph, very ancient in our Sicilian towns, and very important to the people. It is a *festa* that usually lasts one day only, but it shows much tradition. The *festa* falls on the 19th of March; and as spring will be coming in a few days the people, so as to be vouchsafed good auspices, begin to throw out old odds and ends, broken furniture, wood, and so on. These things are collected in the evening, after the function, and together with other wood collected in the countryside, are burned. The bonfire is made in front of the church of the Saint, and its burning is accompanied by shouts and hisses and songs. When the fire begins to die down, the young men begin to jump across it. Whoever can jump higher than the flames is applauded, especially by the women, and is given a prize consisting of bread, wine, and *pasta*, which I have blessed.

'At midday, after the Mass, a traditional meal takes place. They take three poor people, a man, a woman, and a boy, and dress them respectively as St. Joseph, the Madonna, and the child Christ. Then these three are invited to a public lunch, where a richly furnished table awaits them. It's funny, however, that while the three are about to eat one dish, they're suddenly offered another and the first is snatched away, and so on—so that in the course of the meal the three guests may be offered 20, 30, or 40 different dishes, and hardly get a mouthful of them!

'The dishes—either *pasta* or meat, etc.—are given by the peasants out of devotion to the Saint. In the end the "bread of devotion", that was bought with money collected by a small deputation, is divided among the people present at the meal.

'But things are different when it's a big *festa*. There's the principal *festa*, the great *festa*, of St. Antonio. That lasts three days, three days of enjoyment. This *festa* is more costly, and more lucrative. Altogether we collect for it $2\frac{1}{2}$ million lire. Of this sum the best part goes on church expenses, and a lot for organisation of amusements, cinema, horse-races, and so on, and then the offering to the priest, which varies, but which will be, say, another 150,000 lire.

'To the poor? No, they don't give anything to the poor as a rule—sometimes they give them something, *pasta* or flour, but that's up to the committee.

'The *festa* is something providential for us priests; by means of the *festa* the people show us their devotion, and reward us for the teachings we have given to them so liberally.

'Then there are other *festas*, as I said—Easter, Christmas, Corpus Christi, but they are liturgical *festas*, where the earnings are meagre. After Christmas one goes on to the blessing of houses, and usually every family gives something, an offering—but not much, 50 or 100 lire, and very often eggs.

'There are various other functions during the year for which we receive something, for example Gregorian masses.[7]

'On Sunday there's the communal Mass, which is gratis to the people—the offering varies, 10 lire or less, but as there are two Masses on Sunday one always gets about 5,000 lire or more. A lot of people reward us in kind. They give us oil, or cheese, or corn, and so on, and we have to accept these things too, as they also are alms.

'Then there are religious ceremonies for marriage, baptism, funerals, etc. For a wedding? If it's an ordinary one, that is to say without much luxury, 2,500 lire, and if it's a lavish one from 5,000 upwards, and the same applies to baptisms and funerals. Usually a funeral is 5,000 lire, but if anyone wants a funeral with a solemn Mass and ornaments then it can be 20,000 lire or much more still. If the dead man is poor and his family too, then we only give a benediction and send the body to the cemetery.

'Then there are also donations for the soul. Some leave money or goods [land and livestock] to the Church before they die, for the salvation of their souls—what they leave is entrusted to me, for it is the property of the Church. If it is property such as animals or land that is left to the Church, I sell it, and use the money for buying ornaments and robes and so on.

'However, I have to think of the upkeep of a church. It takes a lot of money, a lot. There's a church bank, a country bank, for the assistance of the needy, and anyone can draw money—though not more than 10,000 lire—and only pays the usual interest of 10 per cent or 15 per cent as is allowed by the law. There are other earnings, but they are many, and each of them particular cases, so we won't bother about them here.

'We live by alms, as you see. We aren't rich, as we seem to be; all we have is for the Church. Those are our earnings; if you can call them earnings.

'Every day passes with something to do. We must think always of the Church—she must lack nothing. Then there is the arranging of religious practices for marriage, baptism and funerals—one must be in constant contact with the diocese and the bishop, one must take care of the nuns, helping them, confessing them, and procuring them something to live on. Towards evening there are small functions—benedictions, rosary, etc. There are duties to carry out—saying the office, teaching the catechism to the boys and girls on the days fixed. And the days come and go with the same rhythm.

'We must always be in touch with the diocese and the Holy See—our superiors impress that upon us, and it's very important to us; we have to send money to the diocese according to its orders. We must keep ourselves informed of the dispositions of the Church, accept them, and announce them to the faithful if it's necessary to teach them.

'We obey our superiors, and woe to us if we didn't! To us obedience is the first rule of our calling—to obey, to preach, and to pray are for us our highest duties.

'The bishop is the nearest authority to us. He can only give orders of an administrative nature or occasionally liturgical, but those very rarely, as the Holy See deals with liturgical matters.

'The Holy See, the bishopric, and we priests, all of us live on alms!

'It isn't easy to become a dignitary in the Church—you have to win the title and then to be worthy of it. I don't aspire to be someone in the Church—it's enough for me to look after souls, and perhaps I'm better like that. For a priest like me it's difficult to achieve high office —you have to attend courses of study, and both acquire and deserve ever higher and higher titles—one doesn't get there all at once!

'Certainly anyone who is rich or of noble birth achieves higher rank in the clergy, and also those who have *savoir faire* can become someone. Those roads are closed to me—at most I could become an archpriest, but even that would be difficult. Perhaps staying among the poor and humble is more dutiful, because one must show them the truth and the light. Here almost everyone is ignorant and illiterate, especially the peasants—it's a misfortune.

'They don't know how to read or write; the only way to teach them religion is to explain to them the religious laws according to tradition—introducing superstition here and there—it's the best way to do it. Illiteracy in Sicily is extremely prevalent, and the worst of it is that illiteracy and poverty go hand in hand—when there's poverty there's always ignorance too.

'You ask whether we think about these people? Of course, but one can't claim that, among all the other things an unfortunate priest has to do, he must worry about the poor as well. For me the care of the soul is enough—as it is I can hardly get through my work as I'd like to. The poor think that the priest should help them, even that it's his duty to help them—some almost claim that—but what can a priest give who lives upon alms himself? I think it's absurd to believe that one who lives upon alms can give to others. Already we give a lot—really a lot—if we were paid for our work there would be no higher salary in the world than ours. But unfortunately we're not included among those who get salaries!

'For the people we are the moral, social, spiritual and cultural guides—and political ones too.

'It is our task to illuminate the people's minds in political directions— the people often let themselves be taken in by this or that political party without understanding how and where it's going to finish.

'We want to give the people sane and just governments and rulers, who fear God and know how to maintain the fetters that bind State and Church. We fight against Communism, a party hostile to the Roman Catholic religion. It must not take foothold in Italy—while there's us priests the Communists will have a hard nut to crack. A lot of people—the most ignorant—fall into their hands, but disillusion is not long in coming to them. Then they have faith in us, for they know that we aim at a better life for them. The Communists say they are for the poor, but in reality there is the government for the poor— there are the authorities who provide for their help and maintenance, and there's American aid, too, which is much in evidence.

'But not all the people who would like to be thought poor really are—there's many who enjoy this appellation and profit by it. They cherish it as an ill-justified profession to earn the benevolence of the authorities—and a lot could earn a more honest living. They could but they don't want to—it's better to be "poor" than honest!

'I live with my family—it's the fate of a priest to live with his family. We priests are held to be rich, very rich, and often greedy and blood-suckers of the people; they reproach us with the alms that are gener-ously given to us. These voices come from certain persons who we know well—the Communists—from those, in short, who have little wish to work.

'Perhaps one thing is true, that the person of a priest has prestige in society, because sometimes he can do much—and that is due to the trust we deserve from people of good sense and from the authorities, the Christian Democrat Government. One helps someone when one can and when he deserves it. Certainly one can't help or recommend to the authorities a Communist or one who is against the Demo-christians. Fascism is finished but its wisdom remains—whoever has Demochristian papers works, and whoever hasn't . . . well, it's up to him—or he'll be poor!

'If I wanted to be an archpriest? Well, first I'd have to be parish priest of the Mother Church, and then to have means. Archpriest is already a title—there's more authority, more importance, but more responsibility too. But I don't live to be an archpriest—no, no. I don't want to be either an archpriest or a Pope! It's better to serve God simply. The best thing is to take care of the real soul—I steer my own as well as I am able, and perhaps sometimes I make mistakes, for I'm a mortal too, and I often realise it when I'm forced into being hard or irritable with others. I know I can make mistakes, but you know what they say—"Do what I say, not what I do!" '

CHAPTER THIRTEEN

The Doctor

I DID not know enough country doctors in Western Sicily to say for certain whether Doctor Spinato could be considered typical, though I was assured by my peasant friends that he was.

Among all families who are above peasant level, shopkeepers, small landowners, and others on the periphery of prosperity, there is a well-established set of ambitions for the succeeding generation. If there are three sons—and it is unusual for there not to be at least three —the parents want to count among their children a doctor, a lawyer and a priest, for these are the three professions that have always commanded the greatest respect in the rural communities. The lot of priest falls traditionally to the youngest son, so that he may remain celibate and keep his mother company in her old age, but the doctor and the lawyer may be drawn from any of his elder brothers.

They themselves generally welcome their parents' suggestions, both because they see in these professions a prospect of respect and power, and because as university students they will escape a little of the rigorous discipline of a Sicilian home. In the majority of families a boy up to the age of eighteen may not so much as leave the house without asking his parents' permission, so that he is constantly taxing his powers of invention to find new and plausible excuses. At eighteen he achieves a partial emancipation, but remains much under the parental thumb until he is twenty-one. By comparison, university life seems absolute freedom.

Because the professions are chosen for their prestige-value rather than by reason of any special aptitude on the part of the youth, many would not qualify without influence from outside. 'Influence' may be anything from the mild string-pulling common in all countries to direct threats from the *mafia*, and where—as one of my friends said of Dr. Spinato—the student 'has the smell of the *mafia* clinging to him' the last situation is all too common.

Dr. Spinato belongs to the great body often described as *più o meno mafioso*, and is thus as near as I have been able to get to transcribing the views of a true *mafia* member. As one on the fringe of that body he expects to be *ntisu*—the word so often on Sicilian lips, and implying someone deeply respected and often feared—and at the heart of his frustrations lies the subject of State interference in medical matters that reduces his personal status in the community.

DR. SPINATO

'It's no fun being a doctor nowadays.

'It's a fine profession, agreed, but in these country villages you end up as maid-of-all-work—everybody's slave. You wait so long to become a doctor, you study night and day for years on end, visualising your degree as a dream that will never come true, and then when you finally get your filthy piece of paper and cast your eyes over it— do you know what is written on it? "Go and practice in the country town of Cinisi."

'And from that day you're starting a harder and longer battle than the previous one.

'When I was twenty-one I started at Palermo University. My family told me to be a doctor: "You must be a doctor," they would say authoritatively. My mother would even say "*dottore*" and not "*medico*". And so I obediently enrolled myself in the medical school. I should have spent four years at university, but instead I was there for eight—and thank God it was only eight! I qualified when I was twenty-nine and I have been practising now for two years. I got my degree, but don't run away with the idea that it was due just to my sacrifices; on the contrary, I freely admit that if it hadn't been for the influence which my father exerted on the university big-wigs, I should certainly still be buried in my books at this very moment. It's not enough to work like a beaver at the university—even if I had worked, which I didn't—you need something else—power behind you. For the first years I studied and got good results, but I liked the irresponsible life, and I was very keen on women and amusements. I got my way by telling my family that everything was going well, and when my father heard me say, "in a little while I shall be a doctor", he gave me everything I wanted. I didn't bother to sit for examinations and so I dropped further and further behind. But there came a point when I realised that time was passing and that I was already twenty-seven. All things considered it would take me two years to get my degree. Do you think I was going to put up with two years intense study? Most certainly not. But I had to get a degree, and anyway I wanted one. Only my father could manage to set the wheels of influence rolling. Fortunately for me he's got friends everywhere, influential in every field of activity, even in politics. In Sicilian villages a man like him is well known and respected; anyone who owns a lot of land and animals as he does is bound to have good friends and enjoy prestige. For my father there's always been only one kind of friend— people who wield as much or more power than he does. He has always said to me, "Go around with people more important than yourself, and spare us your expenses." My grandfather was an important member of the old *mafia*; there can't be many people anywhere round here who haven't heard of Don Vincenzo Spinato.

'In things of this kind it's a case of "the King is dead, long live the King"—the son inherits the respect. They tell me my grandfather was a worthy exponent of the *mafia*—he knew his business, and he'd soon slap anyone down who got above himself. Today the real old *mafia* is no longer in existence; there are only those who belong to a new kind of *mafia*, which isn't always on the lines of the old. Let me make it clear that my father is not a member of the *mafia*, many people think of him as one, but he isn't, at least not in the modern sense of the word. He is a man who knows how to command respect; he's well known and he can make men obey him and fear him.

'As I've said, he started to move the pawns of influence for me amongst his friends. Influence is like a chain—if one link fails the whole thing falls to pieces. In my case there were no broken links; my father had chosen them well. Of course, I worked during this period; I couldn't go in front of the professors knowing nothing at all, even if I was recommended. But I wanted to work in the certainty that I'd be passed whatever answers I gave. Before a university professor will pass you in a particular subject, he makes three conditions: either you know your subject inside out; or you've been well recommended; or you've paid him generously. In my case it was the last two conditions: recommendations and generous sums of money. It was only with the Professor of Anatomy, a frightful gossip of a man, that the feathers flew a bit. The Members of Parliament my father approached about recommending me to him refused to do so, because they knew this particular professor wouldn't listen to them. There was only one way to shut that professor up, and that was to send two high-ranking members of the Palermo *mafia* to see him. My father did this—and the professor became as meek as St. Francis' wolf.

'In that way, the only one left open to me, I became a doctor. As soon as I laid hands on my degree I decided to practise straight away, but I didn't realise the obstacles I'd have to face. I ought to have spent six months in clinics and hospitals to gain practical experience, but I needed money and that didn't seem the way to get it. You're not allowed to practice without that six months' training, but fortunately our good friends didn't let anything out.

'In the village there were two doctors practising, the panel doctor and one of my fellow students who had qualified a year before me. Today everyone enjoys insurance against illness. Every family, whether they're peasants, or craftsmen, or ordinary labourers, is insured. The doctor must visit the patient, write out the prescription, and that's that; we don't have the satisfaction of seeing an envelope with money inside it at the end of the visit. Since everyone has a medical insurance card, I now began the hunt. In the village 5,000 of the 7,000 inhabitants are insured; there are about 2,000 to 2,500 insurance cards, and of course they were divided between the two doctors. Neither of them said, "You'll have such and such a number of cards"—they just gave me to understand that I had to manage as best I could, and I began as quick as I could. I started to solicit the cards of my relations, friends, acquaintances, and the relatives of my relatives, and the friends of my friends. At the end of three months I had about fifty cards and about 150 patients. My first salary was 8,000 lire, which was a great disappointment to me. So many dreams as a student, and such a rude awakening. No car, no surgery, no elegance, no real dignity. My family had to buy me all the apparatus for a small surgery, and, to satisfy their dignity, a good car for me.

'I should have liked to go and practise in Palermo, but apart from the fact that my family wouldn't have allowed it, I knew it wouldn't be easy to make a good living. I could only get hold of cards with the help of the usual "great friends", and my father's influence, and then, since authoritative voices had spoken, the cards began to flow in like a river in full spate. I had to make efforts myself all the same, sacrificing my dignity, walking with the common ill-bred people, talking to them, being pleasant even with the roughest of them. After a year of this I had even more cards than my colleagues.

'I still have 300 cards and roughly 1,000 patients. I started giving treatment straight away, though I was full of doubt every time I had to make a diagnosis. I had to compete with the skill of my colleagues, who were more experienced than I was, and very often I sent doubtful cases to Palermo for observation. For the first few months I managed as best I could—none of my patients died. But doctoring today isn't like it was fifty years ago. In those days the doctor was also the obstetrician, the dentist, the occulist—even the vet, whereas today the doctor is only a doctor, and he does only what concerns him. It's practice that makes a doctor, practice and experience, and to try to remember all the various forms of treatment one studied at the university would take too much time and patience. Today there are so many medicines—in a village like this who's in a position to criticise us? Those who can afford it go and have themselves examined by the specialists in the city.

'Today a doctor has lost much of his traditional prestige. I believe that in the good old days a man of the people approaching a doctor would go to any lengths to observe the social distance between himself and the doctor—today that distance no longer exists. They talk to the doctor as if they were talking to anyone else, and none too politely either. Nowadays those who call the doctor don't have to pay him, and so they feel no pain in their pockets, and treat him as if he were a servant. They tell him what to do, and if he doesn't do it they take offence and change their doctor straight away. Time and time again I've been called in by some family: "You must come, doctor," says the mother, "my baby has a high temperature." I rush to the house, examine the baby, diagnose a slightly raised temperature which will soon pass, prescribe ordinary medicines and assure the parents that it is nothing. "But, doctor, I want you to prescribe a good bottle of syrup for the baby and give him injections," and so on and so on. And I have to start talking to a common village woman, explaining why there is nothing wrong with the child, even showing her if necessary. "This or nothing, signora," I tell her angrily. "I'm the doctor, not you." But the wretch, far from being worried at offending me, clinches the argument with: "Very well, I shall go to Doctor Y; he will be sure to give me what I ask for." She goes off to see one of my colleagues and suggests the medicine, and he'll acquiesce this first time so as to get a new card. Not only that—often when we visit a patient he'll say, "Doctor, prescribe these medicines, they will do for my cousin, or my friend, etc., as well." They don't understand that

I can't put down what medicines I want on a National Health prescription, only the ones that are necessary for the illness in question. But if I refuse to do what they ask I risk losing a card. If I do a favour for some poor wretch who isn't on my panel, by putting extra medicine on the prescription, I'm ruined and I can't say "no" to anyone again.

'Most of the people belong to the insurance schemes, it's true, but what does that imply? I.N.A.M. [National Institute for Health Insurance] guarantees medical insurance, but not always pharmaceutical insurance. And according to which category of insurance the worker belongs, I.N.A.M. guarantees medical treatment only to the father of the family, or only to the parents, or only to the children under sixteen or eighteen years of age. But if I have on my panel a family in which only the father belongs to the health insurance scheme, I'm automatically obliged to treat all the members of the family, and to procure medicines for the mother or the children, writing them down as being for the father. So the father is written down as ill for a month with a chill, a month with typhus, a month with food poisoning. I, the doctor, stand the risk of losing my job, because if I was found out I could even be sent to prison. But my good panel patients don't understand that. Where is the doctor's prestige? We are servants and that's the end of it. If the people had to pay every time they called the doctor, you bet your bottom dollar they'd only call him when they were at death's door. There's no longer any difference at all between a doctor and a village lout. They show no finer feelings if the doctor is sleeping, eating, in the lavatory, talking to friends—nothing like that; when they call him he must set off at once without any explanations. All right—we're supposed to look after people's health, but, God in Heaven, we have to look after our own as well!

'We are the victims of the health insurance schemes. For every panel patient they give us between 800 and 1,000 lire a year, and, as I've said, I have 1,000 patients, so I get between 60,000 and 70,000 lire a month. Today a labourer in the city earns 2,000 lire a day, besides his family allowance, so that if he's really lucky he can manage to make 100,000 lire a month—and a doctor earns only half that amount! Is a labourer like a doctor? Has he been to the university too; has he paid out stacks of 1,000-lire notes to get a degree? We no longer get any consideration—but don't think we can't pay them back in their own coin.

'I've been practising for two years and I'm sick of it already. I now know that if I want to be respected I've got to make I don't know how many people understand that I'm a doctor, and that as such I occupy a higher place in society than any other individual.

'I could just as easily not be a doctor, but I must do what I have promised myself I would, and put prestige first. In the town a doctor at least enjoys a certain status, he has a time-table which is respected, and he's paid for his visits to non-panel patients and treated with respect and courtesy. In the country, if you visit someone who doesn't belong to an insurance scheme, they don't pay you, even if they happen to be a friend or relative or acquaintance. If someone wants to pay the doctor he never gives him money: he sends him a basket of fruit, or a chicken, or eggs, and the debt is considered paid. But things can't go on like this.

'It's a problem being a doctor in these country villages today. It's ridiculous for anyone to expect us to have a sense of responsibility as things stand. If you practise your profession here, you can follow one of two principles: either resign yourself to being the servant of the people for always, and leading this life for always; or you can act with complete unconcern, a sense of superiority and indifference to the calls of duty. I admit I've decided on the second alternative. Try and imagine how fed up you get visiting a patient for weeks on end, giving him the best treatment you can, and then being paid a niggardly 1,000 lire.

'If a doctor treats someone and then gets decently paid he gives him fair attention; the very money the doctor receives spurs him on to do his best. But it's not only the poor with their medical insurance who've reduced us to this state—it's also I.N.A.M., which cheats us doctors and tricks its members. The only ones who are well off are the doctors in the towns, those who've won fame for themselves and can charge between 5,000 and 10,000 lire for every consultation. I don't think that they're doing wrong in asking such high fees, on the contrary I think it's an excellent thing, but I don't see why we should get nothing. Haven't we made sacrifices too?

'All the people here are ordinary peasants, artisans, shepherds, and labourers; and so they're poor and needy and miserly, grudging even a farthing. There are masses of them living just as they did two hundred years ago and reacting to modern life with a mentality which is obtuse and completely lacking in common sense. Looking after these folk is something not everyone would do: they're ignorant, and they think ours is a simple occupation like their own. As long as they're in need of anything they behave humbly and submissively, but as soon as it's something which is theirs by right that they want— they're up on their high horse straight away. It's a mistake to give so many benefits to people of this sort—we'll end up by having decently bred people eating out of their hands. Think what you like, but for me there's a great gulf between the educated and the common people. As I told you, when I needed medical insurance cards I was pleasant with everyone, even though it was reluctantly—I even put up with people climbing into my car with their shoes covered in mud. Once when I was driving along the road in my car, I was hailed by five peasants. "As you've got our cards, Doctor, you can give us a lift to the village." I was humiliated, and from that day on none of these bloody country bumpkins has ever got into the car again, and when they signal to me to stop I pretend not to see them.

'We doctors realise by now the game they're playing with us, and we're settling accounts with them. Just because a peasant gives me his card, he feels entitled to consider me a starving beggar, and practically claims my obedience. One needs to be proud, and I certainly can be.

'There's certainly poverty in every village like this, but what's it got to do with us? Everyone talks a lot about this poverty—poverty and scarecrows frighten away sparrows. The Americans say, "Watch out for Communism!" but basically it is they who keep Communism alive and at their expense. And so in Sicily Members of Parliament, bishops, cardinals, journalists, and writers all shout: "Poverty, poverty!" But no one, my good sir, takes it into his head to wipe out poverty, they just talk.

'Under the pretext of helping the poor, the government gives grants of millions, but the very people who make the grants go on to divide them among themselves. The areas where there's poverty get the residue, which in its turn is divided among the most cunning of the administrators.

'I ask myself whether I'm more of a shit than many others—why shouldn't I profit from the situation as they do? Today if you want to get on you have to be a Christian Democrat: I'm a Christian Democrat; tomorrow you may have to be a Communist, and if so I shall certainly be a Communist. Those who are stupid remain onlookers and become more and more stupid. For example there is a lot of monkey business with the public health assistance for the poor. Lots of medical supplies arrive for the poor, and the people in charge put just half of it to the proper use; the rest is sold off by agreement with the chemist. There's a parochial surgery for the poor of the parish, and medicines are sent from various aid centres—but how are they given? when? and to whom? If there's a destitute impoverished man in the parish who's a Communist or a Fascist, he'll die; the parish priest will never give him any medicine. It's not the fault of the priest, he's merely taking advantage of the situation; given a fair reason like that he tries to save medicine. It's the fault of those devils who are Communists and Fascists.

'The medicines are kept, and when there is a fair amount they're sold off in one way or another. There are chemist's shops everywhere, and they're always ready to buy medicines at convenient prices. The priest will say that the money he derives from the sale will be used for the church, and the doctor gets his whack. As for the poverty, and destitution—there's time, yes, there's time.

'Many people kid themselves into thinking that they're enjoying medical insurance, but, as I've said, I.N.A.M. makes fools of both doctors and patients: as a matter of hard fact anyone who is in need always has to pay and if he doesn't, if he waits in the hope of aid from his insurance, he's likely to wait—till he dies.

'I.N.A.M. guarantees free medical treatment, but not always free pharmaceutical supplies. That is to say that every panel patient, no matter to what category he may belong, has the right to be medically examined, but not the right to obtain free of charge the medicines he needs. So if a destitute panel patient shows symptoms of a serious illness, which needs expensive treatment and medicines, I.N.A.M. won't provide them. You can't give any panel patient a prescription for medicine worth more than 1,000 lire, so if some poor devil needs an expensive medicine you can't prescribe it. You just have to give him something else which is only relatively effective, and, for all his health insurance, the patient may die. Don't imagine that, because they're all insured, the poor have been relieved of their anxieties— that's an illusion cherished by the panel patients themselves, and which the government would like to foster. Many patients who enjoy pharmaceutical assistance have to buy their medicines at their own expense, and after notifying the National Insurance Boards they have to wait months before their money, and often only half of it at that, is refunded.

'We doctors don't only have to treat patients but to deal with the necessary forms for refunding the patients' money, hospital treatment, and so on—to put it in a nutshell we do all the small tiresome chores as well. As you can see, on the one hand the people make themselves thoroughly unpleasant, and on the other they sometimes arouse our pity, but after all it's doctors we're supposed to be, not philanthropists. Ours is no longer an independent profession: we're at the command of innumerable people if we want to make a living, and I shall tell you that there are countless unemployed doctors everywhere—more particularly with the crisis we're facing at present. If I ever have any sons, they will study, but they will never go into the medical profession, because it sickens me to think I'm condemned to this life.

'The order of the day here is "Every man for himself". I know only too well by now that my profession isn't what I'd hoped; it'd be too much like hard work if I gave free rein to the voices of conscience and the calls of duty. If a doctor wants to win the prestige and personal dignity which are his due, he must plug his ears, put his duty on one side and if necessary stick out his claws like a cat. In a village like this you need to build up a good side: if you want to get on you have to be in with local big-shots—the parish priest, the mayor, and the chief of police. The first essential is to come to an agreement with the parish priest; at the moment the priests hold the keys of heaven and earth—those black crows are in command everywhere. Not that I like them—I hate them—but the wind's in their favour, and I must show that I'm on their side. I understand nothing about religion. Religion is their business, and they embellish it how they like and do anything they please with it. Popes, bishops, cardinals, priests—they're all one, they make fools first of God and then of the people: the truth of the matter is that they're clever men who have had the wit to dominate the people for 2,000 years.

'I'm not even a Christian Democrat because of political conviction; I've no faith in politics. There's too much chatter—I like real material things. I ought to be a Liberal, as my grandfather was and my father still is; it's well known that the Liberals are the party of the *mafia*, or rather were the mouthpiece of the old *mafia*. Today the party is still impregnated with *mafiosi* and members of the new *mafia*, with landowners, and with people who are *ntisi*, as they say. But although I owe a lot to these people, I'm not a Liberal, because I've come to realise that we don't need an organised *mafia* any more; the old days are over and done with, and everyone's on the make.

'But you've got to be a wolf in sheep's clothing with everyone. I often go to church on Sundays, and I take care that the priest who is celebrating Mass sees me; when he catches sight of me he gives me a little smile from the very steps of the altar; in his mind he hears me say, "I'm still obedient, you see"; but what I'm really saying is "All right, you stinking carrion, you're in command for the moment."

'One does these things in order to live reasonably well, and in a manner befitting your status, even if your prestige is often acquired by hypocrisy. But it's always like that here.

'I'm not yet married or engaged, and I shan't be until I've organised things properly and found a suitable prey. Understand this, I am not going to marry a woman who can buy me nothing; I want a wife who's reasonably attractive, but above all who is rich, a good match, and has personality. I have studied, my family has laid out a lot of money, and even I have suffered; now those are the things I want and I don't intend to renounce them.

'Today we're living in times when rights and duties are being poured out wholesale. The common people never stop arguing their rights and privileges, so much so that one fine day they'll be too grand for us to speak to—it's getting to that point. On their side there's an attitude of revenge, which has been ripening since time immemorial —they're getting their revenge; they want to have the upper hand with the people who've always been their masters. But cabbages won't smell like roses just because you plant them in the garden. So many privileges given to those who have never counted in society—it's incomprehensible. And in the meantime we and our independent profession are turning into a State appointment. Now they've created a Ministry of Health in Italy, and we have yet another minister; let's just hope that this minister Monaldi will keep the demands of the medical profession in mind; if not we shan't be any further forward. The country doctor of today doesn't ask for much, only that his status is properly rewarded, his prestige respected, and that he's treated as is fit and right. That's what I believe is necessary to put matters straight, for in the end we treat people as we're treated.

'I remember when I was a student my father sent me to the fields to supervise the men who were picking the lemons. Well, they didn't do much; as soon as I turned my back they stopped work altogether. In the evening I called over the man in charge and complained. Without a trace of embarrassment he looked at me with his deep shining eyes, ringed with lines, laughed wryly, and then said in sing-song tones, "You pay me enough to live on, and I'll work as long as I don't have to sweat."[1] I realised that my father didn't pay these men very much, and I made no answer, but tried to give a wry smile myself. So I, a doctor, repeat to everyone, rich, poor, I.N.A.M., Ministry of Health:

"'You pay me enough to live on, and I'll work as long as I don't have to sweat."

'Let's get rid of a few of our duties, consciences and responsibilities, by God!

'None of the villages in Sicily is under the supervision of sanitary authorities or Public Health Boards. If some epidemic or other breaks out here you might as well resign yourself to dying, for nobody takes the trouble to deal with it.

'Last year it so happened that the drinking-water became tainted by the sewerage pipes. A real epidemic of typhoid followed, and large numbers of people, children for the most part, were struck down. It broke out gradually, and each case was considered separately. The affected families were generally the poorest. In the space of a few weeks it was a real epidemic that struck at whole families; it became very very disturbing. We doctors notified the sanitary authorities of the exteme gravity of what was happening, but it was as though we hadn't said a word; weeks passed, and we reported the epidemic to the municipal council itself—but it was those paupers who were ill, and it was of no interest to the council. You can imagine of how much interest it was to us!

When several cases got so much worse that the patients died, a little medicine arrived, enough to treat about a tenth of those who were ill. The ones who got the medicine just managed to recover; those who didn't were either cured by the grace of God or their bones were taken to the cemetery. When the epidemic was dying out, doctors arrived from the Public Health department to arrange for the water to be disinfected with chlorine solutions. They were irritated to have been troubled, and astonished that as far as they could see the dangers we'd reported didn't exist. Perhaps they wanted to see corpses all along the street before they'd believe us.

'We doctors had done what concerned us, our duty, so to speak. We'd advised the people to boil all water before drinking it and as far as possible to keep away from those who were affected; we'd handed out our medicines, and treated countless people without even getting any thanks. What more should we have done?

'I.N.A.M. sent all the patients their cards back with the prescriptions we'd made out and stressed that the illness had been an epidemic, for I.N.A.M. refuses medicines in large quantities, especially if they're expensive ones. The chemists were given instructions not to supply the drugs for typhoid unless they were authorised to do so by the Health Insurance Board itself.

'The epidemic came to an end after almost two months; the toll was about ten deaths, three or four old men and the rest young children. Don't imagine the water was changed; it's exactly the same as it was. The sewers haven't been repaired, the water pipes, which were installed about sixty years ago, are as rotten as ever and continually crumbling and turn the water red with rust—but iron is good for the health!

'Hygiene? They don't know a thing about hygiene here—quite the reverse. Many of them wage open war against it: I lost two patients because I ordered them—repeat, ordered—to shave off their children's hair and a lot more because I took other severe sanitary measures. Here filth is the natural way of life; it's usual to see children having great games in puddles of mud, relieving themselves in the middle of the street, walking barefoot, eating everything they come across, playing happily on manure heaps. It's the common thing for a family to have no water in the house, to defecate into a hole behind the door, and to set up the beds in the stables, where the animals sleep.

'And then we mustn't forget the most beautiful symbol of Sicily: the fine large families, the hordes of children that peasant parents bring into the world, the positive barracks-full of babies. In this part of the world it's an absolute disgrace for a family to have fewer than five children—what am I talking about?—fewer than eight, nine, ten or more, I mean! You see parents who look like walking corpses, but they go on churning out children like hens laying eggs.

'Children are a gift of God, they bring to a house riches and good luck; everyone says that if you have a lot of children fate will be propitious and God will look kindly on your family. But the truth of the matter is that the fundamental motive for marriage here is the sexual motive: people marry for the pleasure they'll get in bed, and the rest doesn't matter. Sicilians are made like that; anyone with any sense would think above all, when he got married, of settling down to some sort of companionship, but not they. For them marriage means bed and only bed—the whole family life centres round bed.

'It's not going too far to say that in Sicily the problem of sex looms higher than any other, even than religion. Marriages are very common at the ages of twenty for the man and not more than eighteen for the woman, and a girl married at eighteen will at the age of twenty already have two children.

'People ask us why it is that it's among the destitute that the majority of illnesses are on the increase. As a doctor I can assure you that, apart from poverty and wretchedness, the main reason is in the sexual sphere.

'Here people start to learn the mysteries of sex very early. One out of every two five-year-old children already knows a lot about sex, and from then on till the age of thirty he'll live for nothing else. Here in this very village, where people say that morals and modesty are the most rigid, those standards are utterly lacking. Don't believe the priests or the people who try to hide things and cover them up. I know much more than they do, because I'm a doctor.

'Ninety per cent of the children here learn about sexual intercourse for the first time by watching their parents. "Absurd—ridiculous", a good priest will tell you—but it's the truth.

'It's customary here, because the people are paupers, for children to sleep in their parents' bed until they reach an age somewhere between five and eight.

'Right—what do you imagine a child is going to think in his simple mind when he's woken in the middle of the night and sees this completely new and strange scene? He will think that his father is embracing his mother, but in what way? He will think that he is beating her, but those aren't blows he's giving her. What *are* they doing then? Ignorant of all this, the parents think the child or children asleep, but he's awake, and if he doesn't understand anything that first time he soon will. Innocence turns to cunning; the little brain begins to reason: "What is it that my parents do in the night?" That's the problem that nags him. In his ingenuous curiosity he asks his parents themselves, who try to invent something to put him off the track. They may succeed, but as soon as they've sent the child away from their bed they only rekindle his burning curiosity. Outside he discusses it with his friends, and among them there will be one who is a little older than the rest, who knows more and solves the riddle, and the child's curiosity is terribly and irreparably satisfied. By the time he's eight

years old at the most, he understands everything; he has watched whole
nights of sexual intercourse; he knows now exactly what his parents
are doing; he has an idea of how to achieve sexual pleasure himself.
In a bed where boys and girls sleep together he makes his first experiment. "Why shouldn't we do what Mummy and Daddy do?" And so
depravity is born, and often with the seeds of diseases that are worse
still. In these depressed areas sexual activity begins early: I've come across
small boys who masturbate at the tender age of six years; I've seen
in the genital organs of little girls the marks of sexual intercourse, and
of infections that have begun to develop.

'Naturally these children can't possibly bring forth healthy issue,
they're already worn out and they'll go on getting more so. The whole
responsibility for this rests with their parents, who because they lack
decent moral standards themselves pass on to their children an evil
with endless consequences. And it's here among the poorest and most
ignorant people that there's the most immorality.

'At puberty, when sexual activity is at its height, the immature
consciences of these children are absolutely fogged by conflict, conflict
between desire and religious instruction. The priest says you mustn't
do these things because it's a sin, and you'll go to hell; he says, too,
that you get terrible diseases. And so the most tormenting conflict these
children will ever know boils up in their minds. Boys who come for
treatment never tell the doctor that they've indulged in sexual practices, and even if we notice that they have and begin questioning them,
they deny everything with complete obstinacy. But they tell the
priest. During puberty they live in a state of war with themselves, an
inner conflict that goes like this: "We *must* have a sexual life! it's
good to have it!—pleasant to have it! We must *not* do it because the
priest says so, because the doctor says you can even die from it." The
boys—and the girls, too—without discontinuing their constant sexual
acts—waste away through the torment of this problem, and become the
victims of psychological complexes which often burst out into illness.
The wastage of so much vital fluid at an age like theirs cannot help but
affect their health. Sexual activity is not in itself an evil, it's natural,
but it can become an evil according to the age and social conditions
and environment of the person concerned. What good can the constant
waste of vital fluid do a boy of thirteen who is compelled to live in
poverty, deprived of nourishing food and already physically weak?

'The average boy masturbates twice a day, wasting continuous quantities of vital fluid, and compelling the organism to produce more than necessary. This fluid that's being lost isn't water! Not that I think it comes direct from the brain and the bones as the good priests would have one believe, but I tell the children the same as they do—I've told you already that one must echo the voices of dictators if one wants to live well. Anyway, I believe it's been clearly proved that excessive sexual activity leads to the retarding of bone development and to strain on the various nervous centres, thus encouraging what is called nervous exhaustion. In people particularly addicted to sexual activity I myself have noticed frequent anaemia and heart troubles, apart from visual and intellectual incapacities. But leaving all that aside, what state of affairs would it be if the priest said one thing and the doctor another?

'No boy reaches the age of sixteen without having had intercourse with prostitutes, street prostitutes who are a storehouse of disease. They go to the prostitutes without knowing the enormous risks they're running, without taking the simplest precautions, doing everything blindly, used as they are to living blindly. But they can't escape venereal diseases—by the age of twenty most youths have suffered from some venereal disease three or four times already; many of them also get syphilis, but, thanks to the discoveries of modern medicine, they're able to have treatment for it. Then they go back again as if nothing had happened to them, to the same source of infection.

'This storm of sexual activity overwhelms them all—fathers, mothers, boys, girls, young men, particularly if the environment in which they live is like the ones I'm talking about. This is a section of society—and I say this in all sincerity—that is disgusting, steeped as it is in the mire of immorality, ignorance and poverty.

'It's true that you can't stop their sexual outbursts, especially where young men are concerned; after all I know myself that it's only natural to satisfy the sexual instinct, but just see the rate at which they carry on these sexual activities and with what a lack of responsibility! A child who indulges from his earliest years, who behaves with even greater shamelessness as a young man—when he marries and produces a child, what will that child be like? The product, I say, of his own corruption.

'The "Merlin" Law has now been passed, and it's already in force; no doubt it's been a boon for everyone, particularly for the upper classes, but things haven't taken such a wonderful turn as people imagine. There are many prostitutes walking the streets now, looking for bread. What they're doing, poor souls, is really a job; society doesn't welcome them with open arms, and they can only make a living by carrying on their own wretched trade. Sexual activities have certainly been curtailed by this law, but not rooted out. Today the danger of disease is much more widespread; so many prostitutes are in circulation without medical examination, and they find clients of all ages, from twelve upward.

'I'm of the opinion that if it seems a good thing to prohibit brothels there's another side to the coin. As I've said, the sexual act is a physiological need for everyone, especially after puberty; it can't be destroyed, but it can be channelled into paths of moderation and restraint. Sicily, headed by well-known people such as the university professor Cucco and many others, is in favour of reopening the brothels under a much closer system of State supervision. I'm all for such a decision, which would entail tightening everything up, forbidding access to those under twenty-one, at least—it was eighteen before—and selecting the prostitutes much more carefully. The danger the Merlin Law has brought with it is that the immorality which has up till now been absorbed by the brothels is loosed on the family world, heightening the desires of the young men, who—when they are as hot-blooded as they are here in Sicily—will have no respect for their fiancées or their sisters, unless the homosexuality which is already common among boys begins to spread still further. As a doctor I'm more firmly convinced of one thing than of anything else: that the sexual side of life is the only one dear to the heart of the Sicilian peasant.

'Often I've advised my patients, boys, young men, and newly married men, to suspend sexual activities during their illnesses, but I know perfectly well that my advice might as well have been thrown to the winds. When I touch on these subjects, the patients look at me as if to say, "But what on earth has that got to do with you?"

'But it *has* got to do with me—whose word should be law if not the doctor's? If one man does what I tell him it's because doctor and priest go hand in hand, as far as people can see, anyway, and they fear the priest more than they fear me. That is stupid, because I hold the power of life and death on this earth that they love however much they complain about it, while the priest can only let them into a future paradise. I know that by comparison with some I'm not well read in my profession, and there's probably a lot I don't know about modern ideas, especially on sexual matters—but how much less does the priest

know, who dictates what the views of all in authority must be? The
Apostles taught the men who taught him, long before the science of
medicine was known at all, and their words were too holy to change
with modern knowledge. So the priest's profession is an older one
than mine, and a safer one—and he will always command the respect
I lack, because he can send men's souls to hell with a couple of words.'

CHAPTER FOURTEEN

The 'Carabiniere'

'I'VE served eight years with the *carabinieri*, and I'm resigned to it by now. It's a hard life, ours, under discipline day and night, in blind obedience to superiors who get your goat half the time. Especially here in Sicily the people think of us as cocky and idle, lucky to have a cushy and well-paid job. It's true we *carabinieri* are powerful, here in Sicily and elsewhere; if we'd had a soft life before we shouldn't have chosen to enrol in the *carabinieri* to find a softer one. The reason so many young men join the *carabinieri* is simply unemployment. Unemployment's everywhere; I come from Northern Italy, and I can tell you there's unemployment even there. But there's several kinds of unemployment—at least as far as joining the *carabinieri's* concerned I've recognised three kinds. The first's unemployment in the real sense of the word, that is to say young men with no trade and no occupation to carry on in life and who have to live on land that's unproductive and absolutely without industries that could save the situation. Those ones join up because they hope to find some sort of way of life in it —if not the best at least better than they've got already. No doubt they do find a refuge in the service, but they find out quick enough that their life's not their own any more, they're just tools in the hands of expert workmen.

'The second category is those who aren't too keen on work. In civil life they've loafed about the *piazzas* of their home towns, spending the day in the bars and poolrooms and making love to the loose girls of the town at night. One fine day they wake up to the fact that it can't go on for ever, and look for some way of setting themselves straight. Ninety per cent of them, I assure you, enrol in the *carabinieri*. They're convinced that they'll find the ideal life in the service, a straightening out of everything, and first-class pay. And after a fortnight of it they're putting their heads in their hands and groaning "If only I hadn't done it".

'The third category, I'm ashamed to say, is the one I belong to myself—the famous category of failed students. The failed students

are those who exchanged their school for some haunt of loafers, who
took advantage of the irresponsibility of their teachers and so did sweet
Fanny Adams. When they're nineteen or twenty years old they
realise they can't go on at school—they've never done anything in the
past and they've forfeited their right to go on. I was one of those, and
like ninety per cent of them I'm a *carabiniere* now.

'I come from the mainland—I'm not exactly a *polentone*[1] but what
we call a *medio-polentone*. I'm a Tuscan, from the province of Arezzo,
to be precise. My family are peasant farmers. I was the second-born;
I've got two sisters and a brother who's older than me. My father
wanted me to study, and after I'd got my middle-school certificate
he sent me to the commercial school to become a technician in some
industry. As I said, I did absolutely nothing, and after two years I left
it. I stayed in the town for a while; being a peasant farmer wasn't my
idea of life, and it wasn't easy to find work, because there was no
industry in that district. My father was still a *contadino*, but a *contadino*
over there doesn't mean the same thing as it does in the south. Here
contadini are for the most part poor and needy and at least a century
behind the times. The *contadini* where I come from aren't rich, but
my God they live fairly well in comparison with these! They get fair
payment, and they aren't condemned to live out their lives on a
miserable piece of ground, burnt up by the sun, that can't grow anything, as they are here in Sicily. Here they can live only for the hope
of grain and olives and grapes; they spend their whole lives doing
the same thing in the same little corner of ground—and when they've
got nothing to do, especially in the winter, they pass month after
month just about dying of hunger, them and their families too. It's
not like that over there; the *contadini* are more united, and there's big
farms in the country where they can find work winter and summer
alike when their own little jobs are done. It's like different worlds, the
contadini here and there.

'Well—I got tired of lounging about the town, so I decided to take
the first exam I could, and the *carabiniere* exam was no sooner announced
than I took it without a second thought. I showed the necessary
documents, and after a few months I was waiting for the first interview. My family weren't too pleased that I was going to be a *carabiniere*, but they let me do as I liked. The first interview went all right,
and I had to wait for a second one at which I'd be called up.

'It was about this time that I began to feel a bit discouraged—I

Montelepre, the most famous 'bandit' town in Sicily, and the home of Salvatore Giuliano

realised that I hadn't made a very good job of my life and that in a way I'd disappointed all the hopes of my parents. All my friends were against my joining the *carabinieri*, and they laughed at me too. One evening, I remember, I went into a bar and found several of my friends drinking and having a happy time. "Come on, Sergio," said one, "how's your career going? Have they made you a sergeant yet? or a sergeant-major?" "What, a sergeant-major?" said another. "Don't be crazy, he's a lieutenant!" I tried to laugh; a Sicilian in my place would have pulled out his knife and started a fight, but we take a joke better over there, and we're not so hot-blooded. "Listen, Sergio," said another of my friends, "I'm going to tell you a joke. Two *carabinieri* were strutting along a half-empty street in Rome when they came upon a child blubbering in a corner. "What's the matter, little one?" they asked. "What's wrong?" Between his sobs the boy stammered out: "My father says that if I don't do better at school he'll make me a *carabiniere*!" Well, I laughed with the others, although I felt bitter at heart. But one after the other all those friends of mine became *carabinieri* themselves.

'I was accepted at the second interview, and I was sent from Grossoto to Rome for a course of instruction, a course that lasted nine months before you could be a real *carabiniere*. It was a general course for the new recruits—gymnastics and arms drill and general military instruction; in fact we were treated just like ordinary soldiers; we were paid the same and treated the same. We got practical training in the use of arms, we had to learn and recognise the army ranks, and we learnt army discipline. It's no use telling you about all the lectures we got from the officers about the character and mission of the *benemerita*[2] service—they always said the same things in different words. We had to learn the rules of discipline that we had to submit to, and understand the duties and responsibilities that would rule us all our lives. We don't need to talk about all that—and anyway I don't remember most of it any more. The whole life of the *benemerita* can be summed up in the motto—"Be bold and obey silently and die silently." But to the Sicilians we are "the Godless ones". During that course one catches a glimpse of what one's life will be like in the future; one regrets days gone by and resigns oneself once and for all.

'After the nine months of training you become an actual member of the *carabinieri*,[3] and you're sent to some barracks or other for service. I was in Rome for the first year after my call-up, then I was transferred to Messina and then, after eight months, to Palermo. I've been four years in Sicily now.

'I know plenty about barrack life—it's become my home and my family, and even if it's not a very wonderful life one ends by getting fond of it. That's human nature—you get fond even of the things that get you down. It's easy enough to imagine what barrack life's like; most people have had a spell of it, and know more or less the differences between it and family life. At home you eat when you're hungry, sleep when you're tired, and choose between things you like and don't like. In barracks it's different—you've got to respect discipline and obey orders, and you're not your own master any more.

'In eight years of service I've learnt the two main sides of *carabiniere* life—the city and the provinces, which may be a small town or even a village. There mightn't seem to be all that difference, as we're always under military discipline anyway, but for a *carabiniere* himself there's a lot. In a city, especially in the big barracks, you have to be a *carabiniere* in the strictest sense of the word—you've got to have guts and you've got to keep your arse shut. There's new rules and orders almost every day, and there's never a moment's peace. In a city like Palermo, for instance, you are at the ready minute by minute to go out in the squad car—to chase a pick-pocket, rush to the scene of a suicide or a crime or a strike, or make an arrest, or any other one of the every-day things. And the big barracks have to send squads into the provinces too, often to cope with Sicilian bandits too strong for the local *carabinieri*.

'But there's both the rough and the smooth, as they say, in city life; when you're free to go out in the evening you can pass your time as you like and without spending much, because we don't have to pay in any place of public entertainment, or in trams or buses. When we're free at last for a few hours in the evening and can give ourselves the luxury of going to a cinema or some other place free of charge the people look at us with hatred and mutter "Here's the bosses—the idlers of the Italian Republic". But what do they know of our sacrifices?

'Then there's the life in the provinces, which always takes *carabinieri* of some service, like me. In those small barracks you don't get the harsh discipline you do in the cities. There's not as much to do every day, and you haven't got to be listening to the orders of superiors all the time. You get peaceful times when for a month or more nothing much happens and it seems that every one's made his peace with God and man; and then suddenly in one week you'll get one thing after another, cattle-stealing, murder, rape, knife-fighting—in fact all the famous stock-in-trade of Sicily. Then you get in touch with Palermo and they send reinforcements and you begin a search all over the countryside. There's compensations, of course; the *carabiniere* is a real authority. He's feared, and if he's hated too I've understood that it's because a lot of us give ourselves airs in dealing with these poor ignorant Sicilian peasants. There's no amusements in the country, but that's made up for by a freer life with less discipline and organisation. But the set-up depends on the barracks commander, a *brigadiere* or *maresciallo*, who becomes the local military authority, and, together with the mayor and the priest, rules the district. To be a *brigadiere* in the city is nothing, but in the provinces he's already someone.

'I took up service in Palermo at the biggest barracks, which is the headquarters of all the provincial barracks. At the headquarters there's the famous "*Pepiritu*" barracks[4] where the newly caught criminals are put. It's an interrogation prison, to put it briefly, where the prisoners are made to sing under beating, or under torture if necessary.

'Yes, torture. As a civilian I'd say at once that no human being should suffer these things; I'd say that they're against the moral progress of the human race—but as a *carabiniere* I promise you it's a precious thing and a necessary one, especially in a country like Sicily. Here there's *omeràt* [the code that enjoins silence]. It's the badge of dignity of every Sicilian, and against *omertà* not even the Heavenly Father himself could put up a struggle. *Omertà* is an iron barrier; everyone, guilty or innocent, takes his stand behind it, and to get through it is just about an impossible task. Right, how are you going to destroy a band of criminals? How are you going to make the guilty open up their mouths in prison? With soft words and convincing sermons? They'd never utter. Crime in Sicily could never be destroyed like that, and our presence would be a mockery. But there's the holy rod and holy tortures, things that would make even fishes talk. Our duty is to destroy crime, and we have to do it without bothering our heads about the means.

'You could say that there's so many innocent among the ones that get tortured, and that they share the treatment of the guilty. In a way that's not our fault—it's just the fault of *omertà*, for which both the wicked and the righteous must suffer. I oughtn't to tell you this, but once at Headquarters we were half-killing a man said to be an accomplice of a certain bandit when we found out that the poor wretch was absolutely innocent. He had to stay a month in hospital as a result of what he'd suffered under torture—broken ribs among other things. There could have been a scandal, but even if there had been we'd still have been acting inside the limits of our duty—we exact justice, we act in the name of justice, and justice can't condemn itself. In any case, how could he have made a scandal?—he was only a peasant without powerful friends. People have died, I know, for trying to.

'We use many kinds of tortures—I don't mind telling you what they are now I've explained why they're necessary. About the most general one is called the *cassetta*. The man's tied down on a wooden structure and his head's forced back. You put a gas mask over his face and pour salt water through the tube of the mouthpiece. I'm hardened to seeing it, you have to be in my job, but I must tell you it's not pleasant. His stomach swells till its like a balloon and it hurts him like hell. Then you press on it and get the water out of him and start again. Often its combined with other tortures—the man is naked, and you can do what you like to him. We go for the most sensitive parts— the feet and the genitals. The feet may be burnt or beaten or both— I've never seen toenails pulled out, and I don't think it's done. I don't know why. Twisting of the testicles is almost always used, and sometimes we put electric shocks through them. I've seen one *carabiniere* sticking pins into the head of a man's penis, and even worse things than that, but we won't talk of them. As I've explained, they're necessary. They used to make me feel sick at first, but now I only get worked up about it if it's someone very old or someone who's hardly more than a child. Then I feel I want to spit in the face of God.

'But you need beating and torture in Sicily—if it wasn't for them half the five million people would certainly be criminals. Perhaps I think a bit like all mainland Italians, but at the same time I believe absolutely that to be a criminal is in the blood of every Sicilian. You must know that our offices are full of files listing people whose sympathies are outside the law. Certainly some of those people must be innocent or even downright honest—but who's to say?

'In Sicily there's no difference for us between the guilty and the innocent—if a man is Sicilian he's guilty; they all have a common viewpoint.

'In the provincial towns cattle-theft, robbery and crimes of *vendetta* and hatred and jealousy are the order of the day, and often enough people who are held to be "honest" are involved in them. The machinery of the police gets under way. We *carabinieri* have to risk our lives to find the guilty. It's a hard job getting over the Sicilian country-side with its mountains full of caves and hiding places, and a hard job passing before the stare of all those peasants who look at you with those black threatening eyes that put the fear of death into your bones. Among them there's a guilty one, or an accomplice, or someone who's seen something. But no one says anything, no one knows anything. Then one makes a mass arrest[5]—one arrests everyone one sees in the area and takes them to prison—and there one finds out who knows something or even who is downright guilty. Of, say, two hundred, the half will be released after a day or two, because one finds out that they had nothing to do with what happened. The remainder will be interrogated more closely, and of these half again will be released as they're found innocent, and so on, until at last there's only twenty or so men left, men who during interrogation have answered ambiguously. From these one has to establish who really knows anything or saw anything or is an accomplice. It's only through beating and torture that one can learn the truth—and I assure you that thanks to these methods someone out of the few who are left will talk and the truth will come out. There'll still be some who really have had nothing to do with it, but the job's almost over.

'Besides *omertà* there's the *mafia*. The *mafia* is the real constituted government of Sicily, and the relationship between us and the *mafia* is like that between two great powers in war. There's nothing you can do about the *mafia* and most of the time you have to close your eyes and pretend to see nothing.

'How many criminals and even murderers walk the streets of this town? Don't you believe that if we could arrest them we'd do it at once? The *mafia* protects them—they've asked asylum from the *mafia*, and if they've "deserved" it they're given it. I'm a *carabiniere*, and there's some things I absolutely mustn't see or say, but the facts are so obvious that you probably know them as well as I do. What do you think is the relationship between the *mafia* and our superiors? The *mafia* says "Leave us in peace and there's some money for you", and our bosses reply "We don't know anything and we've seen nothing". And the ones who have to risk their skins after that are us *carabinieri*.

'At the time of Giuliano's band many *carabinieri* lost their lives. Of

course it was the fault of the bandits, but whose else besides theirs . . . ?
I've talked to other *carabinieri* who were at Montelepre, and I learnt
quite a few interesting things. One of these friends of mine told me
that once in the mountains round Bello Lampo in the Pass of Rigano,
there was a gun fight between bandits and *carabinieri*. There were fifty
carabinieri commanded by an officer, and they had surrounded a house
in which there were three bandits. It was the bandits who opened fire.
The officer disposed his men in such a way as to surround the house,
while he himself guarded one side with a *maresciallo* and two *brigadieri*.
Suddenly, while the unfortunate *carabinieri* were closing in on the
house, the bandits rushed out, and by hiding themselves among the big
boulders they managed to escape. One *carabiniere* was killed. The
officer yelled "Why did you let them escape, you fools?"—but in fact
they had made their escape exactly at the point which the officer had
been guarding, and he had given them the signal to come out. That's
one of hundreds of things it's difficult to believe, but here's something
you can see with your own eyes. You know the barracks at Bello
Lampo? Well that little house had just a platoon of *carabinieri* in it;
it was right in the heart of Giuliano's kingdom, and it was attacked
again and again. The wires of the electric light and the telephone pass
within twenty metres of it, but during all that war with Giuliano it had
neither light nor a telephone to call reinforcements. Why? My
friend used to ask himself that and many other things; later he stopped
asking himself questions because he knew the answer—that Guiliano
was being protected, and the *carabinieri* were only there as stooges to
make the game seem real.

'Like everyone from the mainland I admired Giuliano, and I admire
him still. He knew how to be an incarnation of everything that all
Sicilians are. I'm not so simple as to imagine that he was an honest
man, but at least according to him the things he did were for motives
he thought were just. He ought to have been born a hundred years
before, at the time of Italian independence—if he had been there'd be
a monument to him in every town in Italy. He was quick-witted,
strong, impulsive and brave, but he was ignorant like all Sicilian
peasants, and he finished by getting mixed up both in politics and
with big-shots of the *carabinieri*. I've seen the hiding places of the
bandits in these mountains, where so many *carabinieri* died and where
their highest-up commanding officers had card-parties with the
bandits. I'm a *carabiniere*; I know what sort of game we play, and I'm

in it for a living, to send something home to my family. They give me 45,000 lire a month, of which 15,000 are kept back for victualling, and the rest has to do for me and for sending home.

'Not everyone thinks as I do; there's a lot of my colleagues who do it because they like the idea of being policemen. They're mainly young peasants, often southerners, who in the hope of promotion, or the promise of it given them by their superiors, get all sorts of ideas in their heads. They look for difficult jobs to do to get themselves noticed; they play the detective among the ignorant peasants, and give themselves airs in general. They're the blue-eyed boys of their superiors because they save them a lot of work, really, but they make themselves ridiculous, and they make themselves hated. To the people, if one of these types ill-treats a peasant it's reason enough to hate all *carabinieri* for the rest of your life—not only you but your family too. But the main reason why Sicilians hate the *carabiniere* is simply because so many of us don't know how to make ourselves liked.

'Here in Sicily the relationship between us and the Sicilians is like an occupying and an occupied nation. To the Sicilians we are the intruders; the mainlanders shouldn't stick their noses in—it isn't their country, and they haven't the right to give orders. Plenty of peasants have told me that when I'm talking to them on their bits of land. The Sicilians hate the mainlanders, but perhaps we don't see the Sicilians with a very favourable eye either. In my part of the world, it's true, Sicilians are badly thought of; as soon as someone says he's a Sicilian we're on our guard and one has as little to do with him as possible. A Sicilian's always looked upon with suspicion in the North—he'll be a criminal on the run, or he'll have a criminal record, someone who'll pull out a knife at the least offence. That's a weapon Sicilians are famous for everywhere.

'Things have always gone badly between the North and the South, but I think the southerners are much more to blame, because of their character—silent, suspicious, hot-blooded, and ferocious. A Sicilian doesn't think twice about killing somebody—it's no sooner said than done. They're a people who live in hatred and spite, in endless jealousy and suspicion of each other. In Sicily there's want and poverty everywhere, and the more these things get them down the more there grows in the blood of every Sicilian the desire to give himself to crime and express the injustice he thinks has been done to him. Going about Sicily it's terrifying to see these miserable peasants working this dried-up, infertile land. How do they manage to get the necessities of every-day life?

'A peasant here goes to work in the morning with a loaf that weighs a couple of pounds, and sweats away all day, keeping himself going with that hunk of stale bread without anything else to set him up. It's a different thing on the mainland—the peasants aren't rich there, but good God they don't go to work with a hunk of stale bread in their haversacks. They lead a completely different life from the peasants here. They produce all sorts of different crops on their land, while here a man only grows what his father and his grandfather grew before him—corn, vines and olives, and that's all. And the ground's burnt up by the sun, and the peasants know nothing of artificial manures. They don't know that the soil needs certain known substances, or that the crops need certain chemicals against insects and parasites and so on. Over there where I come from they know the right crops to grow and the new methods of cultivation, and the harvests are full and saleable. Here, apart from the fact that hardly anyone ever sells what he's grown, they distrust any medicine to give to an unhealthy plant. Many of them have told me that artificial fertilisers ruin the soil, spoil the natural flavour of fruit, and even destroy the plant itself. And then again, to introduce new products seems to them like a betrayal of their fathers—they must always do as the people did of old, even though they're agreed that things go badly for them.

'And here there's no co-operation between the peasants themselves— one would say that they all hate each other. They aren't trained by a central organisation, each one's different from the next, and they aren't united—that's what it is.

'Their poverty is the fruit of the backwardness that comes from being attached to tradition, and if they go on like that they'll always be poor. The North gets on all right because for a long time past the peasants have managed to break away from tradition, because they've accepted progress in all its aspects and have known how to work together. In the north the caste distinctions haven't existed for a long time now, but here an intellectual blushes to speak to a peasant, and whoever's richer feels socially superior to his poorer neighbour—so a better-off peasant despises one who's dying of hunger although both of them are peasants.

'As I've said, they never get away from tradition. No one in this country thinks of raising farmyard animals—pigs and chickens and bees, things that would give a good result with little outlay. They only keep chickens in the towns, and only for the family's use, not for commercial purposes. But the Sicilian isn't suited to that kind of life—they know nothing about commerce in this country. As a result they don't have the little weekly agricultural fairs we have where I come from, where the peasants can exchange goods and points of view and learn from each other, all of which leads to better conditions.

'But I don't understand why there's got to be so much backwardness here in Sicily. In the towns the want is something awful—almost all the children go barefoot in the streets, dirty and thin and often diseased, and most of them don't go to school because they don't understand the value of it.

'I fell in love with a very beautiful girl here—she was a dressmaker's apprentice, and is still for all I know; our romance didn't last long because of the incredible backwardness of her family. Maria, she was called, and she was in love with me too, and after a little time had gone by we knew our own minds and I thought it would be a good thing to introduce myself to her family.

'I was advised to speak to her relations first and then to her parents, and I did so. When I spoke to her father, a middle-aged peasant and as pig-headed as all Sicilian peasants, he said to me, "Before you enter my house you must bring your parents, and from today on you can't pass through my street again." I was very much upset by this; I wanted to make him understand that my intentions were serious, but it was useless. I told him everything, explaining to him that I could never come to his house again after this. And what does my simple Maria think of doing then?—she goes to the priest and tells the whole story! And he says to her, "A *carabiniere*, my daughter! But think of what you're doing! You know all the mainland people are dirty modern trash who lead girls up the garden path. You mustn't look at him again, and I'll have him transferred from this town as quickly as possible."

'Meanwhile I'd seen the girl's coldness, but I didn't think myself beaten. I sent for a married sister of mine who'd gone to live in Naples. I managed to present my sister to the girl's family, and I tried, too, to explain in front of her that my intentions were serious. It's no use my talking to you about my intimate relations with Maria, because in any ordinary sense of the word they hadn't existed—that is to say in six months of engagement I hadn't once got near enough to her to kiss her.

'After several months of official engagement I was allowed to sit at her side, but always under the watchful eyes of her father and mother. Well, one fine day when I was at the barracks the *brigadiere* commanding the station announced that I was to be transferred. I didn't ask for explanations; it was Maria I was worrying about, because I thought that I'd no sooner be gone than she'd forget all about me. I said this to her one evening, and she replied unhappily, "I knew you'd be transferred soon—it's all the fault of the priest." And then she came out with the whole story, and so I checked and found out that it was just as she said, and the priest had been to see the *brigadiere*. I saw that it was going to be a thankless business all round, and I decided that I'd have to break off relations with Maria as soon as my transfer went through. It was painful, but I did it.

'Now do you see how much power the priests have in Sicily? Do you see the damage that ignorance brings about among these stone-age people?

'As far as the priests are concerned it's enough if all goes well with themselves and they can stick their oar in anywhere. They tell the women not to work out of doors, that it's a sin to do so, and that womanhood is almost a sacred thing in the family. Hardly does a woman start working than the priest tells her it's unseemly, and then she stays whole days indoors doing the same hopeless things every day.

'Where I come from the women even work in the fields without shame, and in the factories, and in the warehouses of agricultural products—they work together with the men. Here it would start an earthquake if a man and a woman worked together! Jealousy and sense of honour; a Sicilian husband chucks his wife out if she's seen speaking to a man in the street. The faintest suspicion, however vague, is enough to start a tragedy—the husband will kill both the wife and her presumed lover.

'A girl can't go out of her house alone; she can never look any man in the face. She's like a sacred object, and if anyone knows that she's been "touched" by a man, she can never get married, never, never. Blessed North, a hundred times blessed, even if it is too modern—there's freedom of thought and action. There a girl can go out with a man without it being thought he's going to eat her; they can go for a walk, they can kiss each other, without all the gossips shooting their mouths off. Here to kiss a girl is just about the same as seducing her, just about the same as taking her sacred and holy maidenhead. Then

again over there a girl can be engaged a hundred times if she wants—
they don't say after the first time that she must never marry anyone
any more. There the woman works to keep the family and improve
its finances—here if the father doesn't work the whole family starves
and she doesn't dare even to take straw to the cows or milk them.

'We in northern Italy don't owe our well-being to the priests or to
the government, but to our fathers, who built it up by their goodwill,
their common initiative and above all by their solidarity. The trouble
about Sicilians is that the Sicilians don't know how to help themselves
and no one knows how to help them. The government ought to do
something, they ought to have done something ages ago, but it's
obvious that if they wash their hands of this island as they do they can
spend their millions in the north where there's the certainty of something
to show for it.

'As I see it the first thing Sicily wants is civilising. Bring a bit of the
mainland life here; show the people that good sense doesn't lie in
tradition or in general hatred of each other, but in working together
fraternally.

'There's one thing I don't understand. In the north all the richest
areas, above all the industrial centres, are strongly under left-wing
influence; they're all either Communist, or Socialist or Social Democrats—Parties, I mean to say, that aren't in power as governments.
Now in all common sense you'd think that here in Sicily everyone,
and I mean everyone, ought to be a Communist, as the Communist
party is the one that brings the working classes together. But in fact
the Sicilians themselves, these poor children of starvation, give their
vote to the Christian Democrats and send them straight to power.
It's obvious that they can't look after themselves; they let themselves
be tricked by the priests and taken in by promises, and pay no attention to those parties who are certainly the only ones really disposed to
help, as they have done in the north.

'I don't go in for politics—I never have done, more especially since
I've been a *carabiniere*. If you're a *carabiniere* it's dangerous to talk
about your political ideas—you'd run the risk of punishment or even
getting the sack. They don't actually say that you've got to be a
Christian Democrat or nothing, but it's well enough understood by all
of us. Perhaps our superiors aren't really Christian Democrats either,
but anyway they toe the line and show themselves as good Party
members.

'We *carabinieri* have one important duty outside our programme—
so as to speak outside our written rules. Just for these bloody politics
we have to be spies as well. In our barracks there's huge ledgers in
which we catalogue with the greatest care the names of every man
whose political ideas aren't Christian Democrat. We, simple *carabinieri*, have the duty of bringing these suspects to light, by catching
them in the act of declaring their political views. I'll give you an
example. After a public speech you'll see the people who applaud
at the end, and the people who go up to shake hands with the speaker.
Well, you mark down those people and enter them on the black list.
They haven't got a clean sheet any more—they can't emigrate, and
they're debarred from many jobs, and there's other things they won't
be allowed to do. A political certificate is required for many things,
and before anyone can get that we have to say what we've written
about the individual concerned. It's not a thing we like doing; perhaps
my *brigadiere* doesn't like doing it either, but it's orders, and to disobey
orders means losing your daily bread. There's "freedom of thought"
in Italy, but it's well looked after by the public security forces, as you
see!

'I haven't got firm political ideas, but perhaps like all the military
all my sympathies go to the Fascists. Mussolini was a great man—
they don't come like that any more. He gave prestige to Italy, and he
made her feared even by the greatest powers. I say I feel this like all
military, because I've found out that many of my superiors say when
they're talking about the Fascists "It's Mussolini we need!"

'Yes, we have to look after political meetings, but we look after
them in a special way if they're Christian Democrat meetings. When
it's *not* a C.D. meeting that's being held in a town not a single *carabiniere*
tries to keep order. The parish priests get together with the other
authorities, including the *maresciallo* of *carabinieri* and send the sacristan
to start ringing the church bells. The church is always in the town
square, where the meeting has to be held, so that no sooner does the
unfortunate speaker begin yelling his convincing arguments at the
crowd than a deafening din of bells cuts him short. He gets furious,
and calls the forces of the law—the *carabinieri*, that is. After a nice
long wait we arrive, saying that we can take no action against the
priest because right now a solemn function is taking place in the
church. The poor speaker goes away; his meeting's gone off at half-
cock. The people start saying, "The *carabinieri* are a lot of shits—they

ought to have stopped the priest ringing the bells. They're tyrants, that's what they are." But what do the people know about it?—we're under orders and we've got to obey. They don't say the priest is a tyrant, because they're too scared of him!

'Here's something that happened to me personally during the last election. There was an order issued forbidding all Parties, including the Christian Democrats, to attach the Party sign to the Italian flag. One evening there was a meeting of the new Fascists, the M.S.I., and I noticed their symbol stuck on to the flag. I didn't want to interfere, but my duty made me go and ask the leader to take it off, explaining to him what the new law was. He did so at once. A couple of hours later there was a Christian Democrat meeting, and they had their sign on the Italian flag too. It was more than duty this time, it was conscience as well, and I was just about to go over to them when the *brigadiere* saw what I was going to do. He called me in a low voice, and told me to go back to the barracks to do some job or other. And the Christian Democrat symbol flew on the Italian flag all that evening. Afterwards he explained to me that if I'd risked taking their symbol from the flag there might have been serious incidents.

'Those people are in command just now, and one doesn't want to say too much, because one has to eat.

'I've mentioned several times the "authorities" that have become authorities as far as we *carabinieri* are concerned too—the clergy, our new bosses. I've already said how much authority they have over the Sicilian people, and at least here in Sicily they've got almost as much over us! We have to bow down to them, and above all about their political views.

'In the various town barracks where we serve we haven't strictly speaking got any religious obligations. For instance I never go to Mass on Sundays, and I don't fuss because one ought to go. Where I come from in the north the priests aren't all that important; they're in command at the moment even over there, but they haven't a fraction of the power they show here in Sicily. In a Sicilian town the priests are everything, and I've found out that they even dabble in banking.

'It's them, too, that are responsible for all the misery down here. After all these centuries they haven't known how to direct the Sicilian people into a new, fuller, more modern life for the common good. But the people keep a blind veneration for the clerical authorities, even while realising that they suffer from them constant outrage and betrayal in every field. But that's the Sicilian way—to hate and to love at the same time.

'The numerous forces of the law in Sicily, the *carabinieri*, P.S., and so on, don't serve, as the Sicilians think and say, to hold down an occupied country, an Italian colony, but to suppress the great running sore of crime that reaches every corner of this island. If this country is ever going to be part of civilised society it's got to wipe out absolutely such attitudes as *omertá*, the too touchy sense of honour, attachment to tradition, and ignorance, suspicion and the absolute rule of the *mafia*.

'The north and the south are completely opposite worlds, and the differences extend to every field of life. You might say that a Sicilian looks at the north as a Tuscan might look at the paradise of America.

'Quite apart from a spirit of pride in one's own home country, I'm utterly convinced that in these matters Sicily will never achieve the well-being of the north. Time may prove me wrong, but as things stand and seem, from all points of view, it's plain that up till now we have been and are their bosses. They would like to live in hope in Sicily, but "whoever lives on hope lives in despair".'

CHAPTER FIFTEEN

The Schoolmaster

'WHEN I told my father that I wanted to go on studying, hardly having taken the certificate of middle school, I never thought to what trouble and hardship I was putting my family. My father had sent me to school hoping that as soon as I had possessed myself of my little certificate I would have been able to go out into the world and look for a job and help the family who had so much need of it.

'Then came the war. There's no point in my telling you how we lived during those years; I'll say only that we suffered, and that's enough. I was twelve, and I was going to the middle school at Partinico. I went to school every morning on an old bicycle, winter and summer alike.

'My father hadn't carried on a profitable trade; he was always suffering, and on account of an illness he could only do light work. He went on being a *spicciafacende*.[1] But how could he have worked in those years? And if he'd managed to find employment, what would he have earned?

'Yes, I was studying, but I was small, and I understood little of my mother's toil and anguish—she died in poverty—or of my father's torments.

'All my father could get was enough only for a piece of bread for one person, and bad bread at that, musty and stale and bitter; we used to divide it in three parts, and we went on being hungry.

'The drudgery didn't end. I managed to get my middle certificate, and I was happy at having gained something already, and proud of myself. "Daddy, I want to go on studying. I want to go on!" That's what I kept on saying to my father, and I insisted, and burst into tears, even while my father was sitting at the table with his head in his hands rubbing his weary forehead.

'I'm certain my words tormented him, as they've tormented my conscience, but I excuse my attitude, because I was only twelve years old. He tried to convince me, by telling me that for the moment it wasn't possible for me to go on going to school, that it cost a lot, that he couldn't even support the family, that my mother was ill, and that for the moment the first thing was to avoid dying of starvation. Many of my schoolfellows did go on studying, even if it was with drudgery and want, but I stayed in the town, and I'm not ashamed to say that I had to work as odd-job boy for a relation of my father's who was a painter. I did this for three years; I worked from morning till night, and in the country too, and I was able to take home a less stale piece of bread, even if a small one.

'But I hadn't forgotten school, and I dreamed of being able to go on studying once those sad times were over—but all the time I was forgetting what little I'd learned.

'The war ended, and I found myself eighteen years old, and confronted with the choice of two paths, neither of them clear but either would definitely be for life; to go on forever being an odd-job boy, or to go on studying and try to achieve something more.

'My father had recovered a little of his trade as a *spiccia*, and I was ready for any sacrifice to get back to school. But what could I do with schooling?—what did I want to go on studying for? I was eighteen, with years of hard work behind me, and I understood that if I was going to study it wouldn't be agreed upon for a long time, because a heavy and serious family duty was beginning to weigh upon me.

'I decided to attend the *magistrale* school in Palermo. In five years I could become a master, probably sooner. But when I was twelve I hadn't wanted to become an elementary schoolmaster![2]

'I had many troubles and hardships to put up with. At night I had to sleep on the pavements—life in the city was too costly and difficult—but in those early days I just adapted myself to everything.

'Then I slept in a kind of boarding-house among fleas and lice. Every now and then a little money or a little bread or *pasta* reached me from the town, and that had to last me a long time—if I wasn't robbed, that is.

'When I was completing my last year to get the diploma—and I really had studied—I lost my mother. She died of some heart disease, and I stayed with my father. Her death was a sad blow to me. To think that I hadn't been able to do anything for my mother was a terrible thing for me, and brought about in my heart a lasting discouragement, a deep rancour against myself. I became embittered—my father was alone and I was far from him but still on his hands—I don't

A mule load of *sommacco*, used in tanning

Ropes of grass for sale in the street, used for stuffing mattresses and pillows

know how I bore it or why I didn't go off my head. But God gave me strength to carry on, and in October 1951 I got my diploma as a teacher.

'My father was proud of me, and told all our friends, relations and acquaintances about it—his fondness for me made him blind, and all his sacrifices found their reward in his great joy.

'But I was still a parasite—I was twenty-three years old, and as yet I'd done nothing for my home or my father. I set to work at once, and began to think of ways to dodge military service, and to make myself known in scholastic circles and to find friends and sympathy. But my misfortunes weren't over—other ones began, and all of them disheartening. My father gave me courage, and comfort too; I understood that he'd made great sacrifices to see me set up and happy. I went on working, and working harder, managing to get enough to live on.

'I never had support or recommendation from anyone; I was always alone in life. I went to many people, looking for work, but there wasn't any; I had to make do with whatever "standing-in" there was going when some teacher was away from school. After two years of that life I got a job teaching at evening school, teaching old and illiterate peasants, fathers of families, and boys and girls too. They used to come to school in the evening, and I had to teach them the basic principles of reading and writing. I used to earn 5,000 lire a month, and that first money was a great standby for me. I remember that first 5,000 lire I made from official salary I took to my father intact, and I was ashamed to give so little, even though I had faith in things getting better. My father refused the money—he said I needed it myself, that it would be useful for me for so many different things; above all I remember he said "because you are young".

'I had to do a lot of bumsucking—presenting myself to this and that bigwig in order to keep even that miserable pittance. After a few years there was a competitive exam for elementary schoolteachers; it took place at Partinico, and there were altogether fifteen hundred vacant posts, but there were more than four thousand entrants. I had to prepare myself for this, and I worked like a nigger, always alone, and I made a deal with myself that if I didn't get through I'd set to work at some other trade. In these exams, as everyone knows, there's always favouritism for the sons of big-shots, for those who've had a word put in for them by the local Member of Parliament or Ministers.

I had no one to put in a word for me—only a little faith in the sacrifices I'd made.

'I took the exam and got through it—I didn't do all that well, but for me it was enough to have passed. Many others in conditions of need like mine were passed over, while many who really knew almost nothing got high marks and promotion. I was really happy to have got through, and in my innocence I thought I'd be set up in life at once, but in fact I had to wait a long time for that.

'When I gave the news to my father he was half mad with joy, and his eyes filled with tears when he looked at the picture of my mother on the wall. After a long time I managed to get in touch with the place where I had to teach. They sent me to a town in Calabria, a very backward town in the Sila mountains. Parting from my father, who was now getting old, from my home where I had suffered so long and swallowed my bitter tears, was a sorrowful thing for me. I'd never been far from home, and I had the terrible idea that I'd never come back again. My father was very close to me; he gave me a lot of advice and talked to me as if I was a five-year-old baby—he put a brave face on it, and appeared almost indifferent to my departure. He was happy, but I knew he'd cry when I'd gone.

'My past is a sad and hard one, and I don't talk about it to anyone, because there's a lot of people who take pleasure in others' misfortunes. I don't let myself think about it, but sometimes I see that it does no harm to remember. I never had any amusements, but I was contented with my life. There were times when I didn't even have a suit, and these arms of mine have worked too; I've suffered a lot, you know— enough to send one off one's head.

'Now I'm earning, and I can budget. I live with my father; I'm not rich, but I earn enough to live on and to give some pleasure to my father, because I'm sorry that my mother's dead. Now I think only of straightening out my life—one wants a family, you know, and a house of one's own; one can't live without a woman. Where would a man's dignity be without those things?

'I've been teaching here in this town for a year. I haven't got a long experience of the school, but I see that my task is a pretty difficult and serious one.

'When I was teaching for the first time in that village in Calabria, I thought myself the unluckiest man in the world. The town where I happened to be, some sixty miles from a city, was more a hamlet than

The Schoolmaster 233

anything else, and the conditions of life were more than uncomfortable.

'Thirty miles away there was a bigger town, of which the village
was a sort of outlying fraction. There were three of us teachers in the
village, a man of forty-five from Reggio Calabria, a young Roman a
little younger than I was, and myself. But I was alone, all the same; the
elder one was pompous and elegant—he used to come to the village
in the afternoon every day in his car. He was the administrator of the
school. He held his lessons in a class of the fifth elementary grade, of
about ten boys and girls. He was well paid, I think, but he ignored, or
pretended to ignore, the meanness of the school. As soon as his lessons
were over he used to go away in his car—he lived in the big town on
the low ground, where life was more comfortable.

'The young Roman was closer to me, but his character was the
opposite of mine—he looked on the school simply as a means of making
money and living comfortably. Lessons became a torment to him,
the classroom a prison, and his programme was carried out with hap-
hazard carelessness. He wasn't in class for half the time I was—one
hour of teaching was more than enough for him. I taught a class of
boys of the first and second elementary grades, and my young colleague
boys of the third and fourth; the headmaster taught the only fifth grade
class.

'But shameful things went on. The place where lessons were held
consisted of two rooms only; I was in one of them and my colleague
in the other, and in the afternoons the headmaster took the fifth grade.

'But that place wasn't a school—it wasn't a sheepfold even, because
even in a sheepfold there's always someone who keeps order. My class
consisted of some thirty-five girls and boys—about fifteen were girls.
There were about twenty of the first grade and the rest second grade.
I had to carry out two programmes in one class in no more than three
hours! I had a blackboard that I had to divide in two with a chalk line,
one half for the first grade and the other for the second. My colleague's
classroom was the same, though he had fewer pupils, and his methods
of work were really shameful—not that I want to say that mine were
all they ought to have been. He let his pupils go very early—or he
went out himself at once, leaving them alone in the classroom. And
where did he go?

'I noticed that sometimes he would go out, closing the door very
gently so that I shouldn't hear the noise. I often saw him, in the narrow

corridor that separated our two classrooms, with some girl or other, and other times I would see him come out of the lavatory with a girl. The situation began to worry and disturb me—I was bewildered at what was going on—I thought of intervening by talking to the headmaster, by telling him at least that someone ought to do something about putting the school straight, and getting other teachers, because we were too few for so many pupils. I did so, but I was disappointed; he said to me: "It's not up to me—just do what you can and don't bother your head with this foolishness." Then he added: "It's something that we give a school to these coarse peasants at all!"

'There was nothing for me to do but resign myself to the sort of things that go on in that kind of school—I pretended to see nothing any more, and gave myself up to working for the pupils.

'Very soon I had another disappointment, bitterer still—the pupils whom I had to teach to read and write and know things were very different from those I'd dreamed of when as a student I'd wanted to be a schoolmaster. What a difference! When I'd studied the principles of psychology and pedagogy I'd dreamed of applying as much as I'd learnt to my pupils, children, that is, because it seemed to me that psychology would be a thing of enormous importance to a good teacher. But the children on whom the theories of my treatises were based hadn't been chosen from rough peasants who were a good deal older. The smallest of them were eight years old, and the oldest, mostly among the girls, were seventeen and eighteen. For the first two years they came to school to learn the first principles of reading and writing, then they used to go home to work, and few of them went on with school after that. In the fifth grade, taught by the headmaster, were the only few boys and girls who understood anything.

'Life in that village was pretty hard for me. I slept in a little room rented from a peasant family—a pot-house really—and I ate only in the evenings, at table with those peasants, because they only cooked in the evening. My colleague lived in the vicinity of a small church, a room conceded to him by the local priest, an old man of more than seventy, who one only saw at Mass on Sundays.

'I ended by resigning myself—I oughtn't to say it, but I said to myself "Put up with everything and don't worry about it." Perhaps I had my reasons.

'But if one thinks that in the year 1953 such circumstances could exist, and such medieval backwardness, one ends by believing that the civilisation we're so proud of is nothing but a superficial illusion. I had to put up with that state of affairs for eight months, and I was fed up and sickened.

'There was no local government representative in the village—that job was carried out by someone entrusted with the work by the administration of the big town; there was no *carabiniere* station, they came to the village every so often, stopped a bit and went away again; there was no chemist, no doctor, no telephone. A tobacconist served the purpose of chemist too—that is to say they sold the commonest medicines there, mostly salts and medicinal herbs, and an old woman was at the same time the doctor, midwife and witch. In the daytime the few streets were full of animals—pigs and hens and geese, and of small children, and on the pavement a few old men sat wrapped in shawls. There was a single *fontana*, and a well where the women drew water that stank. Of course there was no water in the houses. I made no mistake when I said to myself that the set-up was one of a thousand years ago. But, as I said, I resigned myself and gave myself up to the school—if you could call it a school.

'In the mornings I used to go into that classroom and find it empty, full of dust, and impregnated with a pungent stink, a stink that you'll understand later. The desks were old and twisted, the walls damp and the floor cracked, with grass sprouting out of it. I used to come in and open the windows first, doing the job of a serving-man, and sweep the dust off my table, and sit down and read something while I waited for the pupils. They would arrive one by one or in groups; they scarcely ever gave any greeting—they sat down and began to giggle among themselves.

'I put the boys of the first grade in one line of desks and the second grade in another line, but that was no more than a formality, because usually they used to sit down where they liked.

'The pupils had no books—only a slate and a pencil—that was enough! How, and how much, could I teach them?

'I tried to write on one half of the blackboard something for the first grade, and the ones at the other line of desks would begin to mutter and even to shout—whichever lot I was dealing with, the other lot would begin to talk; it was a madhouse. At first I used to try to check them by shouting at them, but it was no good; in the end I told myself not to worry about it so much and to let them carry on.

'In that way they learnt nothing; with people like that you need a

well-organised school and good teachers and strict discipline, which I
wasn't able to enforce.

'Often when I was talking to one half of the class the others would
go out all at once, without asking permission—they just got up and
went away as calm as you please. At first I used to ask them, "Where
are you going?" and they would reply, "To the lavatory."³ After that
I just didn't ask them any more.

'There were girls in the class, as I've said, and to begin with I was
kind to them, but it was useless. They weren't used to our way of
living and they thought everything silly and boring. There were days
when a lot of the pupils didn't come to school at all. Sometimes no
one came. I used to close the shutters and go away, writing in the
register how the lessons had gone and putting my signature to it—
God forgive me!

'I don't want to say how some of the pupils carried on in the classroom in my very presence! At the bottom of the classroom they were
more closely grouped; I had put only boys there, but for them it was
a sort of paradise. I realised it at once—the first time was when I saw
a group of five boys having a (masturbating) race; then one of them
exclaimed loudly, "I've won!"⁴ I intervened then, and asked, "Who's
won what, and what are you talking about?" He replied, "What's
that got to do with you?"⁵

'What ought I to have done? Rebuked them—but they would
never have come to school again; then, too, I was afraid of shocking
the girls, and many times I just pretended not to see. But things
weren't a bit as I'd thought—incredible as it may seem the girls knew
everything, and the older ones knew what was going on at the bottom
of the class and enjoyed it. I was in a fix—I almost went mad one day
when I asked quite a small girl who was giggling stupidly, "What do
you find so funny? Don't you know one doesn't laugh in class? Tell
me why are you laughing?" and she replied, "Nothing, teacher—
Antonino was (masturbating)."⁶ As usual, I was simply stunned; I said
nothing to her, but I was convinced that these people had little understanding of the seriousness of what they were doing, and I proposed to
myself to explain a few things to them.

'So one day I sent the girls out and stayed alone with the boys. I
assumed a serious and sad air, and began slowly to talk to them. I said
that one should not, absolutely not, do these things, and specially not at
school, I said that it damaged one's health, that serious illnesses came

from it, and I invented fairy tales about children who used to do such things and had died of it; I explained to them that it was unseemly and shameful to do it in front of girls, and that it was a sin in the eyes of God. To sum up, I acted the parts of priest and doctor and father. But do you know what they replied? "Hasn't our teacher got one too?"[7]

'I was convinced that whatever I could do was useless, and I was afraid that if I allowed myself any harsh rebuke they wouldn't come to school any more—afraid, too, that I'd get beaten up, for they were quite capable of it.

'At last I tried to talk to the girls, repeating what I'd said to the boys, basing my arguments on religion and modesty. A few were a little put out, and blushed, but they went on giggling among themselves. Then one of the older girls said to me, "Everyone knows about these things—we mind our own business, and anyway we're not so stupid as to make them [mess about with] us."[8]

'I was staggered. I tried to get something across, to explain, but it was useless. "A water melon, cook it how you like, is still a water melon,"[9] as a good Sicilian proverb says.

'Sexual activity was firmly rooted in those young people. I thought their families must know all about it, but as far as I could make out they didn't. Perhaps they didn't attach much importance to the question.

'When I wrote to people at home I couldn't bring myself to say that where I lived was a place of savages, and that my school could have been taken for a brothel.

'Though the girls were interested spectators of these things there was a curious thing about it—they never let a man come near them. I never once saw a girl with a man; when they'd finished their "lessons" the girls went home and the boys went to work in the small-holdings.

'I talked to my young colleague about it, but he laughed.

'It amused him to see me so perplexed, and he marvelled that I should want to stop what was going on. He explained to me that nothing went on between the girl and boy pupils because almost all of them were bound by the ties of kinship or neighbourhood, and it was among themselves that they would afterwards marry.

'School was about to finish, and I was fed up with it. For my colleague, however, that set-up was a veritable paradise. A few of the girls used to go to his house near the church. He said he wanted to give private lessons to coach his pupils better—but I knew well what kind of lessons he was giving those girls; the idea of coaching them was a fine excuse. The girls' families let them go to him—the very fact of seeing him near the church made them think they were dealing with a serious-minded person. I went there myself once or twice to find him, and one of those times, while I was talking to him, two girls arrived, one of them a pupil of mine. I said to my colleague, "I understand that you must give 'lessons' to that other one but as for this one, who is my pupil, I can't see the necessity." He replied, "You give her a good lesson yourself—I'll leave you alone with her, and don't be an idiot; we're here today and gone tomorrow."

'I was left alone with the girl, who was called Nina. She was a dark girl, almost wild-looking, and very sly. I made her sit down, and asked her why she'd come here, and what need she had to study in private if I was able to teach her anything at school. She kept her eyes lowered and didn't reply, while her hands stroked the shawl that draped from her head. Then she said, "To accompany my friend."[10] I heard the girl in the other room laugh as Nina got up and said, "I'm going now."[11] I remembered the words of my colleague. "We're here today and gone tomorrow," and I approached her. . . . A few words were enough—and she wasn't really so ugly. It was a satisfying occasion, and a successful one for me—I knew what I was doing, but I lost my head.

'And that's the kind of schooling I gave! I oughtn't to say these things, because I'm ashamed to think I did them myself—but I think there are others who'd have done the same in my position.

'School finished; I promoted most of them—I failed some of them who really knew nothing. I left the village on a Sunday in the cart of a peasant who kindly wanted to accompany me to the town below. No one had said any last good-byes to me. I had already said good-bye to a few people I'd known, and as soon as I was in the cart I took a deep breath and said, "At last!"

'When we turned a corner of a little street I saw Nina on the side-walk, washing something. I wanted to say good-bye to her; I said, "Goodbye, Nina, and remember me to everyone!" "Goodbye, teacher," she said, "and a happy journey", and laughed in the way she had.

'When I got here my first thought was to get myself transferred to this town, saying that my father was alone and ill. I got the transfer, and now I'm here; I teach here.

'I've had a few postcards from my ex-colleague—he's still teaching over there, and he tells me life is always the same, and that it's like living in paradise!

'But don't think that this school is the same kind as that one in the village—it isn't all it ought to be certainly, but like that one, for heaven's sake, no! But there's some shameful things here too.

'But how can a master like me concern himself with all that goes on? For me, for example, the most important thing is my salary—it's my superiors who carry the real responsibility. However, one's much closer to one's pupils. At the moment I give lessons to children of the third grade, all boys, and they get on well with me.

'I have no method of teaching—I carry out the lessons in the way that seems best; I've completely forgotten the ideas I studied at school, and I'm convinced in any case that theory is a long way from practice. In Sicily, and in the towns particularly, the conception of learning is a strange one, and it is practical only. People send their children to school until they have learnt to read and write only—anything more is considered useless and superfluous. I have a class of thirty children, almost all of them poor and the sons of peasants—half of them have no school books, and others have absolutely no exercise-books or anything else. I've applied to the authorities to have a few books and other materials, and I got ten books and four pounds weight of exercise-books. I divided these among the poorest children, telling those who had no books to study at home with some schoolfellow. But they're children, you know, and when two or three of them work together they get nothing done; they laugh and talk and play—and sometimes with themselves too. But they do have a consciousness of school in their minds; they have respect and even fear for their teacher and their school.

'Naturally there's those who do work and those who can't or won't work, and that lot remain backward. I try to be stern, a disciplinarian, but I finish by becoming a baby too. Do you know what it's like to explain the basic principles of mathematics to children who are completely ignorant of them? It means using every possible method of making them understand, even to setting oneself to play with them. A child needs imaginative examples; he understands them better, and the pictures remain impressed in his mind, so that they're difficult to forget.

'When, for example, I'm explaining the letters of the alphabet or something of that sort, I choose an object or an animal for each letter—

for instance I say P is the sign for "pipe", and M is the sign for "mother", and when the child sees a word with letters like that he remembers at once the sound of the word "pipe" or "mother", and it helps his pronunciation.

'But the teaching conditions are no better than moderate, very moderate. Children need a lot of care—in them are the men of tomorrow, and it's taking a serious risk not to educate them properly. School isn't only the place where one learns to read and write, but where one learns to have decent manners, to know life better, and to know how to behave in society.

'The government concerns itself with the children up to the point it has to, but not all that's needful. What they're keenest about is telling the pupils about the work of the government, about the great strides they've made in progress, what America is—the mother of the Italians—and so on and so forth—it's my job to say these things to the children. And they complain of the days of Fascism, when one had to teach the Fascist doctrine in school—but nothing seems to me to have changed today. Then there was dictatorship, but now we're supposed to be living under a democracy!

'Children of today are different from those of twenty years ago. Now by the time they're seven years old even the poorest of them can talk about rockets and sputniks, about Sofia Loren and Lana Turner, and at five years old they already know as much about sexual matters as twenty years ago they knew at fifteen.

'Progress affects everyone, specially the children, and one ought to give them a clear picture of what it is, because even when they're living in the midst of it they don't know what it is or where it comes from.

'A characteristic of the modern child is his mania for asking why. One said to me, "Why is there a God?" and another, "Is He happy because we're unhappy?" Embarrassing questions that one can't explain in a few words, but I have to satisfy their demands even if I make mistakes in doing so—if I said I didn't know I'd be ruined.

'One thing runs right through the schools of today: one can do the job in two ways—with a couldn't-care-less attitude or with a serious sense of responsibility. Both are common, and one must examine the conditions and the atmosphere which bring them about. However, schools as they exist here in these southern towns need a lot of care. Here illiteracy is rooted in the centuries, and its seeds are planted anew by the authorities, who never exert themselves to heal this open sore. When all's said and done, what can a teacher like me do? The families don't worry about the teaching of their children— I've never once seen the relations of my pupils. They wait till the end of the year and their only thought is whether the boy has been promoted or not. If he hasn't been, they don't send him to school any more; the father takes him to work in the fields—only if he's been promoted does he go on with school and not always then. Many families are so indifferent that they don't even know what grade their own sons are in.

'The people are bound strongly to ignorance, they go on in ignorance, and if the authorities don't take the trouble to eradicate the mentality of idiotic tradition and superstition, now that we're in the twentieth century, in the atomic age, they won't manage it in another two thousand years either!

'I've no ambitions to become a big-wig in the school hierarchy—the big-wigs are the big-wigs, and for someone like me it's forbidden to get on. Perhaps it's true that if one's in a high position, or has power, one forgets a lot of things—and it wouldn't be anything to wonder at if I forgot things too, if I got on. That's why it does me good to talk and remember. But if I could arrange it for just one day! Ah, I'd show them how one should act towards the people!

'Everyone in the south is fed up with politics—by now the people are completely disillusioned; they have understood the *macagna* that's created during elections, they already know all the familiar promises, and they're sick of that carry-on. I've got no politics—as far as I'm concerned all Parties—I say *all*—think only of their own interests; some more, some less, but *all* of them.

'What do ideals and doctrines matter to me? I believe in God and I pray to him to give me good health and to order my life, because I'd like to get married. It's prosperity that counts; when there's prosperity there's everything that matters in life, and when you're married you can go to bed with your wife in the evening, knowing that if children come of it you'll be able to feed them.

'But one must suffer first, that one knows, and above all one must never hope for anything from other people. We have will-power, and it's that that we must use, and then everything may go well.

'And one mustn't believe in the prattle of this man or of that— in the world of civilised man there's a common law: "Every man for himself and God for all."

'When one has done one's duty—if one can do it, because often it's not possible—then pull your own cart, don't give the reins to anyone, and let the others go hang! Don't believe in brotherly love or honour for the next man; Jesus Christ came to speak about it 2,000 years ago, but nothing has changed—and do you think it will change?

'I'm a great lover of proverbs, and I'll end with a very plain one, "*tutta a sciarra e pa cutra*" [literally: "The whole struggle is for the blanket", i.e. each man fights to cover himself and takes the blanket from the others.]'

CHAPTER SIXTEEN

The American

PERHAPS three-quarters of all Castellammarese families have relations in America, who emigrated before the quotas were imposed, and to follow them is the unrealisable dream of all who remained behind in Sicily.

America holds an especial place in the Sicilian mind; it is Utopia, it is Paradise itself. In nearly every village there is some old man who, now an American citizen, has come home to pass his twilight where he was born. He never lacks eager listeners, and his tales are constantly at work enriching a confused image of unimaginable splendours. Don Peppino had spent no less than fifty-two years in the States.

'Fifty-two years! Fifty-two years of America (merica)—that's how long I was there! Go and spend fifty-two years in America yourself!

'America is America. It's a country blessed by God, and you don't find all this shame that you find here. In America one's well off because there's always work, and everyone works, even the women —while here they stay at home from morning to night. Look outside in the street—first of all you see muck and rubbish everywhere. Look how many children are stretched out all over it, and what they're doing thrown down there in the muck. Where do the women here throw out their filth? Look—into the street, where the hens spread it every-where, and the children spend the whole day among it. In the street you see nothing but people begging, day by day, and what's more revolting still is that there are people begging for just enough to buy themselves a piece of bread. Cursed country!

'In Sicily they're born like beasts and they die like beasts—but you go to America as a beast and become a man!

'For fifty years these arms of mine haven't rested, and now, now that I'm sixty-eight, how I'd like to work still, my son—but as you see I haven't got the health, and I'm condemned to live in this lousy[1] country.

'I went to America when I was sixteen years old, when my mouth still stank of my mother's milk, and if you knew how I went there you'd laugh.[2] In those days[3] you didn't need all these documents to emigrate to America—a simple passport was enough, and an address you were going to, and you went. I was young, I hadn't been to school, because I helped my father in the fields, but no one went to school anyway—only the richer people, like now in fact. There was always poverty here, and worse then than now, and all the poor dreamed of going to America to look for work. Among these was my father. Many of those who left the town are dead now—there was Giuseppe Scriba, Minicu[4] Maniaci, Don Raffaele the painter, who died in America after a railway accident—and so many others.

'My father didn't want to take me to America, because the women of the family would be left alone—there were two sisters of mine besides my mother. I thought America was some city near Palermo or Trapani—I thought you could work there during the week and come back home on Saturdays, as if you were working in a distant district.

'The day of departure came, and the evening before my father had charged me to look after my mother and my sisters, and told me to work hard and he would send me lots of things from America. But I was crying, because I wanted to go with him. In the morning while it was still dark all the people who were going to America gathered in the *piazza*. They were all fathers of families, who had scraped together the money for the passage, and each had a bag of his personal belongings. At that time there wasn't a bus to Palermo—there was a carriage which could seat hardly more than ten people. The women climbed on to the carriage, while the men went on foot as far as Palermo.

'But hardly had I seen the carriage leave than, barefoot and carrying my shoes, I set off on a short cut, made it, and jumped on behind the baggage, clutching on and keeping myself low down so as not to be seen. When we got to Palermo and people who saw me asked what I was doing there, I replied cunningly that I was leaving for America. I was hungry and I remember that the one who gave me a bit of bread was Zu Nicola the shoemaker[5]—who's dead now, peace to his soul.

'Then my father came. "*You?*" he said. "What are you doing here?" Shivering and crying, I answered "I want to go to America with you."[6]

'My father almost went off his head trying to persuade me. He said, "But how is your mother going to know? and then you've got nothing to put on; this jacket[7] is filthy—and those shoes, you want to go to America in these shoes?"

'There was quite a scene there at the port, but at last all the other townspeople said to my father, "Salvatore, take this child with you, he'll earn you a lot of money on the way, and we'll each give him a piece of bread.[8] And it was like that[9] that I got onto the ship.

'We got to New York after twenty-three days at sea. There must have been about five hundred Italians on board but most of us were Sicilians. When we arrived we didn't know where to go; some said to go that way and some this way—there was a hell of a mix-up. It was such a muddle that I almost wanted to go home again,[10] but my father would have given me a thrashing if I'd said so.

'At last the American police[11] took us to the Italian quarter, where we found people from our own town and friends of my father's.

'After a few days I and my father were working on the American railway. At sixteen years of age I worked from morning till night along the railroads of America. I saw the mountains from far off, and it seemed to me that behind them must be my home town—I wasted hours and hours trying to make up my mind just where it was and in what direction. I was a child.[12]

'I earned my first money, and I gave it all to my father. But I felt happier; I had got to know a lot of friends, I was learning to speak American, and I was beginning to like the country. Every so often I too sent some dollars[13] to my family, so they could see that I was already earning.

'But a lot of the boys[14] gave themselves up to the good-time life, the Sicilian life—they began to steal. There were still dirtier ones, who gave themselves airs, and formed a kind of *mafia* composed of thieves and murderers and people of that kind. My father never let me out of his sight, and every evening he gave me a lecture, saying that if he saw me with that lot he'd thrash me.

'We were five years in New York and then we went to Detroit, a town which would have made you shiver if you'd seen it then.

'In America it's not like here, they have big railway companies. If I remember rightly, I was with the biggest of them, which was called New York Centre.

'I worked for that company for many years—but I'd also been a bricklayer since childhood—until in 1915 I went back to Italy for the war. I left Italy again in 1920. I'd got married three months after my return from the war—I ran away with my wife, so as not to wait for the whole time of engagement. I was twenty-six years old, and my heart was in America—my father had returned from there, but I'd hardly got married before I wanted to go back again. I left my wife here with a baby, and she was pregnant again into the bargain.

'Even the rocks trembled before me in those days, and as Christ lived no one dared to do me hurt—any one who did paid dearly for it. I worked like a dog in America, and sent home the means of living to my family, which was bigger now.

'I worked in a town called Dodge City as a wagon-driver, and I had to unload sand a couple of miles from the factory. I became foreman of the squad at once. The wagons were big carts drawn by two horses—and what horses! You loaded the sand and brought out the wagons across a road made entirely of sand. But the Americans didn't know how to drive the horses, and they were always upsetting the load on the ground. The boss gave the sack to anyone who lost a wagon-load of sand, and one day I said to him, "Mr. Miller, can I drive the wagons?" "Are you able to?" he asked, and I replied, "Sure I know how!" and from that day it was me who drove the wagons, and without losing as much as one load. I knew horses well in those days and I knew the right way to handle them—everyone was amazed.

'I did this work for two years then I went to work in a shoe factory for a few years, near San Francisco.

'Then I stayed at Grand Rapids near Detroit, and worked as a bricklayer for several years more. I never settled down in one place—as soon as one job was finished I was off to look for another somewhere else. I was in Santa Fé, Los Angeles, at San Antonio in Texas, in Louisiana working in a hide and shoe-sole factory, and then I was a bricklayer again at Sacramento for three years. But for the last twenty years I've been working in the eastern towns, Chicago, Philadelphia, Louisville, and finally Detroit, where I was till the end.

'I didn't want to go to New York any more, because living in that city was a bit dangerous for me—a few years before I'd done a black deed—I'll tell you about it.

'Some fifteen of us Italians slept in one room—there were Tuscans, Piedmontese, Neapolitans, Calabrians and Sicilians. Now I'd have you know that I've never insulted anyone, and I don't like anyone twisting my balls. Every evening I used to come home from work and cook myself something in that room, which was also the kitchen. The evening before I used to leave meat or fruit or *pasta* in my chest of drawers, and also my savings in one of the drawers. But often in the evening I used to find nothing in my chest of drawers, neither meat nor bread nor fruit—and not only that, but the money was missing that I'd put there the day before. I began to suspect who it was I was dealing with, and I said to myself, "This mouse has got to die."[15] I knew who it was all right—it was a Calabrian, who didn't work, and lived by pilfering from our provisions and our earnings. One day I got myself a little packet of poison; I cooked the meat in the evening, and I put some of the poison in each slice, and then I put it in the chest of drawers and went to bed.

The following evening I came back from work, and when I was still on the stairs I could hear a voice screaming "I'm dying!—I'm dying!" I said to myself, "You've had it, you swine!"[16] I went in, pretending to know nothing, and said, "What's up? what's the matter with Mr. Alfonso? Why don't you call the doctor?—but what can he have eaten?"

Mr. Alfonso didn't look at me—he trembled and yelled like a lamb that's going to have its throat cut. I went up to him and asked him what was the matter—but only for a moment. He looked at me, and as if my gaze had killed him he died on the instant. The doctor came, but as I've said, Alfonso was dead. I said at once that he'd probably died of a heart attack, but I think someone there had cottoned on. Weeds must be killed.[17]

'After a few weeks I quit New York, because one's skin is precious —but anyway from that time on I never lost anything more.

'I went to live in Detroit, and bought myself a house there and settled down in that city.

'I returned to Italy in 1935 with my pockets full of dollars. I built myself a fine house here and bought myself some land, but after six months I was off to America again. There were two Italians living in my house in Detroit, a Sardinian and a Palermitan. They used to pay me a monthly sum to sleep there and to cook in the evenings; each was supposed to cook for himself, but often I used to do the cooking for all of us and they would pay me for it. Don't get the idea that in America you eat like you do here! Here a poor worker gets a piece of stale bread and soup in the evening if he's lucky—but in America anyone who's done a day's work deserves to eat and eat well. There you eat meat in quantity, *pasta*, fruit, butter and eggs, and you drink whisky or beer—because there's not much wine there—and in the cold weather you drink strong liquor.

'Ah! America, where are you![18] What a rich country, what a civilised people, what culture there is in America! There's no life to equal it.

'In the morning every one goes to work, even the women; eight hours a day and then home again. Almost everyone has a car, but if you work a long way off you can always take a bus and you're home in no time. Every Saturday morning you get your pay-packet—does that seem to you like here, where they make the poor workers wait months and months to get paid? In America you live happily, you work, and work makes all the day calm and secure. There's nothing lacking in America—you can buy anything you want and you can have every comfort, whereas here if there are any comforts they're for the rich only. You go into an American house and above all you see cleanliness; you find a reception room where you can talk comfortably; the bedroom is separate, and so is the kitchen, leading out of the dining-room. In America there's a whole little room for the lavatory, there's a bath and a shower and hot and cold water—while here the "lavatory" is just a hole behind the door.

'If you don't want to stay at home in the evening, you can go out; there's no lack of places to amuse yourself. There's bars in every street, cinemas everywhere, theatres, variety shows, and clubs where you pay a subscription and go when you like. There's huge parks and gardens where you can go as much as you like, and no one comes to disturb you or to say, "Get out of here and go somewhere else." In the evening everyone goes to some show or other, where you can stay as long as you like and pass the time with your friends. There's everything in that country, except poverty and need—that's the monopoly of the Sicilians.

'And then how can you compare American shops with Italian ones? When you enter an American shop they don't look you up and down to see if you're a peasant or a rich man. You go into a store and they greet you with every possible courtesy—there's girls[19] who come civilly forward, and ask you what you want, and put themselves entirely at your disposal. If you're not satisfied, or if you don't find

what you're looking for, there's someone to apologise first and then to
accompany you to the door. If you go to a shop in Palermo they treat
you like dirt, and if in the end you don't want to buy anything they
give you a certain look and say you've wasted their time for nothing,
and other offensive words. That doesn't happen in America—and
there's not even any haggling over prices; there's one price and that's
all.

'Then again, do you think the city streets are like they are here in
Sicily? On the contrary, the people who pass by mind their own business; and then as for cleanliness, you don't see filth on the ground;
where there's no traffic you don't see children scattered about everywhere; you don't see women sitting on the sidewalks. The streets are
as clean as our rooms, and you could eat off the ground.

'In America all the children go to school, free of charge, and not
like here where you study if you've got money. In America it's compulsory to study for seven years from eight to fifteen.

'Here anyone who's got money feels himself superior to the next
man who hasn't got any. Everyone is noble, or would like to think
he is; you see youths who don't work but lead a life of luxury all the
same—and how do they do it? That's easy—by stealing, that's how.

'Here, if the father of a family wants to breed cows for a living he
can't do it very easily. A poor man, who owns say four cows, has to
fork out his contribution to the *mafia*, and woe to him if he doesn't—
his cows will be stolen, or he may put his life in serious danger. But
look at the American countryside and you'll be amazed. You'll see
green crops without end, animals running free and no one stealing
them, and everyone working—women too, without any shame.

'Who rules in Sicily? There are three rulers; the *mafia*, the Church,
and the police—they are all one body, like Father, Son and Holy
Ghost.

'You want the electric chair, that's what you want in Italy, like in
America—whoever makes a mistake pays the price.

'Here there's no decent upbringing. There's no comparison between
American upbringing and Italian; for example the young men there
give up their seats in a bus to the old and to women, but in the
cities here they sit there like mules. And there's too much malice here
—if a woman walks along the streets she gets no peace for the insults
and looks she receives, but in America the girls walk freely on the
streets without anyone insulting them, it's they who look for men

rather than the other way about, because there's a lot of women in America.

'The girls go to work and aren't ashamed of it—they do everything together with the men without the danger there would be here. I used to work in a factory where there were a hundred or so women, girls and grown women, and nothing happened. There was a scandal or two, but always because of those rough Sicilians without background. When you are working you ought to forget about being a man or a woman—you have a duty to carry out. Here they boast that all the women are virtuous women, the most virtuous in the world. But I, who have travelled so much and by now know something about life, I can assure you that you find virtuous women everywhere, and the other kind too, and it's not true that in America all the women are prostitutes—because I know American life inside out. I can promise you this is true.

'There's too much tradition here, and too much hunger. No one wants to work—that's the truth of the matter. Everyone looks for employment in the city, at some office where there's nothing to do.[20] They get a chit to some Member of Parliament, and he gives the job not to somebody who needs it, but to someone of his own party. You go to some office in Palermo and you find people just standing on the stairs looking at you and holding pieces of paper in their hands, and there's a whole squad of cleaners. If that office has ten real employees there would be a hundred porters and fifty cleaners. These ones earn a monthly wage and do nothing for it—in view of this *camorra* how can other people go out to work? And everyone wants to become a *carabiniere*, so as to say that he's earning too; they go and live in the cities and begin to speak in Italian and to forget their past lives, and when they come back to their home towns and see some wretch still eating bread and onions they say, "But who are these savages?"

'When this sort of thing happens in Italy they say, "Oh, but this is the land of the *camorra*." Sicilians always make themselves out to be poor, especially in front of Americans, and they're always asking for help and parcels—it goes on day by day. From the time the war ended, as you know, all the Americans who had relations in Italy sent parcels to our families. I never sent parcels to mine, always money, but to my relations who used to write to me that there was starvation in Sicily I used to send parcels. In America we used to believe that Sicily was really dying of hunger, and we used to send second-hand things—clothes and shoes mostly. There are still Americans who send parcels, and they still say here that they're dying of hunger—though its fifteen years since the war finished they say things are getting worse and worse. So you see that it wasn't the war that brought the hunger —it was always there and I'm telling you it always will be.

'There's unemployment in Italy—well, that's true and it's not true. Look how many empty mountains there are—why don't they plant them all with woods? Look at this street—why don't they put it in decent order? How many houses are needed for the poor who haven't a roof over their heads—why not build them? How much improvement does the land need—why don't they do it?

'And why does no one go to reap the *sumach* any more, as they used to do? Why does no one go to the *disa* any more—why? Part of it is the fault of the government, but the other part is the fault of the Sicilians themselves, who don't want to do certain types of work, because they're undignified.

'But the government is not the only oppressor of the poor here— no, there's other people! I'll tell you something that happened a short time ago.

'Well, this happened about three years ago, when I was still in America. I was in Detroit, as you know, and at that time a Sicilian priest came there from this town—the priest whom everyone knows, you too, the one who has the central parish of the town. All the Italian families in Detroit were talking about this priest, and saying that he'd come to collect money for the poor people of the town. One Sunday all of us townspeople from here who were in Detroit were invited by him—he sent each of us a note written in Italian saying that he would like the pleasure of meeting us because he wanted to give us news of our relations and our home town and so on. He knew our addresses, as if our relations at home had given them to him. So all of us who had been invited gathered at the place the note said, at the home of a certain family Cosenza.

'In the hope of hearing news of the town, and news of particular interest to me too, I went to that party. With me were my sister-in-law and her children and other friends from the town.

'We all got into my nephew's Ford—a car worth ten of these Italian ones—and we went along to the Cosenza family, near the centre of the town. When we got there we got out of the car and saw that the door of the house was open, and from outside you could hear laughter and general noise. We presented ourselves at the door, and a woman, the householder, asked us to come in, greeted us warmly, and took us through into the big room where all the noise was coming from.

'I knew almost everyone in that room, all American citizens now. At the end of the room a pack of women were bunched round a man, so that you could hardly see his head. I realised that this was the priest, and when I managed to see his long black cassock and his red and smiling face, I decided to approach him as the others had, and did so.

'I introduced myself into the group and turned to the priest, who was delighted to be surrounded by so many beautiful girls. I said, "Excuse me, Father, I'm Don Peppino, the husband of Donna Paola, who lives in 'Mungi Vacche' street, do you remember?"

'The priest pretended to think, or perhaps he really thought, but anyway it turned out that he knew nothing about my family. All the same, I thanked him, and I stayed as a guest at lunch with all the others.

'Meanwhile the priest spoke of the people of my home town. "They're all in a bad way," he said. "There's want and poverty there and we must help them, for they are our brothers, and by ties of blood into the bargain," and so on and so forth. There were a hundred of us at lunch at two long tables in the room, and all of us had a good time. While he was eating, the priest, happy in his gluttony, got up and took a film of us to take back to Italy.

'Towards the end of the meal he got to his feet, made the sign of the cross, and made us recite some prayers for "Our poor brothers of the town", and then began to talk. "I have braved the ocean, oh my brethren," he said, "to come here to see you so that you should be able to give some help to your townspeople who live in want, and whom I assist every day. I beg you, oh my brethren, to send them an offering by me, because, as you know, we priests are the messengers," and so on and so forth. Anyway, that priest managed to move us, and in fact I myself at once took an envelope and put fifteen dollars inside and consigned it to the dear priest. All the others did the same thing. There were some who had nothing to give at the time, but they sent offerings to the Cosenza family afterwards. I didn't give much—there were some who gave fifty dollars, but that's all I was able to give, which if I'm not mistaken would be about ten thousand lire.

'That priest stayed at Detroit for a week and then he went on to other cities where there were many of his townspeople; he went to San Francisco, to Los Angeles, New York, Chicago, and the rest of them. The poor wretch "braved" this journey "by land and sea" to help the poor people.

'He came back from America after three months, and a few days after I got back myself I had the pleasure of seeing what had been done with the help that we Americans had given to the poor. I thought the people might be happier, less poor than before, that at least there'd be a house for everyone as the priest had promised, but what false hopes.[21]

'I saw the priest, fatter than when I had seen him in America, but he didn't say anything—he greeted me and that was all. But now I've seen what was done with our money: the priest got himself a car, bought himself a nice bit of land, renovated his church, joined his house onto it and besides all that put a television into his own house— and, as you see, he doesn't often show himself in the town. Now shall I tell you what that priest has given the poor, the priest who "braved land and sea"? Ah! he'd already shown them the film which he took in America, and he'd brought so many greetings from their American relations—that he had done.

'Do you know what the priest says? He says the Americans gave very little, and that the money was spent on the voyage and on the film, and a small sum was spent on restoring the church. First comes God, and then the poor people! Now the people here don't know the real set-up, and they believe the good priest—that the Americans were mean with him.

'Tell me, when you think of all this don't you think there's a lot of filth in Sicily? What, me go to the priest and ask him what he did with the money? Me? and who am I? He tells me this and that, he tells me he didn't bring back much money. He tells me that he showed our poor relations his film and that amused them for a whole evening —but he will pray to God for them that they may always be kept in poverty so that he, messenger of God, can brave the ocean in a boat yet again.

'This is land flowing with milk and honey!

'Tell me, now, what concern of mine are the poor people? They can't live! They haven't got a house? They're dying of hunger? But they go to work and they earn their daily bread like everyone else—

there's work enough, but the poor don't want to work, they want to live on the shoulders of others, and so many people worry about them.

'But my life's already over; I've worked, and I've done my duty. Now I'm waiting for the summons; I've hardly arrived on this earth before I must leave it, and good-bye to everyone.

'But, old as I am, I would like to go back to America! Ah, Detroit, New York, San Francisco, Grand Rapids, California, Louisiana, I would like to see all those places again. How many friends I left there, and how many years of hard work I've passed there. I would like to die in America and be buried in an American cemetery; because, you see, in America even the dead are all equal. Here when someone dies, if he's rich he's buried in his family chapel, or else in a church, or a *congregazione* at the cemetery—but if he's poor they bury him under the ground. For a rich man here the priests celebrate sung Masses, and say special prayers to make them go to paradise—but for a poor man there is none of that—he's left to his fate. In America rich and poor are equal, and they're all buried under the ground. But we are in Sicily, and to be any good this land would have to be buried by the sea that surrounds it—it would have to stay a thousand years under the water and then rise beautiful and purified and restored like new. That's what's wanted.

'Why did I come back? Because at a certain age there's something all of us need; I was alone and I was getting old too. I had reached pensionable age and I couldn't work any more. My family wanted me to come back. My wife's here and my children, and the house that I built with the sweat of my brow. I sold everything in America, I left many things as remembrances to my relations, and I came back to this town. I live on the pension that I get from America—it's not a big sum there, but I gain on the exchange, and I live quietly. I get seventy-five dollars a month, which brings me nearly 50,000 lire.

'I'm enjoying the last days of my life. I'm certain not to die of hunger; I can buy meat every day; I can buy medicine when I need it. All this I owe to no one but myself—I've worked in my day!

'It's true that I find myself in Italy, but I'm not an Italian. Look at this document here—it says that I'm an American, an American citizen.

'Here I don't know the priest nor the mayors nor the sergeants. Why do I despise Sicily and the Sicilians? Why ask why? Who has given me work all my life? Who has given me the means to bring up a family? Who has assured my old age? Isn't it America? And who has shown me kindness? So why should I love a country of want and dirt and rudeness, and forget one where I lived for fifty-two years?

'If you have the luck to go to America and live there—I'm not saying for long, but at least two years—and then come back again to Italy, to Sicily, to this town, just see how you feel. You'd go off your head. So now think of me, who's lived there fifty-two years—should I love this country which has given me nothing, or the one that gave me everything?'

Notes to Chapters

Notes to Chapter Two

1 A *spicciafaccende*, usually shortened to *spiccia*, is broadly a man who does odd jobs that involve the ability to read and write; he may take letters at dictation or fill in forms or advise on what authority should be approached about this or that problem. He rarely has specialised knowledge or qualification beyond his literacy.

Notes to Chapter Three

1 CHI SACCIU IU COSA VÒ FARI TU CU CHIDDU CHI TI DICU.
2 IU SUGNU POVIRU.
3 LU SIGNURI VOLI ACCUSSÌ, IDDU VOLI ACCUSSÌ.
4 MINCHIA C'ERA UN CAVURU.
5 PISCIAZZA.
6 NNI MIA.
7 PUVUREDDI.
8 NUAUTRI.
9 SIDDIA ALZARCI.
10 MINCHIA,QUANNU C'E FRIDDU ASSAI NUNNI VULISSIMU SUSIRI MAI.
11 AGGHIORNA.
12 The age of call-up for military service is 21, and the subject undergoes his medical in his twenty-first year. Exceptions are made in cases where there is only one parent; where the father is unable to work either by reason of sickness or age; where the subject can otherwise be shown to be indispensable at home, or where he is already at a University by the age of call-up. The period of service is a year and a half in the case of the Army or Air Force, and two years for the Navy. The rate of pay is approximately 1s. 6d. a day.
The following note on conscientious objection is taken from *Moral and Pastoral Theology* by Henry Davis, S.J. (*nihil obstat*) 1952:

'Those who "conscientiously" object to all war, even if it be just—a supposition which, of course, pacifists do not admit—are the victims of gross error. The State need take no notice of their objections, since it is not obliged to respect erroneous consciences.'

13 LI RINI LENTI.
14 VACCARU.
15 CARRUBBI.
16 CUMMATTIRI.
17 APPUZZO NNÀ MINNA.
18 NOVARE.
19 SCHIFIARI.
20 PICCIRIDDI.
21 RACINA.
22 FICURIGNA.
23 CHIANCHERI.
24 E CHISTA È LA VITA CHI FAZZU.
25 PASTUREDDE.
26 PASTURIDDIATA.
27 SUNNU COMU A RINA DU MARI.
28 AFFÁCCIA BÉDDA
E SÉNTIMI CANTÁRI
CÀ LÁ ME VÚCI TI
TÓCCA LÚ CORI.

QUÁNNU NASCÍSTI TU
NASCIU NA RÓSA
L'ARÚRI SÍ SINTÍA
DI LÁ ME CÁSA.

L'OCCHI TÓI SU CÓMU
DU CÓCCIA DI LÚCI
QUANNÚ TU MI TALI
TUTTÚ M'ABBRUCI.

ISAVU L'ÓCCHI NCÉLU
E CHÍ VIRÍA
NA STÍDDA MI PARÍU
LA BÉDDA MÍA

CIURÍ MA TRA LI CIÚRI
DI GERSUMÍNU
TU SÍ LU MÉGGHIU CIÚRI
DU MÈ JARDÍNU

L'OCCHÍ TOI SÚNNU
CÓMU DU LANTÉRNI
CA FANNU LUSTRU DINTRA
LI CAVÉRNI.

SI PÉNSU CÀ CU MÍA
VÚCI A CHICCÁRI
CU TÍA N'UN MI VULÍSSI
CHIÚ MÁRITÁRI

AMÚRI AMÚRI
CHI M'A FATTU FARI
LA BÉDDA MÍA
VÓLIMI TRADÍRI

CIÚRI MA TRA LI CÚRI
DI VILLÚTU
AMARI A C' UN TI VÓLI
TEMP' É PIRDÚTU

NU' MI LASSÁRI NÓ
OSINNÓ M'AMMÁZZU
LU SÀ CÀ IU PI TÍA
DIVÉNTU PÁZZU

LU SÁI PICCHI'
IU LÚNA TI TALÍU
DDA TROÍA DA ME BÉDDA
MI TRARÍU

E ÚNA DUI E TRI'
NGRÁSCIÁTA D'ÓGGHIU
CU TÚTTA A TO' MPURTÁNZA
CHIÚ N'UN TI VÓGGHIU

PRIMÁ D'AMÁRI A TÍA
N'AMÁVU CÉNTU
A TÍA IU TÍ TINÉA
PI PÁSSATÉMPU

AFFÁCCIA BÉDDA
E PÍSCIAMI NTÓ N'ÓCCHIU

QUANTÚ TI VIU TUTTÚ
LU BÉDDU STÍCCHIU

MMÉNZU LU MÁRI C'ÉRA
UN MÁZZ'I CÁNNI
E TU BÉDDA TI CALÁSTI
LÍ MUTÁNNI

SI TÚTTI SÁNNU CÀ
DI MIA SÍ TUCCÁTA
PI LA TO VÍTA ARRÉSTI
NA TABBÚTA

QUANNÚ A LU SCIÚMI LÁVI
UN TI CALÁRI
TI VÍU LI MÍNNI E PÓI
MI FAI SBRÚGGHIÁRI

L'ARMÁLI IU CI VURRÍA
ÁVVIÁRI
NTÀ LU VÓSCU CÀ MMÉNZU
LÍ AMMI TÉNI

STÀ NOTTI CCA' M'ARRÉSTU
NTÀ NA RÚTTA
SI VÉNI SÚLA TU
TI SPÁCCHIU TÚTTA

and as a closing verse:

MI ZZÍTTU BÉDDA
CÀ C'È TRÓPPA GÉNTI
PÍ TIA CHISTÍ STURNÉLLI
SUNNÚ TURMÉNTI

29 ATTACCAMU NÀ STURNILLIATA.
30 CHI VÀ CANTÁNNU TÚ
NTÀ STÍ PARÁGGI
N'UN VÍRI CÀ COMÚ
UN CANÚZZU ARRÁGGI

E TU CU SÌ CÀ DÓCU
TI LAMÉNTI
PARÍSSI CÀ TI DÓNNU
TUTTÍ LI RÉNTI

CANTÁRI N'UN SÁI
METTÍCCI MPÉGNU
VATTÍNNI MA ALI STÚRI
DI PALÉRMU

A MIA RÍCI CÁ
N'UN SU CANTÁRI
VATTÍNNI MA ALI STURI
DI MURRIALI

N'UN CÍ PASSÁRI CHIÙ
DI STÚ VADDÚNI
TUTTÍ TI L'ANNU RÍTTU
CÀ SÌ TÚRDÚNI

N'UN CÍ PASSÁRI CHIÙ
DI STÀ VANÉDDA
TUTTI TI L'ÁNNU DÍTTU
CÀ SI PUDDICINÉDDA

QUANNÚ NASCÍSTI TU
D'ARRÉRI À PÓRTA
A MIA TU MI PARÉVI
NÀ CANÚZZA MÓRTA

QUANNÚ NASCÍSTI TU
NTÀ LA ME STRÁTA
C'ERA ÚNA PÚZZA DI
MMÉRDA VAGNÁTA

MMÉNZU LU MÁRI C'ÉRA
UN LÍGNU SÁNTU
CROZZA DI MÓRTU SÍ
DU CAMPUSÁNTU

MMÉNZU LU MÁRI C'ÉRA
UNU ÁNNIÁTU
DI L'ÓMINI TU SÌ
LU CHIÙ CURNÚTU

LA FRÚNTI L'AIU LÍSCIA
E MÍNNI GORU
LI CÓRNA IU TI LI FÍCI
CU TÒ SÓRU

CU VÒ MBUGGÍHARI TÚ
CÁNI FITÉNTI
SÚTTA LI CAÚSI N'UN
CI TÉNI NÉNTI

STÀ FÍRNICÍA TI LA
FAZZÚ LIVÁRI
CALÁTI LI MUTÁNNI
E FATTÍ NCULÁRI

PUPU DI PÉZZA E PUPU
DI LINÁZZA
L'OMÍNI COMU A TÍA
SUNNÚ MUNNÍZZA

MUNNÍZZA SÚGNU SI
MA COMU L'ÓRU
IU SI CI LA FICCÁI
MA A TÒ SÓRU

TUTTÍ LU SÁNNU CA
SI UN GARRÚSU
CI PÉNZI TI NTRUMMÁI
LU CATUSU

TI FÁZZU VIRÍRI
SI MI LA MÍNI
CÀ T'ÍNCU LI SACCHÈTTI
DI SPACCHÍMI

INCÚ LU PIGNATÚNI
DI QUAGGHIATA
SI TU MI VÉNI A FÁI
NÀ MINÁTA

VITTÍ NÀ PICCIUTTÉDDA
A LU CANNÓLU
MÍNCHIA CHI CÚLU AVIA
ERA TÒ SÓRU

ME SÓRU CÚLU PÌ
TIA N'UN NNÁVI
CU NÀ GRAN PÍSCIAZZÁTA
TI FA ANNIÁRI

VIU CÁ LA TÒ VÚCI
VA FINÉNNU
LI TÒ STURNÉDDI CHIÙ
N'UN VÁNNU E VÉNNU

N'AIU PI TÍA E PÌ
L'AMICI TOI
POZZU ARRISTARI CÀ
QUANTÚ CHI VÓI

N'UN PÓZZU CHIÙ CANTÁRI
CÒ N'ÁIU CHIÙ VÚCI
L'AIU PÉRSU IERI SÍRA
A LÍ FURNÁCI

TI NZÍGNU UN GRAN SIGRÉTU
PI CANTÁRI
AZZÚPPA NTÀ LA ME MÍNCHIA
E FORTI À SUCÁRI

LU CÁZZU MIU PI TÍA È
TRÓPPU DÚRU
STRINCÍTI FORTI A CHÍDDU
DI LU MÚLU

SÉNTI CHI TI RÍCU
FAMMÍNNI IRI
LI TÒ STURNÉDDI MI
FANNU LANZARI

TRA LI VACCÁRA
SI LU CHIÙ SCHIFIÁTU
COMU UN CANÚZZU SCÁPPI
VASTUNIÁTU

31 NTÀ LI MEI SFURTUNI.

32 LU SUPICCHIUSU.

33 A SÈ ANNI CI IVI.

34 TESTUNI.

35 SCICCAREDDU.

36 SCICCAREDDU
DA MÈ SCOLA
CI SI TÙ
E LA PAGGHIA
DÙ MÈ SCECCU
TI LA MANCI
TUTTA TU.

37 SACCIU.

38 PICCHÌ, PICCHÌ.

39 PER IDDE MINCHIA NU'USA
ASSAI.

40 BÀ LASSAMU IRI STÌ COSI, STÌ
COSI NUN SI DICINU.

41 PIENA LU NFERNU.

42 LU STICCHIU.

43 NTUPPATEDDI.

44 SI NCUCCHIANU LI VIDDICA.

45 AVOGGHIA.

46 NÀ RAZIUNEDDA.

47 SPIRDI.

48 VATTINNI DI NNI MIA CÀ
SUGNU FIGGHIU DI MARIA.

49 CHÈ CUMPLICATA STÀ VITA.

50 TOSTU, SFIRRIGNU.

51 SCIUSCIAVU U MANTASCIU.

52 ADDIU PERI Ì FICU — literally
'goodbye to the fig-tree'.

53 SCICCHIGNU.

54 FUTTUTE.

55 LU LIGNU S'AGGRIZZA QUANNU
È NICU.

56 PICCIOTTI.

57 FUIUTI.

58 CORVA NIVURI.

59 NCÚMPÚNÉNNA.

60 CAVULICEDDI, GIRI and VUR-
RANI—three edible herbs.

61 LU SANGUI DI LI POVURI È
STATU SEMPRI DUCI MA PÌ
QUANTU?

Notes to Chapter Four

1 ZA 'NTONIA.

2 ANNI LONGHI E MALA VIC-
CHIAIA.

3 MÈ PATRI.

4 VIDDANU.

5 IAVA.

6 AFFANNARI PANI È DURU, LU
PANI È DUCI.

7 NCÀ LA MANU DI DIU LO VÒ
GHIUNCIRI.

8 LI MUGGHERI.

9 LI BUTTANI.

10 LU PUNTU D'ONURI.

11 FURBICIARI.

12 OGNUNU AVI LA SÒ STIDDA,
LA MIA È STATA NÀ MALA
STIDDA.

13 CU NUN PORTA LA SÒ CRUCI
L'ARMA SUA NFERNU CUN-
NUCI.

14 AFFANNATU A SURURI DI
SANGUI.

15 LI LAUSI.

16 ADDU MUNNU.

17 ARMA E CAMMISA L'AVEMU

DIVISA, OGNUNU SI TIRA Ù
SÒ CARRETTU.

18 NTA LI TANTI MISTERI.

19 SMORFIATORA.

20 ARMUZZI.

21 ARRIZZARI LI CARNI.

22 DI ME NANNA.

23 SMORFIA.

24 Gesu Giuseppe e Maria
Viniti prestu ni mia
Micheli, Gablieli, Isaeli
Curriti cu spati nfatali

Viriti stu criaturi
Nun voli nun devi pinari
Satana l'avi li catini
Dimoniu di tanti ruini

Santi di lu paraddisu
Ancili iu vaiu chiamatu
Curriti cu spati nfatali
Apriti li vostri gran veli

Vattimmi dimoniu alu nfernu
Rammilla chist'anima a mia
Vattinni nca tutti vennu
L'ancili a scacciari a tia.

25 SIGNIRUZZU CHIUVITI CHIU-
   VITI
   LI CAMPAGNEDDI SÙ MORTI
   D'ASITI

   FACITINNI VENIRI UNA BONA
   SENZA LAMPI E SENZA
   TRONA.
26 SANCIUVANNI.
27 Ù LAMPU.
28 LU SANTU PUTENTI.
29 CURNUTIASSINU.
30 MA ACCUSSÌ LA TIMPESTA NUN
   FINISCI.
31 CUNTICEDDU.
32 NNÒ PAGGHIALORU.
33 SAN CIUVÀ, SAN CIUVÀ,
   MPARARISU VI VOLI GESÙ,
   ACCHIANATI A CASCITEDDA
   E DI POI ACCHIANATI VÙ.
34 O CUORE AMABILISSIMU
   DEL SACRO MIU GESU
   PI NÀ VOTA MI FUTTISTIVU
   NATRA VOTA U'MI FUTTITI
   CHIÙ.
35 ARTAREDDI.
36 ANGELU DOMINI NUZIAVITI
   MARIA PATRI NOSTRI
   AGNIULU DEI CHIE DOJE
   SPICCATA MUNTI MISER-
   ERE NOBI.
37 U SULARU.
38 ASRACU.
39 ASCIU.
40 RETRÈ.
41 NMARRA.
42 LU CANNOLU, CU LI QUAR-
   TARA.
43 ALLA VIDDANA.
44 CASSI NCÀ VENI L'ARMA A
   COCIRI.
45 ARRISITTARI.
46 SIMMULATA.
47 COMMARI.
48 SCHETTE.
49 BRACERA.
50 QUASETTA.
51 SPICCHIAMU FAVI:
52 CANTARANU—the Cantaranu is the
sign which distinguishes a poor family
from a rich one—it is found only among
the poor.

53 L'ABBIANCHIATURI:
54 U FALARI.
55 SCIALLU.
56 SCIALLINA.
57 DI SUCARINNI LU SANGU A
   NUATRI POVIRI.
58 MASTRA.
59 LU PANNIZZU — the bride-cloth
is preserved secretly for the rest of one's
life—an ancient custom that is beginning
to disappear, but it remains in the case of
the poorest people, the peasants.
60 COSA RUCI.
61 CUCCIDDATA.
62 SCANATURI.
63 COSA DA ACCUMMURARI.
64 U CHINU.
65 LU MIRCATU D'L'ORNAMENTI.
66 LA LIANZA.
67 CHI SU BEDDI STÌ DU OCCHI
   SUNNU BEDDI COMU U MARI
   NNI VULEMU ARRIPARARI
   SUTTA Ò MANTO DA CARITÀ.

   A LU QUINNICI D'AUSTU
   CE NÀ ROSA SPANPINATA
   E MARIA DI L'ASSUNTA
   E DI NCELU SINNACCHIANÒ.

68 PICCIRIDDI.
69 I VARICEDDI.
70 PARRINI.
71 MASCULIDDI.
72 LI BUMMI NNALLARIU
   LA BELLA ALLIGRIA
   E VIVA MARIA
   E CU LA CRIÒ
   E SENZA MARIA
   CAMPARI NUN SI PÒ.
73 CHU CERCA LU PICCHI NTÀ LI
   COSI TROVA SPINIANZI CHI
   ROSI.
74 CUMMARI DI SANCIUVANNI.
75 PI LU SANCIUVANNI
   CH'AVEMU.
76 SAPURCRI.
77 Madonna:
   LASSATIMI MURIRI LASSAT-
   MI VIRIRI
   LASSATIMI ABBRACCIARI
   CHIANGIRI E VASARI
   NTÙ NTÙ NTÙ RAPITI STI
   CANCELLI.

Chorus of Jews:
A, CU, A, CU, A, CU È DOCU.
Madonna:
IU SUGNU LA SÒ MATRI
SFURTUNATA.
Jesus:
MATRUZZA MIA UNTI POZZU
RAPIRI
NCA SUGNU MMENZU L'ODIU
E LI JUREI.
Madonna:
JUREI NCA VI TINITI A GESU
MIU
LASSATICCI NCA PU MINUTU
VIRI

LA MATRI DI LI PENI E LI
SUSPIRI
NCA CHIANCI E GRIDA AMURI
E CARITÀ.
78 NTÀ LI AVUTRI I PUVVREDDI
SEMU IGNORANTI.
79 NZA MÀ DIU.
80 LA CRUCI NCELU CONNUCI.
81 IU A DIU NU' MMU CANCIU.
82 'NTONIA SI LO VÒ CIRCARI LU
PANI NTÀ CHISTU E CHIDDU.
83 LAVANNARA NASCIVI E LA-
VANNARA È MORIRI.

Notes to Chapter Five

1 ZU NICOLA U CARRERI.
2 QUANDO LU MUTURI SI
SFASCIA.
3 LI MEI SUNNU IORNA.
4 DI STA VITA NENTI N'AVEMU.
5 CUNNIGGHIUNI.
6 SANCIU PIRREDDU.
7 PI LI VIOLA.
8 O LÚNA LÚNA BÁTTÁGGHÉRA
SAI IU CHI T'E DIRI STÀ SIRA
NCÁ CONTRU LÁ ME MÚLA
UN CI PÓNNU CENTU SCHERA.
9 CE LU PRUGRESSU.
10 AMICO DEGLI AMICI.
11 ORBU, SURDU, E MUTU.
12 MA QUANNU MAI.
13 CURA DI CAVALLO.
14 CU LU SIGNURI.
15 SANTA MISSA.
16 I MIEI SONO IORNI IN QUESTA
TERRA.
17 MINNIACCHIANU.
18 CU BONA VITA FÀ NCELU SINNI
VÀ.

19 In Sicily it is usual to leave, before one's death, a sum of money, or a house, or an animal, or a piece of land, in exchange for which the priest will say for the deceased 15, 20 or 30 Masses, according to the sum left, so that the soul shall go to Paradise. These Masses are called Gregoriane. This is not a specifically Sicilian tradition as most Sicilians believe. The

following extracts are from *Moral and Pastoral Theology* by Henry Davis, S.J., 1951, carrying the *nihil obstat*, and are for general use by Roman Catholic priests in all countries.

'The Gregorian Masses for one deceased (thirty in number) are piously believed to have special efficacy. They may be celebrated at any altar, but must be said by the priest who undertook to say them, or his substitute, on thirty consecutive days, one Mass only to each day. . . . If the series has been unavoidably or inadvertently interrupted, in default of condonation by the donor of the alms for the Masses, application may be made to the Holy See for dispensation.' And again: 'If the series has been illegitimately or inadvertently interrupted, it must be repeated from the beginning, unless condonation by the donor of the stipend can be reasonably presumed, or a composition obtained from the Holy See.'

20 FRATI MIU.

21 In Sicily it is an indignity to be buried underground; *congregazioni* are above-ground mausoleums in which the dead are placed on ledges and sealed over. The following extract is from Henry Davis, S.J., op. cit.

'The sacred congregation of the Holy Office issued (July 1, 1949) the following replies to queries on Communism:

(a) Is it permissible to be aggregated to the Communist faction, or to show it favour?

No, for Communism is materialistic and anti-Christian. The leaders of the Communists, though sometimes professing that they do not oppose religion, do, in fact, show themselves by their teaching or activities, to be hostile to God, true religion and the Church of Christ.

(b) Is it permissible to publish, defend, or read, or write in the books, periodicals, magazines, leaflets, which favour the teaching or activity of Communists?

No, for they are forbidden by law (c. 1399).

(c) May those Catholics be admitted to the Sacraments who knowingly and freely do what is stated in nn. 1, 2?

No, in accordance with the ordinary rules of refusing to give the Sacraments to such as are not disposed to receive them.

(d) Do Catholics who profess the materialistic and anti-Christian doctrines of Communists, and do those especially who defend them and contend for them, incur excommunication specially reserved to the Apostolic See, as being apostates from the Catholic faith?

Yes.

22 The old-time school hours were from 8 a.m. till 3 p.m.; now they are from 8.30 a.m. until 12.30 p.m.; always a total daily duration of four hours, whether morning or evening.

Notes to Chapter Six

1 The word used for a bad harvest is TINTA; it is curious to note that the same adjective is used to describe an impure act.

2 STIMATURI.

3 LIAME.

4 SALUTAMU—OGGI SI METI DUMANI MANGIAMU.

5 E CHISTA È VITA CA SEMPRI FACEMU.

6 A LU NNOMU DI DIU IAMU PICCIOTTI.

7 IEMMITI.

8 REGNA.

9 CHIUITI LA VUCCA, RAPITI LI MANI
OGGI SURATI, CANTATI DUMANI.

10 SI LEVA U CAVURU E NNI METTI U FRISCU.

11 VULEMU FURMENTU E NENTI ORIU.

12 U RISSI A BEDDA MATRI DI PONPEI.

13 PICCA PICCA TINNI À FARI SEI.

14 DISSI U RE A REGINA.

15 NÀ FICCATA OGNI MATINA.

16 E CU ERA U ZU NNIRIA?

17 QUELLO CHE PESAVA ICUGGHIUNA CÀ STATIA.

18 SPILLONGU CURNUTU A CU È CHIÙ LONGU.

19 SPICCURTU CURNUTU A CU È CHIÙ CURTU.

20 AH SIA LUDATU DIU.

21 SCHITTU.

22 ZOTTA.

23 ALL'AIA MAREDDA.

24 ALL'AIA MAREDDA
NCÀ LA PAGGHIA E BEDDA

AAH CHI SU MASSARI
STI MULA DU ME CORI
IU SULU L'E TALIARI
IU SULU L'E TALIARI.

VIVA SANTA RUSULIA
LA PAGGHIA E PÌ TIA
LU FURMENTU E PÌ MIA
FELICI E CUNTENTI
NCÒ TRAVEGGHIU E NENTI

STA MULA GIRA E VOTA
COMU NÀ PICCIOTTA CHIANOTA
MENTRI LU FERRU E CAVURU SI STITA
O SANTANTUNINU TALIACI LU CAMINU

SUPIRATI STU TURMENTU
PÌ TIA C'È PAGGHIA E PÌ MIA FURMENTU!

25 COMU VOLI DIU.

26 LA PALIATA.

27 CIRNIGGHIU.
28 ZIMMILI.
29 NTISU.
30 U CUNTU.

31 IDDI ARRISTARU FELICI
CUNTENTI.
32 E NUAUTRI NNI MUNNAMU LI
RENTI.

Notes to Chapter Seven

1 O TI MANCI STA MINESRA O TI
ECCHI DA FINESRA.
2 APPIZZARI.
3 SCANATURI.
4 CU LA GRAZIA DI DIU PASTA TI
VIU.
5 LONA.
6 A LU NOMU DI LA MATRI
DIVINA.
7 JAMU A LA BEDDA RACINA.
8 O STA BEDDA RACINA
PETRI PRIZIUSI PARI
MI FAZZU NA CULLANA
PÌ QUANNU ME MARITARI

SAI M'UCCA CHI TEGNU
UN COCCIU RUSSU E DUCI
VUCCA DI NULLI VASI
DI N'TA ATTIA METTIRI LU
VOGGHIU

LU COCCIU MI LA DARI
DIN TA LI MANU MEI
M'UCCA TI PÒ ABBRUCIARI
LI GUAI SUNNU TUI.

9 RUSSU
COMU LU SANGU NOSTRU
BEDDU
COMU LU BAMMINEDDU
DUCI
COMU MELI DI L'API
TU SI, TU SI
OH OH TU SI, OH OH TU SI!

NUN C'E TAVULATI
NTÀ GRAN PRINCIPATI
SI IN GRANNI ABBUNNANEA
LA BEDDA PRISENZA
DI VINU N'UN C'E.

OH OH VINU OH OH VINU
TU SI
VERU LU RE
VERU LU REEEEEE.

10 MALASENA. MALASENO means
a big shed—in Italian FONDACO.
11 A LÀ PICCIOTTI JAMO JAMO!!
12 L'AMURI È N'FOCU CA NUN FA
FAIDDI
PICCHÌ NTÀ L'ARMA CUVA E
NUN SI VIRI
CCHIÙ CAPRICCIUSU DI LI
PICCIRIDDI
FA SPACINZIARI RIRIRI E
SUFFRIRI

LA PICCIUTTEDDA CA TI FÒ
CCHIÙ BENI
SULU N'SICILIA TU LA PÒ
TRUVARI
LU CORI AFFLITTU D'AMURUSI
PENI
IDDI SULTANTU SAPI CONSU-
LARI
OH OH OH OH L'AMURI.

13 E LU VINU VINIA CHI MELI
D'IN TÀ LI BUMMULA
D'ISTRAELI
E GESÙ CRISTU RIRIA RIRIA
CU LA SÒ BEDDA MATRI MARIA
—and everyone repeats in chorus:
E GESÙ CRISTU RIRIA RIRIA,
etc. . . .
14 U PIGNATUNI. (PIGNATA is Sicilian for PENTOLA, a cooking pot, and
PIGNATUNI is a large PENTOLA.)
15 The stove is the usual form of heat-
ing in Sicilian houses; it is round and
usually made of copper.

Notes to Chapter Eight

1 NÀ VITA DI ZAPPARI
CHI VALI
SI NUN CHIANTI PERI D'ALIVI.
2 LA TIERZA RAZIA.
3 L'ACQUA LU MUNNU CUMMIG-
GHIAVA
NCELU VINEA NA PALUMMEDDA
DIN TA LU PIZZU PINNULIAVA
NA RAMUZZA D'ALIVA BEDDA.
4 PUTRUNI, ARRISPAGGHIATI,
MINCHIA CHI SI LAGNUSU,
AMUNÌ
È TARDU DURMIGGHIUNI.
5 E CI TUCCAU LA TESTA
E LA BEDDA CI DISSI DI NO
NO NO SIGNÒ DUTTURI
LU MALI N'UN È CÀ
CHIÙ SUTTA STÀ CHIÙ SUTTA
STÀ

E CI TUCCAU LU PETTU
E LA BEDDA CI DISSI DI NO

NO NO SIGNÒ DUTTURI
LU MALI NUN E CÀ
CHIÙ SUTTA STÀ CHIÙ SUTTA
STÀ.

E CI TUCCAU LA PANZA E
E LA BEDDA CI DISSI DI NO

NO NO SIGNÒ DUTTURI
LU MALI NUN E CÀ
CHIÙ SUTTA STÀ CHIÙ SUTTA
STÀ.

E CI TUCCAU LU STICCHIU
E LA BEDDA CI DISSI DI SI

SI SI SIGNÒ DUTTURI
LU MALI STA PROPRIU CÀ
STA PRUPRIU CÀ.

6 ALIVA DI SALARI.
7 PATRUNI TRIMAMU
LU PANI VULEMU
CÀ FIGGHI SEMU
VULEMU MANCIÀ

E SI NU CI LU RATI
U SIGNURI SI LAGNA

ALU NFERNU VI MANNA
ULLU VIRITI CHIÙ

CHIANCIRI UN PUTEMU
CÀ L'OCCHI SU FRIDDI
SEMU PICCIRIDDI
FACITINNI QUARIÀ

O SAN' TANTUNINU
ALIVI FACITI
VIRITI VIRITI
COM'AMU A TRAVAGGHIÀ

FICU E CARUBBI
NNI RATI A MANCIARI
COMU L'ARMALI
UN VULEMU PASSÀ.

8 TIRA, FORZA, PIGGHIA, E UNU
DUI E TRIIIIIII A LU NOMU DI
MARIA STA RAMA FIRRIA.

9 A MIA MI FICI GENIU
U FIGGHIU DU TAVIRNARU
E TUTTU CHINU D'ORU
E RICCA MI FARÀ.

A MIA MI FICI GENIU
UN GIOVANI CU MUSTAZZIEDDU
UN GIOVANI MECCANICU
CÀ MIA MI RISSI SI.

L'AMURI E COMU U FOCU
CÀ L'ACQUA O VENTU MORI
SI RICCA VÒ CAMPARI
RICCU TI LA PIGGHIARI

L'ACQUA DI LU MARI
NUN MI LU PUÒ ASTUTARI
NE CU LI SORDI TOI
PIGGHIARIMILLU POI.

10 AVANNU NUN SI FICI NENTI
SEMU CASTIATI DI DIU.
11 O TRAPPITU.
12 EIH ZU TURI VINITI VUI ARRIS-
BIGGHIATIVI QUALE' LA
VOSTRA ALIVA?
13 ZU TURI LU NUOZZULU LU
VUOLI?
14 E LA CRUCI MI LA FICI.
15 LI PUVUREDDI
A SUFFRIRI AVEMU
SI CAMPARI VULEMU.

Notes to Chapter Nine

1 TRAPPETI.
2 CHESA PARATA.
3 LI PARATURI.
4 COPPULA.
5 CILECCHU.
6 AMMUCCIUNI.
7 MINCHIA CHE BONA.
8 TALE CHI MINNI.
9 Ò TIREPPAPPITI.
10 LI TIRRUNARU.
11 LU CALIARU.
12 LU GELATARU.
13 IAMO O BERSAGLIO.
14 MANCIATEVI O TIRRUNI.
15 I SANZALI.
16 SIGNURI MEI
FACITI ATTINZIONI
DANNI N'UN PAHA
LA DIPUTAZIONI

NUDD'AVI A LASSARI
LU POSTU SOU
CU MORI MORI
A CUNTU SOU

QUANTU VULITI
PUTITI GRIRARI
MA L'OCCHI NCELU
SENZA ISARI!

17 ALLA CARRETTIERA.
18 CÀ TI VOGGHIU UN TI INNIRI
NO PEZZU DI CURNUTU

PI FISSA NUN MI CI PIGGHI!
ATTENTU COMU TI METTI

PORCO D'UNU STICCHIU LASSA
IRI, TI SCANTI HA HA TI
SCANTI

FIGGHIU D'UNA BUTTANA
LIBERA VI FAZZU LICCARIA
TUTTI MMERDA CHIÙ SUTTA
AVITI A SCINNIRI

DI CÀ NUN MI MOVU, AC-
CHIANA TU.

19 GIANNETTI.
20 DA BANNIERA.
21 CALAIO.
22 DEI PAREDDI.

23 CURSI NZACCATI.
24 CURSI ANNURVATI.
25 NTO CASSARU.
26 BANNERA.
27 CÀ VI VOGGHIU CA VUCI UNNI
LASSU IRI FINU A DUMAI
MATINA.
28 FACITI CHIÙ FICCA U CAMUR-
RUSU IU SCINNU SI SCINNINU
L'AUTRI.
29 ATTENTU COMU TI METTI VIRI
CA LI MEI CUGGHIUNA SUNNU
CHIÙ GROSSI DI LI TOI.
30 STÀ BANNERA STÀ VOTA UN SA
PIGGHIA NUDDU DI VUAU-
TRI! PORCU DI . . . ST'ANURI
E MIU E MI LU TEGNU.
31 DON TOTO, STATI ATTENTU
DDU CURNUTU APPENA VU-
TAMU L'OCCHI LASSA DIRI
LU CAVADDU ATTENTU AT-
TENTU AH AH AH AMUNÌ
AMUNÌ LASSA' LASSA' AA.
32 NOOOO! TE FARI CRIPARI
LASSU QUANNU RICU IU!
SCINNI CHIÙ SUTTA TU
CHIUTTOSTU PEZZU DI
CURNUTU.
33 AH AH AH VIA AAAAA! NO,
NO, NUN VALI, NUN VAL-
IIIIII!
34 PEZZU DI CAFUNI.
35 CURNUTU DI PATRI E DI
MATRI.
36 STA BANNERA TÀ VÒ RISTARI
MUCCA.
37 AHA AHA HAH VI PIGGHIAI
PI FISSA CU PIPPINU DI
PALERMU NUN SI BABBÍA.
38 BIDDAZZU QUANNU RICI TU A
FINISCI PORCO DI . . . BUT-
TANA DÀ . . . SCINNEMU
CHIÙ SUTTA SI LASSA IRI CI
RUMPEMU LI CORNA.
39 ASPITTATI CA M'ADDUMU NÀ
SICARETTA. UN VI SCANTATI
UN LASSU IRI MA CHI? VI
SCANTATI? SITI RUSSI CO-
MU TANTI MIN . . .

40 E CHI SEMU TUTTI MUTI VIVA
SANCIUVANNI PICCIOTTI.

41 A FELICITÀ PÒ VENIRI DU-
MANI.

Notes to Chapter Ten

1 SPERDUTO.

2 CALIARU.

3 TALE CHI TI MISIRU I MORTI
U PUPU CU L'ANGHI TORTI
U SURCI CA BALLAVA
E A ATTA CHI SUNAVA.

4 CALIA! CALIA! NUCIDD-E-E-E!
AIU LA CALIA CHE CAVURA-
A-A!

5 TASTALA CHE DUCE-E-E!

6 SI NUN SAI L'ARTI CHIÙI PUTÍA,
E LA MINCHIA NTÀ LU CULU
ARRESTA A TIA.

7 SPACCHIMI.

8 CHISTU VENI A DIRI NASCIRI
SENZA PATRI E MATRI!

9 M'ASCURA U CORI—literally 'it
darkens my heart'.

10 NUN LU RAMO Ò CULO PURO
NOI?

11 U SCULU.

12 VO SAPE PURE QUESTA?

13 VA TIRA A CAMPÀ.

14 MOCCIOSELLO.

15 MACCHETTA.

16 UNNI C'È CAMPANI C'È BUT-
TANI.

17 BEDUINI.

18 The following are the articles of the
Merlin Law under which there is no
further licensed prostitution in Italy.

ONE: The tenure of brothels is pro-
hibited in the territory of the State and in
the territories under Italian administration.

TWO: The houses, lodgings and all
other places where prostitution is practised, declared brothels under the law,
must be closed within six months of the
coming into force of this law.

THREE, FOUR and *SIX* set forth the
penalties for those who continue to keep
brothels, incite women into prostitution,
or exploit them, after the new law is in
force. The penalties which had been
previously proposed are made consider-
ably heavier.

FIVE and *SEVEN* are particularly
important from the point of view of the
protection of personal rights. Article
Five declares that any person of either sex
who, in a public place, or place open to
the public, incites for a libidinous purpose
in a way which gives offence or annoy-
ance will be penalised; likewise any person
who follows another inciting him by word
or deed for a libidinous purpose. It then
proceeds: 'Any person caught contraven-
ing the provisions here cited may not be
taken to the Police Station if they have in
their possession the prescribed identification documents. Any person who is
taken to the Police Station for infraction
of the provisions of the law in question
may not be submitted to medical examination. The proceedings of the contra-
vention will be referred to the judicial
authorities.'

SEVEN: Neither the Police, the Public
Health Department, nor any other
administrative authority may resort to any
direct form or indirect form of registra-
tion, even by the issue of medical certi-
ficates, of women who practise, or who
are suspected of practising prostitution;
nor compel them to report periodically.
The furnishing of the said women with
special documents is likewise forbidden.

EIGHT: The Ministry of the Interior
will see to the protection, help and re-
habilitation of the women who leave the
brothels as a result of the law in question,
by providing for the establishment of
special institutions, besides assisting and
subsidising those already in existence which
satisfy the demands of the law. The
institutions envisaged above will provide
shelter and help both to women from the
brothels abolished by this law, and to
those who have started on a life of prostitution and who wish to return to a decent
way of life.

NINE: The Ministry of the Interior will

268 *Appendix*

supervise the provision of the necessary means for the institutes mentioned in the preceding article to carry out their activities: the money will be drawn from the fund set apart in the Budget as provided by the law in question.

TEN: Minors under 21 years of age who habitually draw their whole means of subsistence from prostitution will be repatriated and taken back to their families, when it has been previously ascertained that the latter are willing to receive them. If, however, they have no relatives willing to take them in and able to offer a sure guarantee of morality, they will by order of the President of the Tribunal be entrusted to the institutes dealt with in the preceding article. They may also enter the institutes by their own choice.

ELEVEN: The deficit of taxes previously derived from prostitution will be met in the Budget, up to a total of 100 million lire, by the revenue provided for in the law of 9th April, 1953, number 248.

TWELVE: A special body has been set up which will gradually and within the allowed limits replace the Police in those functions which have to do with the services of morality and the prevention of juvenile delinquency and prostitution. Their organisation and functions will be determined by Presidential decree on the advice of the Minister of the Interior.

THIRTEEN and *FOURTEEN* declare null and void the leases on the brothels and the monetary obligations contracted by the women.

FIFTEEN: All decrees which are contrary to the law in question or in some way incompatible with it, are abrogated.

The following profile of Signora Merlin is taken from *L'Ora:*

Of medium height, sturdy and young-looking, with extremely bright eyes, Angeline Merlin's age is not betrayed even by her grey hair. She is 67 and appears little more than 50. She looks like the housewife she likes to call herself, and has the quick but affectionate ways of the teacher. Teaching was in fact her vocation and for some time her career. She took a degree in French language and literature when she was very young, and devoted herself to teaching, turning at the same time to Socialism, chiefly because of the fascination which the writings of Turati had for her. She became an official member of the organised movement after the war, in which she lost two of her brothers. One of them, Mario, was awarded the gold medal for his heroic action at Bainsizza.

In the Party she became at once an active member, devoting herself to organising the women in the district of Padua. In 1924 she became secretary of the electoral committee of Venetia. In 1926, having refused to swear allegiance to the Facist regime, she was dismissed from her teaching post; she then took refuge in Milan in order to escape political persecution. After being arrested and released, she was again arrested in Padua, and as a result of the second arrest was imprisoned. In 1928 her sentence was reduced to three years as a result of an amnesty.

In 1930 she instituted an aid committee for political victims and two years later began her clandestine activities. She collaborated with the Garibaldino movement during the Resistance; then, after the Liberation, formed the first nucleus of the Women's Socialist Movement. Immediately after the war she was appointed vice-Commissary of the Lombardy C.L.N. School. She entered the Assembly with the Italian Socialist Party Union Proletariat and remained in the Nenni bloc after the split. In April, 1948, she was elected Senator and a few months later presented her now famous draftbill on prostitution. She is a Secretary of the Senate.

19 LA REPUBBLICA.
20 PE OGGI CI PENSO IO, DUMANI CI PENSA U SIGNURI.

Notes to Chapter Eleven

1 LA PIA OPERA ASSISTENZA—the Bank of the Vatican City.

Notes to Chapter Twelve

1 PARRINU E FATTU COSI TINTI.

2 PARRÌ PIRDIVI

3 PARRÌ SUGNU SCIARRIATU CU CHIDDU, CI FAZZU PACI?

4 A surprising number of English Catholics are unaware of just how restrictive the teaching of their Church may be upon these subjects. For example: 'Modelling and painting from the nude for public exhibition is to be condemned. Nude statuary of the ancient artists can be tolerated, but there is no artistic need of multiplying such nudities.'
Henry Davis, S.J., op.cit.

5 MINCHIA CHE BONA!

6 Every parish priest is paid by the State a monthly stipend under Concordat, ranging from 15,000 to 25,000 lire according to his status; for example the priest of the principle parish of a town will receive the higher payment. Further State funds are paid in the form of assistance, such as maintenance money for the church, poor relief funds, and others.

7 The 30 consecutive masses celebrated for a soul. See note 19, Chapter V. For these 30 masses the fee is 20,000-25,000 lire —tradition holds that after 30 masses the soul will go straight to Paradise.

Notes to Chapter Thirteen

1 'In the unmarried, even the slightest amount of sexual activity that is deliberate, whether it is sought, or accepted when it has arisen, is a grievous sin.
Henry Davis, S.J., op.cit.

Notes to Chapter Fourteen

1 POLENTONE. This word derives from *Polenta*, the northern equivalent of *pasta*, made from a finer, yellowish coloured flour. *Polentone* means 'polenta-eater' and is a mildly abusive term used by Southerners of Northerners.

2 Literally, 'praiseworthy' or 'deserving'; among the various branches of service this word is only used of the *carabiniere*.

3 CARABINIERI. The principle *carabinieri* ranks are:
(a) Rank and file:
  1. Carabiniere semplice.
  2. Carabiniere scelto (after so many years' service and good conduct).

3. Carabiniere Appuntato (after nomination by commissioned officer).
(b) Non-commissioned officers:
  1. Vice Brigadiere (after a 9 months course and examination).
  2. Brigadiere (after further course or direct promotion).
  3. Maresciallo di Alloggio (corresponding to Quartermaster-Sergeant).
  4. Maresciallo Capo (corresponding to colour sergeant—office work).
  5. Maresciallo Maggiore (corresponding to Sergeant-Major).

(c) Commissioned:
1. Sottotenente
   (2nd Lieut.)
2. Tenente
   (Lieutenant) } Classe Ufficiali inferiori
3. Capitano
   (Captain)
4. Maggiore (Major)
5. Tenente Colonello
   (Lt. Col.) } Classe Ufficiali superiori
6. Colonello
   (Colonel)

7. Generale di Brigata
   (Brigadier-General)
8. Generale di Divisi-
   one (General) } Classe degli Ufficiali Generali.
9. Generale di Corpo
   d'Armata.

4 PEPIRITU. In Piazza Papireto. Often called 'Pipiretu', or just 'Pipi', possibly a play on the fact that a man may urinate under torture.

5 RASTRELLAMENTO.

Notes to Chapter Fifteen

1 See note 1 to Chapter 2.
2 See Appendix II.
3 A PISCIÀ.
4 A VINCÌ.
5 A LÈ CHE CI NI NPORTA?
6 PE NIENTE, PROFESSÒ, TANO STAVA A MINÀ.
7 CHE A MINCHIA NUN CI AVE PURU LÈ PROFESSO?
8 A CHE CERTE COSI NUN SE SANNO? NUIE CE FECIMU E FATTE NOSTRE, E POI NUN SEMO TANTO FESSE È FALLE CHIAVÀ.
9 CONZALA COMU VOI NCA SEMPRE E CUCUZZA.
10 PE FÀ COMPAGNIA A ME CUMPAGNA.
11 MÒ ME NE VADO.

Notes to Chapter Sixteen

1 PIDUCCHISIA.
2 TI FUTTI DI RIRIRI.
3 TANNU.
4 DOMENICO.
5 U SCARPARU.
6 VOGGHIU VENIRI A MERICA CU TIA.
7 BUNACA.
8 TURRIDDU, PORTATILLU A STU PICCIUTEDDU, CHISTU TI GUADAGNERÀ UN SACCU DI SORDI, AMUNÌ PORTATILLU CI RAMU NUAUTRI PER ORA UN PEZZU DI PANI.
9 ACCUSSÌ.
10 IAMU CA IO MINNI VULEVA VENIRI ARRERI.
11 PULISI.
12 PICCIUTEDDU.
13 PEZZO.
14 PICCIUTAZZI.
15 NCHIARRARI AVI U SURCI.
16 NCHIARRASTI, PEZZU DI CUR-NUTU.
17 LA MALA ERBA SÒ VÒ SRARICARI.
18 AH MERICA, UNNI SÌ.
19 CHELLE.
20 DUCI FARI NENTI.
21 MA CHE BENESSERE D'EGGITTO.

The Educational System

At two or three years of age a baby is sent to infant school; usually a large premises with spacious rooms and often a small garden. Here girls, and often old women, look after the children for almost the whole day, organising their play and teaching them the rudiments of acceptable behaviour, prayers, and songs.

There are three main types of infant school:

1. A Government school, where the children may be sent gratis. The staff are legally qualified and authorised to carry out the work. There are very few of this type in Sicily, and those few are in the cities and large centres. The children spend the whole day there, eating what their mothers have sent them with.

2. A parish infant school, to be found in all Sicilian towns. The school is in the church precincts, and the priest chooses women from Catholic Action to look after them. A charge is made for each child—never less than 2,000 lire a month. The children always bring their own food from home. On an average a parish infant school consists of from 70 to 100 children.

3. The third type is almost the same as a parish infant school. It is run by, and located at, a convent, and the fees are higher than at the parish infant school.

Because of the deeply religious nature of the people these Church establishments are highly thought of, but the poor are unable to pay anything to an infant school, and the majority of Sicilian children spend their days in the streets.

At six years of age school becomes compulsory, but the obligation is rarely enforced.

Elementary school lasts five years and is made up of five grades, the whole course taught by a single teacher. Daily lessons last four hours, from 8.30 till 12.30 midday, after which the children are free. They learn the basis of the Italian language, simple mathematics, national history, and so on. The charge for elementary school is not high (some 300 lire annually) but it is often more than a destitute family is willing to pay. Very many poor families do not send their children to school, because they are needed to work and to help the family.

After five years boys are given a certificate stating that they have completed elementary school, but this certificate is valueless for future employment.

At the end of elementary school the boy who wants and has the opportunity to go on studying enters middle school, of which there are two types:

1. First Agricultural or Professional (*Avviamento Agrario o Professionale*), in which boys receive practical instruction in their future profession. The course lasts three years, and the syllabus comprises the elements of a foreign language, the theory of algebra, mathematics, the Italian language, science, and above all the basic principles of botany, agriculture, zoology, etc. There is an annual fee for attendance of 3,000 lire, and the boy must provide his own books, which will usually cost more than 10,000 lire every year. At the end of the course the boy, who is now thirteen or fourteen, is given a certificate by which he may obtain employment of a lower order.

2. Middle School (*Scuola Media*) is also

a three-year course. Admission is through a minor exam, and the course differs from the above in that:

(a) the fee is higher (7,000 lire a year) and the books required are more costly (20,000 lire or more).

(b) Latin is included in the syllabus.

(c) There is no technical teaching, and the boy is directed to the literary side.

(d) There is the possibility, having completed the three-years' course, of continuing education at a higher level.

At the end of the three years a certificate is granted which has the same employment value as the *Avviamento Agrario o Professionale*. With this certificate, the *Licenza Media*, the student may also enter any of the various higher level schools:

1. Normal School (*Instituto Magistrale*).
2. Technical School (*Instituto Tecnico*).
3. Agricultural School (*Instituto Agrario*).
4. Geometric School (*Instituto per Geometri*).
5. Nautical School (*Instituto Nautico*).
6. Scientific School (*Instituto Scientifico*, or *Liceo*).
7. Commercial School (*Instituto Commerciale*).
8. Industrial School (*Instituto Industriale*) —and several others.

These, with the exception of the *Liceo*, are all five-year courses; the fees are upwards of 8,000 lire a year, and the necessary books will cost from 40,000 lire a year upward. In the fifth year the student undergoes an examination and having passed it he receives a diploma, for example as a middle-school teacher in one of the above subjects.

Only from the Scientific School, or *Liceo*, is it a simple matter to go to University, but having obtained the *Licenza Media* there are other ways of entering the *Liceo*. Some boys when they obtain the *Licenza Media* go on studying at the *Ginnasio*, or Grammar School—a two-year course in preparation for the principal studies of the *Liceo*, classics, and then go on to the *Liceo*. The main subjects of the *Ginnasio* are Latin, Greek, literature and science. The lessons last an average of four or five hours a day. After the two-year *Ginnasio* course a boy gets the Grammar School Certificate, and with this he may enter the *Liceo*.

The *Liceo* is a three-year course, of which the hub is classics, but science, mathematics, physics, etc., are also taught. Having obtained the *Liceo* certificate the boy has three choices before him; to seek immediate employment, to enter the army as a career, or to go on to the University.

Often boys who have obtained a certificate from one of the other schools, such as Agricultural, Nautical, or Commercial, try to go on to University, but it is not easy. They must pass very stiff examinations before acceptance, and thereafter they may only study the subject of the school from which they have come—e.g., a boy with a certificate in geometry may only take the engineering course at the University.

Travel books
from Alan Sutton

ALPS AND SANCTUARIES
Samuel Butler

Butler always spent his holidays in Italy. Using this book it is possible to find sanctuary in this beautiful region, to delight in the heartsease afforded by his loving description and sketches and to capture the flavour of that far off time.

336pp 198mm × 127mm Illustrated
ISBN 0 86299 283 4 (paper) £5.95

THE BIRDS OF SIBERIA:
TO THE PETCHORA VALLEY
Henry Seebohm

In *The Birds of Siberia* Seebohm's narrative skill is put to good use in describing the birds he and Harvie-Brown found, together with vivid descriptions of their exciting experiences in this remote and hostile territory.

256pp 122mm × 114mm Illustrated
ISBN 0 86299 259 1 (paper) £2.95

THE BIRDS OF SIBERIA:
THE YENESEI
Henry Seebohm

Seebohm was anxious to carry his ornithological and ethnological researches further eastward than those described in *To the Petchora Valley*. In this he was entirely successful but it was a long and adventurous journey. Truly a classic of travel.

272pp 172mm × 114mm Illustrated
ISBN 0 86299 260 5 (paper) £2.95

THE ENGLISHMAN ABROAD
Hugh and Pauline Massingham

'These pages can be seen as a painless armchair journey. No bother about tickets', write the compilers of this amusing anthology of personal descriptions through the centuries. Famous, infamous and unknown islanders write of their experiences 'across the water'.

Sovereign
256pp 216mm × 138mm
ISBN 0 86299 143 9 (paper) £5.95

EVERYTHING IS POSSIBLE
Our Sudan Years
Margaret and Alick Potter

A beautifully illustrated account: that rare thing, a travel book which combines past and present, anecdote, personal experience and a feeling for place in a way that takes the reader right into the country it describes.

192pp 248mm × 172mm Illustrated
ISBN 0 86299 125 0 (cloth) £9.95

THE GENERAL
Travel Memoirs of General Sir
George Whitmore
Edited by Joan Johnson

The life of a man who was at once soldier, architect, archaeologist, brilliant diarist and accomplished artist. This book covers Whitmore's travels in Britain, Malta, the Mediterranean, West

Indies and on the Continent in the early part of the nineteenth century including many of his remarkable watercolours.

256pp   246mm × 172mm Illustrated
ISBN 0 86299 277 X (cloth) £14.95

A GIFT OF ISLANDS
June Knox-Mawer

A worthy successor to *The Sultans Came to Tea*, providing a rich, complex and human picture of the author's years in Fiji, some of the loneliest and most beautiful islands in the world.

Sovereign
256pp   216mm × 138mm Illustrated
ISBN 0 86299 196 X (paper) £4.95

GOLDEN INTERLUDE
The Edens in India 1836–1842
Janet Dunbar

A detailed account of the Indian adventure against the background of the Eden family, together with biographical portraits of Emily and Fanny in their early and later years.

272pp   216mm × 138mm Illustrated
ISBN 0 86299 229 X (paper) £5.95 AC

HIGHLANDS AND ISLANDS
A Nineteenth Century Tour
J.E. Bowman

An eventful journey through Scotland in 1825 providing a fascinating comparison with Dr. Johnson's sojourn of over fifty years before. The perfect travelling companion for any living in or visiting Scotland.

256pp   219mm × 157mm Illustrated
ISBN 0 86299 275 3 (cloth) £10.95

HIMALAYAN VILLAGE
Geoffrey Gorer

A revised, first paperback edition of Geoffrey Gorer's unique book, taking the reader into the fascinating world of the Lepchas of Sikkim – a world which has almost certainly vanished forever.

Sovereign
520pp   219mm × 157mm Illustrated
ISBN 0 86299 178 1 (paper) £6.95

MISS FANE IN INDIA
Edited by John Pemble

Here published for the first time *Miss Fane in India* reveals the private lives of the sahibs and memsahibs in the 1830s.

224pp   216mm × 138mm Illustrated
ISBN 0 86299 240 0 (case) £10.95

ON HORSEBACK THROUGH ASIA MINOR
Colonel Frederick Burnaby

An adventurous ride of 2,000 miles across wild, inhospitable country in the winter of 1876/7 by the author of *A Ride To Khiva*.

324pp   172mm × 114mm
ISBN 0 86299 231 1 (paper) £3.95

PARIS AND THE PARISIANS
Fanny Trollope

The Paris of Chateaubriand, George Sand and Franz Liszt brought vividly to life by the author of *Domestic Manners of the Americans*.

544pp   172mm × 114mm Illustrated
ISBN 0 86299 219 2 (paper) £3.95

KNOW THE MIDDLE EAST
An A-Z
John Laffin

The only book of its kind. The perfect companion for the business man, traveller, tourist, politician, journalist and anyone otherwise interested in the complex and volatile area we know as the 'Middle East'.

192pp   192mm × 127mm
ISBN 0 86299 215 X (paper) £3.95

THE LADIES OF CASTLEBRAE
A. Whigham Price
with a foreword by Eric Newby

The remarkable story of two Victorian blue-stockings who journeyed across the Sinai desert to a remote monastery and there discovered an early Siriac version of the Gospels.

224pp   216mm × 138mm Illustrated
ISBN 0 86299 228 1 (cloth) £10.95

MEMOIRS OF A MOUNTAINEER
1. Helvellyn to Himalaya
F. Spencer Chapman

In one of the classics of travel and adventure of the thirties, Spencer Chapman thrills the reader with the story of an expedition to the Kanchenjunga district of Northern Sikkim. His travels through this vast region are related in vivid detail with an eye for the spectacular beauty of the mountains, the changing light on distant peaks, foot-hills carpeted with flowers, and always the weather.

Sovereign
192pp   198mm × 127mm Illustrated
ISBN 0 86299 144 7 (paper) £4.95

MEMOIRS OF A MOUNTAINEER
2. Lhasa: The Holy City
F. Spencer Chapman

This book tells of his six months residence in Lhasa, the Holy City, and the journey through Tibet as a member of the British Diplomatic Mission 1936–7.

Sovereign
288pp   198mm × 127mm Illustrated
ISBN 0 86299 145 5 (paper) £5.95

NOTES FROM AN ODD COUNTRY
Geoffrey Grigson

Notes from an Odd Country is a celebration of living and of the natural world and the response it evokes in man. In particular it is a celebration of one special place, the French village which the English writer and poet Geoffrey Grigson made his second home.

240pp   216mm × 138mm Illustrated
ISBN 0 86299 122 6 (paper) £4.95

WEDDING TOUR
January – June 1873
Emily Birchall
Edited by David Verey

The six-month journey of the 'Victorian Squire' and his bride through France, Italy, Sicily, Vienna and Hungary, brilliantly conveyed by the perfect travelling companion.

224pp   219mm × 157mm Illustrated
ISBN 0 86299 208 7 (cloth) £9.95 SMP

THE WEST INDIES AND THE SPANISH MAIN
Anthony Trollope

Trollope's journey through the West Indies, Central America and British Guiana in 1858/9 is full of personal anecdote told with all the detail and colour of which he was master.

352pp   172mm × 114mm
ISBN 0 86299 220 6 (paper) £3.95